Regulatory Worlds

Cultural and Social Perspectives when North Meets South

Mark Findlay

Professor of Law, Singapore Management University, Singapore, and Professor of Criminal Justice, University of Sydney, Australia

Lim Si Wei

Postgraduate Student, Law School, University of Leiden, the Netherlands

Edward Elgar

Cheltenham, UK • Northampton, MA, USA

Published by
Edward Elgar Publishing Limited
The Lypiatts
15 Lansdown Road
Cheltenham
Glos GL50 2JA
UK

Edward Elgar Publishing, Inc.
William Pratt House
9 Dewey Court
Northampton
Massachusetts 01060
USA

A catalogue record for this book
is available from the British Library

Library of Congress Control Number: 2014941542

This book is available electronically in the ElgarOnline.com Law Subject Collection, E-ISBN 978 1 78347 031 0

ISBN 978 1 78347 030 3

Typeset by Columns Design XML Ltd, Reading
Printed and bound in Great Britain by T.J. International Ltd, Padstow

Contents

Preface

The age calls for vision, for the sort of critically engaged social science of which Karl Polanyi is an outstanding representative.[1]

Sally Randles correctly observes that the key target for Polanyi's critique of dis-embedded economic and social arrangements was not markets per se, but an ever-expanding market society in which not only does market myopia render modes of non-economic reproduction invisible to scholars and policymakers alike but '... such heightened levels of planetary economic interdependence create the conditions for a fall. A fall, when it does come, is of ever-increasing severity and brings large-scale social dislocation'.[2]

This book tackles market myopia and regulatory invisibility from a South to North World perspective. The purpose of this critical inversion is to interrogate the possibility for radically repositioning regulatory principle and reconsidering regulatory relationships and outcomes motivated by social sustainability rather than individualized wealth creation. As Polanyi foreshadowed this will require returning economy to society; a massive project were it not for the impetus from prevailing global crises in immediate need of new and creative regulatory intervention.[3]

We live in an era wherein if homo economicus exists he has a fast diminishing terrain.[4] This all-knowing self-interested decision-maker no longer enjoys even economic conditions for uninhibited rationality, if ever these were his to enjoy beyond the exploitation of those without the luxury of choice. His essential capacity for efficient, gain-maximizing decisions which combine considerations of opportunity cost, marginal utility and price is now a hostage to fortune: fortune based on fictional commodification and exchange in a world of market societies where risk rules above sustainability. However, against the reflections of organic social bonding that the book will advance, perhaps this is a North World/regulatory state malaise. In a South World social context economy

---

[1] Dale (2010), p. 250.
[2] Randles (2010).
[3] Findlay (2013a).
[4] For a discussion of *homo economicus* read von Mises (1972).

is not necessarily adrift from society. Market liberalism wherein markets are imagined as free to attain their natural unfettered state and hence function effectively, remains essentially subject to vital organic social bonds where economy is but one frame governed by and working for sustainability.

The pleasure of homo economicus relies on fictitious commodities and exchange, dislocated from socially sustainable productivity, and it comes at a cost. As economy critically dis-embeds out of society and replaces organic social bonding with mechanical market conditions, those who are unable to mirror the homo economicus livelihood look to the support of social welfare policy instruments (themselves mechanical in operation). Society is kept compliant within the market, for the have-nots at least, through a protective social impulse which Polanyi referred to as the double movement. Today governance through autonomy has turned on welfare, in a dangerous celebration of unsustainable neo-liberal, and rabid individualism. The double movement is dissipating, and the welfare it promised is without purchase.

Economic austerity in response to the excesses of international financial dealings over the past decade undermines welfarism as a wasteful luxury or at worst a refuge for the feckless. Armies of unemployed are increasingly alienated from the fictional market of wage labour. Generations are now being forever disenfranchised from forms of wage-based economic survival. Autonomy has conspired to undermine the essential preconditions of its economic promise, producing pressures in the North World as well as the South for prolonged welfare when the public sector cupboard is bare.

The truth is that in the South World the double movement never kicked in. South World developing economies suffer from strains on the dominant cultural primacy of community through the selective availability of private property, and capital-strapped imposed cash economies. Traditional systems of reciprocal economic production are bought out and the negative social impact is not ameliorated through restorative welfare policy. The consequences of dis-embedded market societies are yet to deliver their full economic significance as global warming advances and global financial crisis remains unaddressed. Where is effective regulation in all of this?

Prior to the questioning of the neo-liberal economic model which followed the international financial crisis in the first decade of this century, little was written in the mainstream economics literature concerning market economies as the problem. Wade exposes this short-sighted scholarship as the reason for the failure of economists to foresee the collapse, or even provide advanced warning of its inevitability. He refers to a letter written by a group of thirty British academic economists explaining this blindside as '… a failure of the collective imagination of many bright people … to understand the risks of the system as a whole'.[5]

In the context of what he suggests as the 'art of paradigm maintenance', Wade castigates the modern economic discipline for much more than imagination deficit.

> The (neo-classical conceptual) framework generated theories which justified and celebrated the structure of Western economies – a structure which generated rising levels of financial fragility; and it occluded the impending collapse from the sight of almost all professional economists. As the self-styled queen of the social sciences, the discipline has betrayed the trust of society in its expertise and professional ethics.[6]

Socio-legal regulatory scholarship faces a similar denunciation. In the wake of the attack on regulation in any form launched through policy wars such as the 'Washington Consensus', where were the critical voices of law and society defending the social necessity of principled regulation?[7]

Lest the reader decides to discard our book at this point for what might be perceived as a disenchanted and defeatist tone, be assured that what follows is anything but. We argue in the cause of repositioning regulatory principle and the governance of market economies towards social sustainability. We see this as attainable in the sustainable circumstances which are set out in detail. For this task, which we deem achievable through consideration of markets, morality and mutuality, the role of law, its regulation of property relations and the social value that it can imbue offers up an immense potential to change the way we think about social bonding. Shifting the regulatory paradigm requires our analysis that combines the rich capacity of socio-legal and socio-economic thinking, together with fundamental concepts of law as building blocks in a just, fair and sustainable society.

Mark Findlay
Lim Si Wei
April 2014

---

[5] Wade (2014).

[6] The detail of his acerbic and challenging critique is contained in Wade (2014).

[7] An exception was Braithwaite (2008).

1. Reimagining contemporary regulatory principle – fragmented regulatory space

INTRODUCTION

From a North World perspective we believe that the economic suffering of the South is an inevitable consequence of the absent or failed regulatory state. This book endorses the more organic position that when economic interests and market frames no longer serve essential social needs then state or no state, the regulatory agenda (in principle, relationships and outcomes) is toxic for sustainable social bonding. The challenge is to design a regulatory thinking for a global future beyond exponential economic growth and individual wealth creation that is crucial in a fast-approaching age after materialism, modernism and regulatory myopia.

An early motivation for this project was, in an applied sense, to identify the alternative regulatory cultures in the South World that might assist in understanding the possible social location of economy without the regulatory state. Despair surrounding the prevailing global economic model attends disillusionment with global economic regulation as the North World descends further into financial crisis, and the South suffers livelihood consequences far from its own making. Whether North or South, and across the divide, we live in fragmented regulatory space.

A better understanding about the problematic future of global regulation lies in revealing the different reasons for fragmentation within and between very different regulatory spaces. For a start in this regard, the chapter will suggest a nexus between social embeddedness, mechanical/organic regulatory form and differential culturally located values, all of which influence essential social bonding.[1] Where the analysis advances the embeddedness debate is through revealing the forces at work for and

---

[1] In our other work we employ a device that advances such a causal consideration in order to break free of any obligatory comparative reference to consolidated states and to explore in regulatory environments where social bonds

against social bonding, which then profoundly impact both the sustainability of regulation and of what it regulates.

Previously we have suggested that the motivations for human satisfaction are forcibly shifting from wealth creation to sustainability, creating an economic and social epoch within which analysts can more effectively make vibrant critiques of regulatory principle – recognizing the significance of transition in principle brought about by valuing conditions of social bonding and solidarity, and vice versa.[2] To enrich this analysis, the chapter suggests looking for different ways of regulating that relate to essential cultural location rather than being bound to phases of state development. In so doing, we ask whether a method which goes beyond a structural approach to regulatory difference enables an acceptance of alternative fundamental phenomena that influence regulatory challenges, options and outcomes (such as concepts of fairness, the significance of efficiency, the importance of loyalty for bonding central social units).

> Judging from the current debate in international relations theory, we live in a period of 'transformation' and 'transition' … it is advisable to use the concept of transformation … in which modern society is understood both as a result of market expansion, and as the self-protection of society against the disruptive and destabilizing effects of the market.[3]

Like it or not (and we don't), the development of arguments in favour of repositioning regulatory principle quickly lead to a recognition of the largely economic conditions and existing institutional constructions which stand in its way. That principles should critically inform regulation for our analysis is a given,[4] even when proponents of regulation see principle *and* self-interest as compatible. That regulation should operate in a principled environment or even produce principled outcomes is more contestable. Braithwaite (2005), using the comparative case-study of tax evasion, proposes that markets can be flipped from the *vice* of tax avoidance to markets in the *virtue* of tax integrity.[5] It is a bold theoretical assertion in keeping with the thesis that the right sort of regulation can better achieve the right economic model for thinking about the variety of human exchanges which take place. For us it is not so much the nature of the proposed transition that assists our argument, but rather that a

---

are deeply embedded, what counterbalances state disaggregation. See Findlay and Lim (forthcoming).

[2]   Findlay (2013).
[3]   Hettne (2006).
[4]   Grabosky (2012).
[5]   Braithwaite (2005).

fundamental transition can occur when the essential social bonds from which the market originates are reformed to correspond with the spirit of regulation.

The analysis of regulatory principle as a means for repositioning regulatory discourse and thereby in turn enabling a fundamental shift in regulatory principle will, we argue as this book progresses, achieve its purposes in two ways. The first is to return to forms of sustainable principled regulation that we see in the societies and cultures where social bonding remains organic (see chapter 6), which are not trumped by profit maximization. Initially for the purposes of our analysis, principled regulation will be considered as an organic[6] phenomenon, required to seek its essence in social embeddedness (elaborated upon in chapter 4).[7] This distinction is not to suggest that valid and even valued regulatory principle may not be a mechanical and externally imposed influence over regulation. However, our interest in the transition of regulatory principle is away from the more mechanical North World frames, concentrating instead on principle which flourishes in more organic contexts of embeddedness and social bonding. The danger here, as some might consider is well exhibited in Trobriand anthropology,[8] is presenting a pastoral or naïve reflection of subsistence societies wherein it is assumed that primitive market arrangements better reflect and support valuable social bonding. Armed with this warning we restrict our cultural reflection to conditions of sustainability stimulated by the very real recognition North or South that global crises are largely premised on the consistent devaluation of sustainable lifestyles. In chapter 3 we detail the 'downsides' of more organically bonded societies (and even the problems associated with a simplified organic/mechanical duality when addressing social bonds). In particular, in chapter 6 in the context of sustainable market/society synthesis, we investigate the dangers associated with 'knowledge deficit' commonly apparent in subsistence and transitional societies where organic social bonds allow for dependency and restrictive

---

[6] The distinction between organic and mechanical regulation draws from Durkheim's analysis of *mechanical solidarity* and Weber's *communal solidarity*; see Durkheim (1893); Weber (1947).

[7] For a discussion of social embeddedness in the context of the history of criminal liability and penality as regulators, see Melossi, Sozzo and Sparks (2011).

[8] The cultures of the Trobriand Islands some might say have been disproportionately influential in social anthropologies celebrating tribal social embeddedness. The lives of these islanders have become emblematic of anti-market economy cultures; see for example Polanyi (1944), chapter 4.

structures of obligation. If the market supports, but makes reliant, social bonding, then dependent sustainability arrangements can be as problematic as the resilience of the market frame.

In market situations specifically, a transformation in regulatory principle will contemplate new expectations about what we want to regulate economies for. As the values of global society are currently inevitably shifting from wealth creation (regenerative and sustainable[9] or otherwise) to resource sustainability,[10] the economic *new deal* speaks in terms of social responsibility ahead of individual profit,[11] determining the most appropriate reasoning behind global regulation as a high order normative task on which, we argue, the nature of global governance may depend.[12] This determination will be assisted by, the chapter asserts, examining motivations for regulation emerging out of social and cultural settings in which modernization may not be a dominant motivation. In a later section we explore, as examples of culturally located principles, some approaches to social cohesion which are culturally independent of materialist mechanics.

The second approach to contesting contemporary global regulatory motivation is to redirect the *what for* question. The analysis to follow will suggest a mechanical process of global ordering benefitting from embeddedness impulses, in which regulation will play a key role, and from which critical connections can be drawn between socio-economic regulatory principles and sustainable regulatory outcomes. To assist in this progression, the book moves through two opposing case-studies that exemplify either:

- organic social bonding and the promise of sustainability as an alternative regulatory principle to redirect regulatory perspectives from the South to the North Worlds; or
- mechanical bonding in transitional economies where market prioritization and dis-embeddedness hold the promise of eventually devaluing the economy and returning it to less materialist social conditions, but not without disorder and dysfunction.

Reimagining regulatory principle requires even a cursory survey of the novel normative social and economic values, besides wealth creation and

---

[9]   United Nations General Assembly (1987).
[10]   Anon (1999).
[11]   Borzaga and Becchetti (2010).
[12]   Findlay (2013a).

exponential growth, which provide social cement in cultures and communities not recent products of neo-conservative or neo-liberal political mechanics.[13] This chapter will assert that in modernized, materialist economies, perpetual economic growth and expanding production in pursuit of maximum private profit as motivators for, and evaluators of, good regulation can now be (and should be) challenged. Here again, the South/North repositioning offers the chance to disconnect regional and global regulation from its economic obsessiveness.

The timing of this book is fortuitous. Recent global financial upheaval has relieved us of the struggle to justify regulation as valuable and viable for socializing healthy market conditions. Social disorder, as a consequence of dis-embedded labour markets, even in repressive societies, is on the rise (see chapter 5). Contemporary possibilities for our wider critique of prevailing regulatory principle (or lack of it) have been afforded to critical scholars and policy makers by the cracks appearing in the Washington Consensus assault on commercial regulation, and the not unconnected emerging interest in regulatory contexts beyond the North World.[14]

CONTEXTS FOR THE ANALYSIS

In order to confirm our analytical platform there is a need to empirically research the anthropology of culturally sensitive regulatory principle.[15] The purpose of such an enterprise is not only to better understand the nature and development of regulatory principle beyond a North World paradigm. It also advances a nexus between social embeddedness and regulatory principle, so that a richer analysis would offer practical opportunities for examining regulatory dimensions within cultures where the state is disaggregated, civil society is resilient, non-government organizations fill many regulatory voids, and multinational commercial incursion is often rapacious. In the case-studies provided later in the book (chapters 5 and 6) we take the contexts of transitional economies and societies as a backdrop to evaluate the dis-embedding tensions in mechanical market economies and the potential of markets to integrate and bond otherwise commercially (and even culturally) unsustainable societies.

---

[13]   Harvey (2005); Leys (1980).
[14]   Findlay (2013a).
[15]   This analytical framework is being tested through empirical research currently funded within Singapore Management University.

With the intention of analyzing market location and social sustainability in mind, some preparatory and prevailing questions include:

1. How are regulatory challenges culturally specific?
2. Are regulatory challenges and regulatory alternatives perceived differently in the South/East and if so, how and why?
3. How does regulation become influenced by mechanical/organic social bonding?
4. Is there a potential to identify significant cultural characteristics which will individualize regulatory policy through social bonding?
5. Why does the language of regulation, when directed towards the South/East World, still focus on the role of the regulatory state?
6. If not as the principal comparative referent, how and why should regulation in the South/East World avoid taking into account the dysfunctional influence of disaggregated states?

The answers to these questions may depend on a range of social and economic assumptions from which we work. Generally put and contestable, for the purposes of our analysis they are proposed as contextual *givens*, and include that:

●   *Regulation is fundamentally a question of community/social bonds.* Regulation as perceived by any South World society can assist our understanding of regulation as a question of community/social bonds.
●   *Social bonding is culturally specific.* Unlike what has been presumed in contemporary regulatory scholarship, the nature of regulatory principle and project cannot be more cogently appreciated beyond economic and market conditions without a consideration of cultures and related South World contexts.
●   *Regional and global regulatory crises are currently enunciated from a Western/Northern focus.* The subject of regulation policy and commentary itself is a Western conceptualization (or at least viewed from an irredentist perspective) and many of the theories and techniques discussed in regulatory scholarship are building blocks for a theoretical, state-referential model assumed to be superior to, or at least dominant over, those other cultures and societies.
●   *Contemporary regulatory policy literature is written from a Western/Northern point of view.* This historically and commercially prevailing single perspective from which current regulatory scholarship is constructed cannot be said to apply universally or consistently across all cultures if considered from anything but a Western/

Northern location, divorced from recognizing degrees of modernization and economic development.

- *Regulatory techniques and regulatory theory which influence global and regional policies come primarily from a Western/Northern focus.* This dominance stems from the one-time more economically dominant Western hegemony in global affairs, coupled with the cultural insensitivity of global regulation discussed earlier that distorts the eventual determinations of regulatory challenges and their respective solutions. It does not take into account local regulatory needs, responses and principle.
- *Regulatory academic and scholarly knowledge are directed towards regulatory challenges in consolidated states.*[16] As a result, small and disaggregated states in the South World that do not conform to governance models to which the Northern states subscribe, are assailed for their unconventional (and even comparatively dysfunctional) governance techniques and policies. Little of the literature from a non-North regulatory origin examines the contribution of post-colonial, or commercially imperial pressures from the North World which add to, or profit from, the disaggregation of South World state institutions and processes.
- *Many serious global and regional regulatory problems emerge from post-colonial power and commercially imperial imbalances caused by often predatory multinational influence in developing states.* International organizations regularly extort promises of regulatory reform from South World governments in exchange for monetary or other benefits, while multinational conglomerates complicate the dependent domestic investment landscapes and economies in their rush to industrialize.
- *Transitional states (economically/politically/culturally and regulatory transitional) are augmenting regulatory alternatives to suit their domestic contexts.* Given that these regulatory alternatives are constructed with a Western/Northern focus, they may be incompatible with such domestic contexts, and these transitional states often struggle to keep up with reform as according to contemporary Western regulatory literature.

Along with these contextual considerations run connected critical theoretical assumptions regarding social embeddedness, on which we rely for

---

[16] For a detailed discussion of our use of this notion see Findlay (2013a), chapter 1.

the suggested value of organic social bonding as a preferred context for the development of sustainable regulatory principle. Granovetter identifies the 'argument of embeddedness' in these terms: '... that the behavior of institutions to be analyzed are so constrained by ongoing social relations that to construe them as independent is a grievous misunderstanding'.[17]

Granovetter emphasizes the inextricable relationship between institutional behaviour and the forces of social bonding. If the latter, we argue, are organically maintained then institutions and their behaviour will depend for their value on the manner in which they complement and reflect the principles of social bonding. Regulatory principle should be so located.

In order to understand the manner in which the analysis of regulatory principle repositioned from a South World gaze employs social embeddedness, there is a need to discuss our interpretation of how such embeddedness is achieved (or indeed undermined). We will develop these preliminary thoughts more critically in chapter 3.

MECHANICS OF EMBEDDEDNESS – HOW 'SOLID' IS SOLIDARITY?

Like regulation, social embeddedness is both a force for and a product of social bonding, or in other words social *solidarity*. In making this assertion it becomes immediately necessary to seek out and establish a convincing theoretical frame for what we will call the mechanisms of embeddedness. To do this it is useful to explore our particular interpretation of the organic/mechanical dialectic.

In any investigation of the relationships enduring social bonding, external mechanical structural forces can be as influential or more so, than are original bonds of cultural connectiveness. We would accept this assertion particularly in modern North World economic and regulatory arrangements. However, we later argue that as the predominant economic integrative mechanisms move from politically determined distribution in complex stratified societies (where labour, land and capital are commodities) towards those which are rich in socially embedded forms of exchange in small-scale symmetric communities, then the *rules of the market* are not regulated for in all spheres of human activity, particularly when and where social structures are more redistributive and reciprocal.

---

[17] Granovetter (1985).

Along with this transformation, social bonding becomes more organic in that it grows out of and relies on socially protective reactions rather than socially distracted structural mechanics. It is what precedes the need for Polanyi's *double movement* (see chapter 3) as markets are socially supportive rather than dislocated.

Durkheim argued that social order is maintained in societies based on two forms of solidarity: mechanical and organic.[18] He proposed that primitive and small-scale societies are typically characterized by mechanical solidarity. It is homogeneity between individuals that allows social order to be maintained – people feeling connected through similar work, education and religious training. In such societies, the structural ties are weak and individuals do not depend on one another to have their needs met. The links between them can be easily broken. For Durkheim, on the other hand, modern and industrial societies are characterized by organic solidarity. Social cohesion comes from the interdependence of individuals on each other in performing different tasks (occupational specialization) and having different values and interests. Because the economic system in particular is one of integrated functions, the ties between individuals are very strong.

Understanding what drives the process of social bonding may be complicated further by its *chicken and egg* characteristics. Particularly in societies where economies are stratified but fundamental economic relations may still be influenced by organic cultural conventions, mechanical structural forces such as workplace security and hiring conventions (discussed critically in the context of dis-embedded markets in chapter 5) can be critically mediated by organic bonds such as firm loyalty and predictable employment progression. Perhaps a more realistic way of engaging with social bonding is to look at the dynamic influences (organic and mechanical) that move towards or away from embeddedness (Figure 1), and these can work in tension with each other and require resolution with the help of regulatory principle. Our interpretation of the embeddedness/dis-embeddedness dynamic, we later explain (see chapter 3), answers the criticism of Polanyi's use of these concepts being too unidirectional and simplistic.

Durkheim accepted that modern society was, at his time, in a transitional phase, demonstrated by an inevitable move from mechanical to organic solidarity with increasing division of labour. In this context social bonds represented through devices such as laws will change a society with mechanical solidarity, transforming through a heavier reliance on

---

[18]   Durkheim (1893).

organic solidarity. In this process of change, laws are reflective of a society's dynamics and rules and regulations are outcomes of people's interactions (discussed critically in chapter 4).

As we will develop later, there is no essential correlation between degrees of market morality and a progression from organic to mechanical solidarity. This is an important observation when in chapter 3 we advance the significance of social embeddedness in determining a realignment of regulatory principle, as some of the more mechanical dimensions of individual wealth creation become subsumed by the risks that fed their profitability. Looking at markets and their behaviour, Durkheim was circumspect as to the satisfactory distinction between organic and mechanical behaviours and relationships. He observed that the rules of supply and demand no longer brought into alignment the moral evaluation of services, remuneration and commodity exchange. Whatever the view of economists, Durkheim suspected that particularly in thinking of differential salary scales, and their exponential growth up the salary chain, for instance, 'lay people felt that it was unfair'.[19]

Turning away from solidarity which holds society together, to reflect on the types of solidarity in social relations – communal and associative[20] – in post-Fordist economies (discussed further in chapter 3), it is apparent that social relationships moulded through the division of labour are no longer universally built on coordinated interests (if they ever were). Associative labour relationships are now more likely to be forced externally and mechanically imposed. Times have changed and where we diverge from Durkheim's treatment of the mechanical/organic dialectic is initially by questioning the contemporary relevance of his version of the division of labour as 'the supreme law of human societies and the condition of their progress'.[21] Weber would no doubt as an idealized interpretation of the forces behind such a division, favour Durkheim's interpretation that mechanical solidarity constructed through law may constitute imposed devices to control social behaviours and relationships that 'offend(s) strong and defined states of the collective conscience'.[22] Indeed in post-Fordist capitalist economies we would argue that as a result of the unnatural nature of labour division (and more importantly dis-embedded market arrangements which sustain and are sustained by its artificiality), mechanical rather than organic solidarity prevails due to the recurrent failure of Durkheim's belief in the resilience of meritocracy.

---

[19] Durkheim (1897), p. 226
[20] Weber (1978 edn), chapter 1.
[21] Ibid.
[22] Durkheim (1893), p. 39.

A complex division of labour as he saw it meant that people were allocated in society according to merit; therefore moral regulation and economic regulation are needed to maintain order, for people to 'compose their differences peaceably'.[23] Contrary to this view, in a global setting, the violence entailed in maintaining the post-colonial North/ South economic divide suggests that discriminatory economic ordering requires mechanical enforcement if the oppression of discriminatory peace is to be maintained.

Merit is not an organic discriminator where labour prices are depressed, skill retarded and opportunity constrained in the South for the economic benefit of the North (see our later discussion of the migrant labour market, in chapter 5). Poverty-based discrimination between the world divide questions the real market reasons behind socio-economic developmental *failures* of South World countries, so often used to justify colonialism. The provident North image suggests that only the systematic adoption of the values, practices, and resources of modernization can overcome the absence of social capital to establish the necessary preconditions for greater material prosperity in the South.[24] This places a large amount of focus on nation states and transnational corporations, and rational individuals and firms, to lead the South to economic prosperity, while overlooking the vital role of domestic civil society and other institutional arrangements (developed later in chapter 6), appropriately resourced and regulated, that can and should mediate the space between states and markets. In this regard pressures for autonomy (commercial in particular) which feature in North World development models devalue the significance of economic embeddedness,[25] in favour of atomized markets and autonomous productivity paradigms, mechanically maintained.

We argue that it is this economic and regulatory myopia that ignores the significance of socially embedded economic relations for a South

---

[23]   Ibid, p. 60.

[24]   Woolcock (1998), p. 153.

[25]   In this chapter, *social embeddedness* is employed as a critical tool for unlocking the analysis of regulation as a question of community/social bonding. The embeddedness of economic behaviour refers to how economic transactions are embedded in the social relations within that society. The necessary implication is that economic activity is but one category of social activity, and therefore economic growth as the only measure for regulatory effectiveness cannot continue to persist. Through an interrogation of the principle of mechanical/organic solidarity which maintains social order, the organization of social life and social activity takes on a form and meaning that explains legal relationships, or for us, the purposes, and outcomes of regulation.

world development model likely to avoid the exacerbation of discriminatory mechanical ordering which underpins the North World development dominion. In order to add detail to this revision we engage Granovetter's concepts of *embeddedness* and *autonomy*.[26] In his argument, all economic action is inherently enmeshed in social relations of one configuration or another (with which we agree), and development brought about a change in the kind, not degree of embeddedness. Three claims of this embeddedness thesis demand:

1. All forms of exchange are inherently embedded in social relationships.
2. Embeddedness itself can take several distinct forms – e.g. social ties, cultural practices, and political contexts.
3. Embeddedness within a network can bring benefits as well as costs.

A recurrent theme throughout this book is that to effectively advance a regulatory anthropology employing social embeddedness as an indicator of whether regulatory principle reflects and relies on more organic frames of social bonding the enquiry needs to range across diverse forms of social engagement and not just economy. Locating economy, as we later do (see chapter 3), within more embedded social conditions will enable a measure of the degree of embeddedness and not simply its occurrence, and when sustainability is the regulatory outcome then empirical specificity is even more possible (see chapters 5 and 6). As a dynamic social state it is critical to know how variations in embeddedness influence the transition of regulatory principle, and vice versa. As with the mechanical/organic dialectic itself, and stages of development, considerations of embeddedness are more transitional than static. In an economic sense this is exemplified in the shift from informal exchange (primitive) to more sophisticated exchange networks (modern). Crucial to any such transition (especially in post-colonial socio-economic frames) is the emergence of new institutional forms, particularly those to guard against corruption and exploitation. As is common in transitional economic and cultural contexts (discussed more fully in chapter 3), these institutions and their positive influence for social embeddedness can be determined through the extent that they are maintained by organic rather than mechanical social bonding.[27]

---

[26] Granovetter (1985), p. 493.
[27] Findlay (2007).

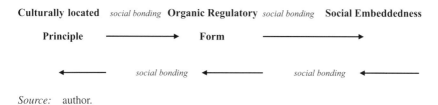

Source: author.

Figure 1.1 Social bonding in regulation

The analysis of regulatory principle in transition, *depending on its cultural relevance and location*, recognizes that an unyielding emphasis on the consolidated nation state model as a referent for regulation misses the global reality that most societies live within fragmented state frameworks and much of the local regulatory activity in these environments, particularly that emerging out of civil society, is an effort to supplement, sublimate or sustain the state's regulatory failings.[28] This redirection of analytical focus should not be taken as a venture in pastoral communitarianism which Cohen warns against when particularly examining social control.[29] We do not suggest that culture-centred principle will always have more regulatory impact or a greater value in motivating regulation than many mechanical regulatory frames (as demonstrated through international conventions and covenants on human rights). To do so would leave us open to a charge of *cultural absolutism*,[30] which we eschew. Culture, and relativity to it, is employed here as an analytical device and not as a preferred normative location although with the right social bonding and regulatory conditions, it could be both. As the title of this chapter suggests, whether it is a North or South World cultural context we have a shared interest in *fractured spaces* in which regulatory principle can have a more sustainable impact. From a perspective of cultural relativity, what this book strives to establish is a positive (in social bonding terms) relationship between principle, organic regulatory forms, and social embeddedness. This enables a critique of regulatory principle and of cultural location in terms of social bonding. Once connected, it is possible at least to interrogate regulatory principle and its transition as forces within and products of social bonding.

Relativity is also a useful approach when searching for the moral relevance of regulatory principles, their relationships and outcomes. In a

---

[28] Scherer and Palazzo (2011).
[29] Cohen (1985).
[30] For a discussion of this notion see Howard (1993).

moral context relativity may neither be culturally nor temporally constrained and a moral lens can temper the essentialism of cultural and
contextual analysis when regulation is to be approached as a more
universal consideration. Like we will discuss more fully in terms of
moral economy, economic and social motivations, relationships, actions
and outcomes can be evaluated morally, an approach which is different
from the one dominating the prevailing discourse. When such an evaluation is interactive and measured against considerations of embeddedness
and sustainability then morality can be both subjective and reflected
against uniform considerations of social good, and not profit and
individual wealth creation.

SEARCH FOR CULTURALLY LOCATED PRINCIPLE –
MORE THAN PROFIT

Searching for fundamental, culturally grounded regulatory (social bonding) principles might be seen as a celebration of the primacy of popular
culture. In an effort to limit any such suggestion this analysis accords
with Samir Amin's assertion that 'Culture is a mode of organisation of
use values… the direct apprehension of use values, without the inter-
mediary of exchange values… the embryo of a social science based on
the dialectic of use value/exchange value… in which commodity
exchange performs decisive (although not dominant) functions'.[31]

In this sense cultural location is directed specifically at a more
embedded context for economy. We are limiting culture for the present to
the demonstration and manifestation of values, valuing principles, relationships and outcomes alternative to the dominant economic paradigm.
In so doing we could be understood as attacking economic populism in
North World materialist valuing. Specifically, market economies in a
South World situation are not essentially connected to exchange value.
The populism in the South World economic sense is bonded through
sustainability more often than through surplus exchange and wealth
creation. If this is so, would regulatory motivation and outcomes not also
represent a different popular valuing? And how would South World
discourse reveal its alternative principled regulatory populism?

Populism as we employ it requires a socially located understanding,
whether it concerns regulatory preferencing, or otherwise. With the
paucity of an indigenous South World scholarship concerning regulation

---

[31]   Amin (1974), p. 190.

in its own perception, it is necessary, for any subsequent empirical research, also to search for regulatory themes and engagement in literature coming from different disciplines. This is enriching for analysis but has the negative tendency of being hard to locate and to consistently employ understandings arising from any uniform language of analysis. In addition to such empirical challenges there is the more fundamental concern about what narrative reveals the essence of culture? And how does interpretation through external (economic) analysis play a role in understanding that essence?

From as far back as Aristotle, the distinction has been drawn between production for subsistence and production for gain. Achieving production for market exchange, within this distinction, need not destroy self-sufficiency as long as the cash crop would also otherwise have some social embeddedness in subsistence considerations. Amin talked of *economic alienation* and Karl Polanyi referred to the *dis-embedded economy* when impersonal market forces and impersonal state technologies for production subordinate man's societal and cultural needs, and not desires. With the growth and significance of disembodied market capital, and the rise of those who have power to profit transnationally, impersonally and without apparent socially embedded consequences, dependent societies in the South World are left to assert protective principles against externally dictated deflation and social disintegration. It is against these principles that our analysis determines its comparative interest, reflecting between the existential polarities which Polanyi identified as:

- Fact and value;
- Empiricism and normativity;
- Society and community; and
- Science and religion.

Polanyi saw these distinctions being 'oscillated as they were tested in life, thought and history'.[32] Preceding the empirical extension of this analysis, in our consideration of comparisons to follow it is necessary to construe principles as being responses to the regulatory incursions (North to South Worlds or within these worlds), as well as themes for injecting a normative or theoretical *reason* into regulatory processes and behaviours designed to accord with or enhance social bonding. Fact is essentially

---

[32] Polanyi-Levitt (1990), p. 117.

informed by value; the normative (principle) directs the empirical (motivation and outcome); economic community recedes back into society; regulatory religion bridges regulatory science through culturally grounded principle. Employing the pathways between such polarities, the empirical researcher then is charged with investigating particular principles, their cultural location, and the forces behind their transition (to influence social bonding) in order to confirm how regulatory principle is revealed through motivations and outcomes not dependent on state referents or North World hegemony.

How would such comparison of principle through harmonizing polarities progress? Grounded enquiry might proceed by turning the comparative exercise to culturally idiosyncratic regulatory paradigms like the Chinese principle of *face*. Two variants of face exist in the traditional Chinese context: *lian* and *mianzi*. *Lian* means the confidence of society in the integrity and moral character of the particular person, while *mianzi* refers to a person's reputation achieved through success and ostentation in life.[33] The loss of face occurs through a violation of the moral order of the society and it brings with it a subjective experience of guilt by the individual who has failed to meet his obligations or by the failure of others to act in accordance with his expectations.[34]

In many East Asian cultural contexts, following and endorsing such norms are core cultural goals that foster group harmony and subscribe to the collectivistic cultural tradition.[35] The notion of loss of face is not easily grasped as there are a range of situations in which even actions not aimed directly at the individual can cause her a loss of face – for example, a lack of deference shown to friends, relatives or subordinates. We can trace this subjective experience of guilt to the individual bearing some sense of responsibility, and then collectivize the motives and outcomes of the principle of protecting face as an organic regulatory mechanism.

There exists great potential for regulation to grow out of the value accorded to face by Chinese society, particularly in the collective network of social bonds which give value to face and to its maintenance. Recognizing the loss of *lian* amounts to, and produces, a social sanction in the enforcement of moral standards.[36] As a result, individuals find themselves, in the course of their transactional exchanges, subject to what is essentially a form of social bonding that alters their behaviour in

---

[33]   Hu (1944), p. 45.
[34]   Ho (1976).
[35]   Hsu (1948).
[36]   Bedford and Hwang (2003).

such a way as to conform to the moral standards promulgated by a shared consensus amongst those who they value and respect as comprising the critical hierarchy and authority of their society. The value identified through face empowers a much more influential regulatory principle (control through reputation and shaming) in Asian society than might be claimed by external mechanical regulatory frames such as laws of defamation, because the value of face and the shame from its loss are organic regulators, having grown naturally out of the interactions between critical cultural actors within institutional social bonds such as the family, the workplace, or the local community.

As such, face is an organic regulatory mechanism that particular societies themselves have developed, enunciated and valued/devalued in order to simply, individually and mystically, regulate behaviours that offend a certain set of collectivized moral standards. The motive is individualized, the outcome is collective, and the regulatory principle is embedded in the individual and social psyche.

At the social and cultural level as a regulatory principle, *conformity* or the unwillingness to cause others to lose face is an important consequent value because conformity and harmony grow out of an active and collective acceptance of the value of the regulatory principle. The existence of such communitarianism means that regulation generates initially from individualized responsibility, and is not imposed from the top, much less from the state. Regulatory principles such as this not only shift the regulatory dialectic away from its current state referent, but precede and exist above and beyond the state. This example of organic regulatory principle clearly breaks any comparative endeavour away from state institutionalism and locates it centrally within networks of deeply traditional social bonding.

The analysis to follow (see chapters 4, 5 and 6) anticipates a more empirical consideration of the relationship between variation in culture-centred principles which underpin social bonding, and intends to reveal the possible connection of socially embedded principle with more organic and embedded, principled regulation. Towards the end of the brief introductory discussion in this chapter we proffer *trust* as an exemplar of a regulatory principle which has varying regulatory impact depending on its degree of social embeddedness. Trust can be individually focussed, trust in our lives and the lives of others, or in a wider sense of social bonding it is trust in those factors which ensure livelihood; where economy is an essential social relationship and a socialized outcome.

LIVES AND LIVELIHOOD[37]

As emphasized above, it is essential not to neglect the cultural context that surrounds and motivates systems for producing goods and services in embedded markets. However, because of the economic ethnocentrism which has infiltrated North World regulatory discourse, this wider cultural lens has not featured in any helpful application of South World experience when interrogating the transition of regulatory principle. The factors that promote or allow such ethnocentrism devalue or even ignore the importance of historically specific analysis of regulation within culture.

All economies – that is, all the material aspects of human cultures – involve the provisioning of human purposes by the technological trans-formation of nature. In all but the most primitive societies, there is also a division of labour with the concomitant necessity of integrative insti-tutions to coordinate economic activity. These institutions have at least superficial similarities – market places, trade, monetary objects, and accounting devices. The presence of these categorical generalities sim-ultaneously makes it fruitful to draw trans-cultural comparisons and establishes the need for methodological discipline so that fundamental and instructive differences are not swept under the rug of hasty general-izations and ethnocentrism.[38]

Market economies are the focus of much North World regulatory discourse. In this section we advance our comparative method (elaborated on more fully in chapter 2) by exploring a little further the distinguishing features of market economies within particular market society conditions. The purpose of this perspective is to appreciate why market economies neither need to nor do stand apart from more encompassing social frames in the South World which determine life well beyond the determinants of economic-only livelihoods. In so doing we need to challenge the prevail-ing dogma that market culture must legitimate self-gain and subordinate powerful features of traditional obligation, to individualist pecuniary success. For such dogma, social relations are dealt a heavy blow by market economy, and we want to find ways where this need not be so, one being through the differentiation of regulatory principle. For instance, labour force mobility waged against family obligation and located social bonds will create tensions in the measure of life cost/benefit balance (noted in questions of migrant labour sustainability

---

[37]   This juxtaposition is interestingly explored in Stanfield (1990).
[38]   Stanfield (1990), p. 199.

canvassed in chapters 5 and 7). The use of economic progress to justify the destruction of historical built environments and established local communities, wildlife habitats, traditional labour skills, and small business foundations of towns and communities, requires critical evaluation (detailed in chapter 6).

In short, the effects of a market economy tend to permeate all aspects of life. Politics, family life, education, the arts, settlement patterns, religion and so on, must comply with, or at least not impede the attitudes and actions necessary for the operation of competitive markets.[39]

Need this be so? In reality, either due to social embeddedness or contesting regulatory principle the same cannot be said of South World economic frames. The pervasive and pernicious impact of market economy modes is a natural consequence of paradoxical market assumptions which substantially question the relevance of the model, such as:

(a)   Scarcity and Choice – the Core of Sustainability

> … scarcity of means to satisfy ends of varying importance is an almost ubiquitous condition of human behaviour.[40]

An axiomatic foundation of modern economic science is that decisions about the allocation and distribution of productive capacity will be calculated choices regarding both scarcity and maximization. From Marx's perspective on capitalism's class society, these decisions regarding investments of capital and its timing and direction lie in the hands of the capitalists, that is, those who own all of society's accumulated means of production. It is them who determine which industries or segments of the economic market will expand or decline.[41] In a similar fashion, if this process is viewed through a Northern ethnocentric lens, then scarcity is dependent on the capacity of the South to fuel the North, where conditions and opportunities for choice are in no way as constrained as those that prevail in the South. The difference here is in the exploitation of embedded economies by the dis-embedded markets of the North. For the vast majority of societies in the South, economy is invisible because economic behaviour is interwoven with the general fabric of social, political and religious life. It would be fair to say in these cultures, economic activity is significantly motivated by social obligation and

---

[39]   Pearson (1977), p. 12.
[40]   Robbins (1935), p. 15.
[41]   *Capital*, Vol. I, chapter 10, in Tucker (1978), p. 365.

regulated by the moral context that governs social life in general.[42] In these societies there is no distinct behaviour which is economic by virtue of specific economic motivation or social constraints. Dis-embedded economies, by contrast, became governed by the institutional complex of supply and demand. As a result the distinctly economic motivation and formal rationality for the autonomous sphere of 'economy' became autonomous gain. This leads to a consideration of market economies which trumped all other social motivation through a single-minded emphasis on individualized pecuniary success.

Repositioning regulatory principle as part of the facilitation of social embedding will bring regulation hard up against the formalist axiom, the value prevailing in market societies, that more is better. This value in turn promotes dis-embedded, calculative economy which disrupts collective or mutualized society and stunts individualized social development in the name of mobility, rationality, allocative adjustment, all for the purposes of market efficiency and dislocated productivity.

(b)   Market Societies or Markets within Society?

From a sustainability and communitarian perspective, the economy is an instituted process or culturally patterned arrangement wherein human society sustainably provides for itself. In this vision economic motivation is self-sufficiency in social reproduction, and the substituted instrumentality of the economic process *for the life process*. Economy, therefore, reasons and is given reason by its specific social embeddedness. The analysis of economic behaviour in this context requires cross-cultural economics, and challenges the ethnocentrism of North World economic modelling, or the a-cultural envisaging of market societies dislocated from any and all societies.

The regulatory framework which sustains embedded economies and markets will approach economic institutions and processes as cultural traits; as expressions of human values stemming from definite patterns of social interaction'.[43] Moving the consideration of regulatory principle as it imbues economy towards the socially embedded promise of substantivism, will be possible through the empirical examination of South World non-exchange or pre-capitalist economies without being contained within the rigidity of dis-embedded marketing presumptions about universal

---

[42]   Appleby (1978), chapter 3.
[43]   Stanfield (1990), p. 204.

economic relations. The interaction of economy and society is a regulatory principle valuing lives above livelihood. Regulation is as such responsible for the subordination of economy to the lives (rather than the markets) it is meant to serve.

(c) Nature as an Object

A destructive characteristic of North World modernization has been the commodification of all things natural and social. Everything has its price, even life itself. A consequence of universal commodification has been the overemphasis on production and as suggested above the unhealthy fixation on exponential and inevitable economic growth.

Sustainability is forging back into the valuation of economic relationships. The influence of this on motivations for regulation and outcomes is already a feature of North World politics and consumer preferencing. However, this process of recognition is not without pain or economic cost and as such is portrayed as an *unnatural reconfiguration of market relationships*. Interestingly, by comparison, in economies where commodification has been much more selective and production has not been unbuckled from substantive social interests, sustainability is the natural regulatory principle and as such nature is the context rather than just an expendable object within market transactions.

(d) Primacy of Industrial Production

Econocentric culture, with its inextricable bonds back to industrialized production, is where meaning is read in a capitalist context from the process of market exchange. The analysis of embedded economy and supportive regulatory principle is a study of social reproduction. Initially then the exploration of embedded economy should proceed from a critical evaluation of North World economic regulatory principle and its impact on specific societies (North and South), polities and cultures when commodity production rather than social reproduction is the paramount motivation and outcome for regulation.

Industry, wage labour and capitalist market arrangements, within regulatory relationships where sufficiency rather than productivity is principled, become processes wherein livelihood facilitates rather than fabricates lives. Once this principled redirection is achieved then considerations of efficiency and productivity no longer value ends over means. The meaning, place and function of human economy are repositioned so that industry is at the service of society and not the other way around.

(e) Metaphor of Growth

Development is one of the oldest and most powerful of western ideas.[44] Central to this perspective is the metaphor of growth. Development is conceived as organic, immanent, directional, cumulative, irreversible and purposive.[45] Critical to this emphasis was the identification of *growth* with the modern idea of *progress*.

In the past, North World socio-economic development has predominantly focused on the economic. Polanyi suggested a new departure for the understanding of growth in socially embedded terms. It offers an alternative definition of economy, another method for economic enquiry, and most important for this chapter, the means to create an alternative standard of value which vests economy (and society) with human meaning. The cursory consideration of central *market society* characteristics renders a limited opportunity for that exercise. Economic growth developing out of industrial production in which the commodification of nature and society is essential and inevitable will move the market away from its substantive social bonds. This then will create conditions in modernization which require counterpoint if markets are to return to their social roots and thereby gain relevance and resilience. The nature of that counterpoint may be discovered in the stories of regulatory principle and social bonding in cultures where social embeddedness is (or was) not unnatural, not commodified and not subservient to the exponential growth of production.

NEW WAYS OF SEEING REGULATORY PRINCIPLE – PROTECTING SOCIAL EXISTENCE AGAINST MARKET IMPERATIVES

What Polanyi referred to as an 'obsolete market mentality' is entrenched through economic formalism which represents both the economy and the market as separate from society. In an effort to see what would happen if markets and economies can become socially embedded, or in exploring cultural locations in which socio-economic interaction is given and natural, regulatory principle can be seen as being grounded in and

---

44   Nisbet (1969), p. 233.
45   Hettne (1990), p. 209.

reflecting this synergy rather than advancing economic or market para-mountcy. Associated with this is an essential need to reconsider economy not only, or simply, in technological or material terms.

So far we have explored the manner in which the cultural location of principle could be understood in terms of organic regulatory forms within socially embedded market conditions, and have identified different prior-ities and purposes in social bonding as suggesting the nature and impact of such principle. It remains to make some projections on the likely transition of regulatory principle if released from its institutionalization within Northern/Western market economies, and given rein in more organic South World locations and interests. If we see the transformation of regulatory principle in this way as engaging with counterpoint thinking, then how can this transition avoid the criticism that it represents a vague ideological protest against the role of regulation in perpetuating Northern hegemonic economic institutionalism?

To take this further we again borrow from Polanyi's thinking by critically juxtaposing his three modes of economic institutionalization (market exchange, redistribution and reciprocity) in order to envisage different motivations and outcomes for transformed regulatory principle.

In the methodology for engaging with counterpoint we return to the comparative project, but this time using mainstream Northern/Western developmentalist thinking as the referent against which counterpoint can be historically and contextually manifest. While earlier in the chapter we criticized regulatory scholarship constantly reflecting on consolidated states and North World economic paradigms, here we need imagery to counterpoint and in so doing to suggest the possible strengths in the belief systems and cosmology which can spirit a transformation in regulatory principle.

Clearly, it is difficult to comprehend what characterizes one's own society: an outsider has certain advantages of objective perception. Until such times as North–South intellectual relations become more symmetric, and Southern anthropologists flood the Northern metropoles, we have to be content with a few relevant Western contributions that attempt to transcend the Eurocentric tradition and look on Western development 'from outside'.[46]

Some degree of comparative objectivity will help ensure that the consideration of counterpoint is not romanticism, utopian or nostalgic. The populist foundations of counterpoint as we see them in the trans-formation of regulatory principle may challenge the instrumentalist world

---

[46] Ibid.

systems and regulatory relationships which confirm Western liberalism. However, as the recent social media mobilization in *the Arab Spring* disappointments retorts, new methods of populist arrangement are nothing if not culturally located and deeply political.

Market exchange in a populist sense can be understood in different social locations by searching for the threads of economic reciprocity which, in more embedded societies, have a redistributive dimension. Populism in such socially embedded, reciprocal contexts can be seen as:

- Reactions in self-sustaining or embedded market societies to capitalist penetration
- Alliances between organised labour and the small business classes against multi-national colonization
- Small-scale farmer capital fighting against urbanization and finance capital
- Anti-bureaucratic movements in static or fragmented one-time provident states or failed centralized economies.

Populism need not oppose all technological progress or external direct financing, just that which undermines cultural and social embeddedness. However, a problem with populism as a counterpoint to the autonomy of modernized market societies is the claim of 'over-socialization'. Clearly evident in modernized Asian commercial communities, or in those governed by more centralized economies, is the over-socialization of social units such as the family within modernizing economic frames. The significance of consensual values and compliant reaction to authority even in modernized economic environments can tend to confuse simpler measures of embeddedness, wherein its indicators are obscured by concerns about the loss of *face* and the importance of hierarchies of obligation.

MARKET MYSTICISM

Before moving on to a consideration of market aphorisms, such as perfect competition, and natural market balance, it is necessary to confront morality. An essential paradox lies in the conventional economics that markets are essentially objective and neutral while at the same time certain market arrangements are *good* while some are *bad*. Competition is good, protectionism is bad when in reality oligopolistic cartels in the financial industry are good business. While not wishing to labour the 'good/bad' dichotomy (and its pretence) we consider it important at the outset to align regulatory principle with apparent *morality* in an age where certain economic behaviour is critiqued at least in popular culture as immoral.

To take this course we risk a range of criticisms, not the least of which would focus on the subjectivity and partiality of moral grounding. We counter this by saying that at the very least, in the current problematic discussion concerning the taxpayer's obligation to repay sovereign debt as a moral/democratic obligation, we are invited to critique regulatory austerity in simple moral terms (which will be expanded upon in chapter 4).[47] Economic morality is a difficult case to put when for centuries the poor have been represented as indolent and the dangerous classes, and the rich through wealth have esteem and respect. However and despite the distortions of popular wisdom it is clear that economies are shaped by moral dispositions and the beliefs demonstrated by the individuals and institutions which govern them as much as they are determined through any objectivist maze of techniques and numbers.[48] These dispositions emerge from individual and collective political and economic interests and need to be disentangled and responsibilized as such. For instance, enhancing collective moral responsibility in order to collaboratively ensure against risk has been demanded of the banks that till now, some would say, have immorally benefitted through taxpayer bail-outs.

In the North/South economic tension, debt and its ownership stands as a contemporary form of slavery, with more demoralizing consequences than the human enslavement of the South's colonial past. The moral dimension of the slave trade is beyond question. Now global debt is coming under a not dissimilar gaze. Whether contracted individually or impersonally and interpersonally, it is debt as a relationship of power which demands moral engagement, and as such moral motivation in regulatory principle. The rapid divergence in economic trajectories, North to South, have awakened old enslavement and the cruelty of cultural stigma, applied to entire populations, and as in the Eurozone crisis, echoing ghosts of violent pasts.

Aligned with the consideration of economic morality is the counter argument in favour of social atomization. From here, we are told, lies the capacity for the uniquely 'moral' (or at least laudable) market context of perfect competition. The analysis of the paradox of market competition reveals much about the suspect morality of the market and ushers in a revised consideration of regulatory principle.

---

[47] For an interesting consolidation of moral themes regarding economic morality or moral economy see Sayer (2000).

[48] Fourcade and Woll (2013), p. 603.

'SOCIAL ATOMIZATION IS THE PREREQUISITE TO PERFECT COMPETITION'[49]

In the under-socialized account of modernization featuring dis-embedded markets, atomization results from the narrow utilitarian pursuit of self-interest. In the over-socialized account behaviour patterns are internalized and ongoing social relations as a consequence have little more than a peripheral effect on individual behaviour. Reconciling these interpretations in order to reflect on the utility of embeddedness for analyzing regulatory principle requires a return to considering market exchange, redistribution and reciprocity. In so doing we suggest that these variants be employed not so much in functional terms (i.e. what they produce in under or over-socialized settings) but rather against what motivates their attainment. We will take up the challenge of identifying a regulatory principle which separates atomism from embeddedness so as to explain market conditions like exchange, redistribution and reciprocity in either organic (embedded) or mechanical (dis-embedded) terms. The principle is trust (see Figure 1.2).

As the recent public backlash against banker's bonuses in times when the taxpayer was bailing out bank default, it is unconvincing to assume that one's economic interests generally are pursued through gentlemanly means. If competitive forces in a self-regulating market are meant to diminish force or fraud then trust in either that market model or the motivations of its principle players has recently been shattered. Imperfectly competitive markets and the micro-analysis of entrepreneurial motivation have profoundly shaken faith in trust as a market bond when social embeddedness does not feature.

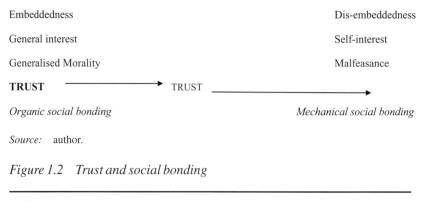

Embeddedness	Dis-embeddedness
General interest	Self-interest
Generalised Morality	Malfeasance
TRUST ⟶ TRUST	
Organic social bonding	*Mechanical social bonding*

Source: author.

Figure 1.2   Trust and social bonding

---

⁴⁹   Smith (1776), pp. 232–3.

To paint such a gloomy picture would be to ignore the organizational reality that even in dis-embedded market arrangements much commercial behaviour relies on trust.[50] From this position we make two fundamental concessions regarding our preferred trust continuum.

1. While trust relationships are present in all market forms they are neither as essential or transparent in dis-embedded market frames; and
2. Trust is a defining organic mechanism for the social bonding indicative of embedded market frames.

Granovetter identifies a distinction between 'functional substitutes for trust' (which in dis-embedded markets could involve external mechanical regulators) and 'concrete personal relations and structures (or networks) generating trust and discouraging malfeasance'.

> The widespread preference for transacting with individuals of known reputation implies that few are actually content to rely either on generalised morality or institutional arrangements to guard against trouble ... social relations rather than institutional arrangements or generalised morality are mainly responsible for the production of trust in economic life.[51]

At the same time he accepts that social relations may penetrate irregularly and in different degrees into economic life, and indeed social relations may create conditions for malfeasance which may eventually endanger trust. It is necessary, therefore, as we have suggested earlier, to study patterns of concrete social relations to see when their influence towards embeddedness generates trust or otherwise. Another critical key to exploring the nexus between trust and social relations is to look at how the embeddedness of one significant system such as the market is in turn embedded within broader systems of social relations. One way of doing the latter is to return to our consideration of motive and outcome and ask to what extent is a particular social transaction overlayed by more embedded, dense and long-lasting social relations which bridge different frames of engagement.

If as Mccaulay suggests, 'one doesn't run to lawyers if one wants to stay in business because one must have to behave decently',[52] then it makes sense that this will hold more commonly in certain cultures rather

---

[50] Arrow (1974).
[51] Granovetter (1985) pp. 490–91.
[52] Mccaulay (1963), p. 61.

than others. Granovetter persuasively establishes this point in relation to different cultures of the firm, evidenced through various structural conditions. If the organization of production and labour prefers or is constrained to operate with different structural conditions (determined by (among other factors) social relations) then it follows that cultural conditions, more generally, will influence the proliferation and valuing of trust.

In the regulatory context, the resolution of conflict within particular market frames may influence the importance of trust as a regulatory principle. In this respect a higher order of regulatory influence can be offered to essential market relations, if the market is embedded with social relations which spread beyond the market and into other critical fields of social bonding. Such vertical integration means that conflict within the market can be moderated in terms of other significant and valued market principles going beyond more narrow market imperatives. Cultures providing a more natural vertical integration for market embeddedness may then be able to manage conflict within the market by implicating higher order regulatory principles with more pervasive social value.

CONCLUSION

Granovetter is right to caution that the 'causal analysis adopted in the embeddedness argument is a rather proximate one'.[53] Without the benefit of empirical work which interrogates broad historical or macro-structural themes regarding the characteristics which promote or retard embeddedness, one is left begging the question about the connection between culture, social bonding and regulatory principle: what produces the embedding which means that organic regulatory principle evolves more naturally? Granovetter posits that it is the impact of social change on social relations in which economic life is embedded that is a pathway to understanding why particular cultures display the social structural characteristics they have and why these change.

Take for instance the common observation that traditional Chinese family bonding affects the motivation and outcome of wealth creation in modernized societies where Chinese family values predominate, or the conventional Japanese view concerning firm loyalty which may have prior to 'Abenomics' uniquely influenced Japanese firms' recruitment

---

[53]   Granovetter (1985), p. 506.

policies. The regulatory principles behind wealth creation in the earlier instance or employment practice in the latter could not be adequately understood without interrogating the embedding potentials of filial relations or employee/employer loyalty. Certainly in terms of the Japanese example tortuous changes in this underlying principle, determined by demographic and commercial shifts within the Japanese employment environment, has led to transformations in regulatory principle and the strength of social bonds and embedding in modern Japanese social frames.

Weber reminded researchers that economic action should be seen only as a special, if important, category of social action. Accepting this, then both sociological and anthropological interrogations of the place of economy within societies are not only instructive, they are essential. This chapter has advanced both approaches, with the analytical assistance of embeddedness, to suggest that the cultural relativity of social relations has a particular relevance for understanding the economic pre-occupation of modern regulation. If economy is more organically embedded within wider social relations in a particular culture then the principle behind regulating economy will be equally dependent on wider and embedded social relations.

2. Redirecting analytical focus – South to North Worlds

> Human society appears to have taken the disturbing form of 'desperate children trapped in a wagon careering helplessly towards a precipice'.[1]

INTRODUCTION

In the preceding chapter we called for a redirection in regulatory principle that can be understood against imperatives for social sustainability ahead of economic growth and individualized wealth creation. In the context of contemporary global crises we see this and an inevitable repositioning of economic imperatives within social worlds experiencing severe strain.[2] This chapter lays out the methodological pathways (and a few hurdles in the path) to evaluating and charting this process of redirection, specifically through reversing the direction of critical gaze.

Our analytical interest in regulatory principle emerged initially in trying to understand why global and regional regulatory discourse is focused on the global North/West, and what influence any such predisposition has over understanding regulatory problems in the South/East World. Taking our enquiry beyond revealing the misunderstandings of South World regulatory failure and governance needs (discussed in chapter 6), this chapter suggests employing regulatory principle to reveal the weaknesses of the North World regulatory state model which has made regulators too often blind and deaf to the problems underpinning negative comparisons South to North.[3] In particular, the chapter will argue that breaking free of the regulatory state referent when approaching South World regulatory (and broader social) conditions would serve as a starting point in identifying the limitations of the regulatory literature as it currently stands. The analytical deficit North to South is keenly

---

[1] Dale (2010), p. 23 (quoting Polanyi (2005), p. 149).
[2] Findlay (2013a).
[3] Black (2002).

apparent when scholarship and policy endeavours to address the inescapable need for change in the way the regulatory state as a configuration of governance has been constructed exclusive of crucial South World social forms.[4]

The chapters to follow (particularly chapter 4) develop the thesis that dis-embedded North World economic regulation, in particular, has dislocated principle from surrounding social bonds and has infused regulatory analysis and discourse with a narrowing econo-centric approach to principle, its relevance and utility. Accepting that there is good sense in both policy and scholarship terms to rehabilitate regulatory principle from the constricting conditions of market economies and consolidated regulatory states, the chapters specifically interrogate other cultural locations offering more than econo-centric motivations and outcomes. The present chapter suggests the methodological backbone for such a shift in focus and foundation.

Analyzing principle, and regulation at large, should be as dynamic as are the forces for regulatory change. A more developed analysis which builds on our interrogation of methodology will need to wrestle with the impact of transitions in regulatory principle on specific economic motivations and outcomes, and the significance of their perception relative to cultural location.[5] This approach will necessitate a shift in addressing and utilizing the innumerable social and cultural variables which characterize the differences, South to North, including and transcending narrower economic paradigms. The pervasive methodological theme in our comparative project is the importance of considering the role of context unburdened by the conviction of North World predominance and enlivened by the South World qualitative conditions that direct principle, which in turn affects social bonding. In the chapter following we will identify some exemplars of these conditions and their transformational potential.

Regulatory principle is culturally relative. *Cultures of the market*[6] which are currently over-represented in prevailing North World regulatory discourse (such as corporate capitalism) within a dominant economic paradigm, we argue, are responsible for the atrophy of regulatory principle. Like other features of North World regulation, principle has dis-embedded from significant social bonds beyond economy (discussed

---

[4] Findlay and Lim (forthcoming).

[5] For instance, if a society values economic efficiency over social fairness, this will bring pressure on the construction and direction of regulatory initiatives.

[6] Dale (2010), pp. 137–87.

in chapter 3). It is through the investigation of more diverse context-centred principles in more embedded market frames that the richer potential contribution of regulatory principle for social cohesion connects principled South World regulatory priorities to the pressing regulatory challenges in the North. These dominant challenges now also paradoxically and consequentially disadvantage the South, and require new regulatory approaches to deal with mechanical market dis-embedding – not previously a South World economic condition.

An essential precondition and a critical outcome for our analysis of North/South regulatory intersection is the redirection of conventional regulatory discourse in terms of analytical view. Global regulatory state alignment or mirroring has been peddled by the North (and much of its scholarship)[7] as an answer to the difficult incline faced by South World societies endeavouring to reach the economic potential offered by the developmental goals dictated from the North. We prefer to employ the differences in the two worlds (and the place of the market and society in particular) as an opportunity to explore imperatives of social sustainability and communitarian construction as alternative regulatory principles.

In offering a consideration of contemporary global regulation South to North, we are not simply engaged in a restorative project. True it is, and we reiterate this in other parts of the text, that for too long regulation scholarship and policy has almost entirely ignored the significance of South World context, except as either the 'problem' for advancing a uniform, modernized global regulatory agenda, or as a political and economic opportunity for the colonization of the regulatory state.

This chapter is not so much an explanation of, or an exclusive argument against this irredentist state of affairs. Accepting that any attempt to reposition the analytical perspective of global regulatory analysis is a worthwhile exercise (and indeed we will hope to establish that it is an essential endeavour if the demise of modern market economies is to be understood) (see chapter 4), it becomes immediately necessary to engage a number of important methodological challenges which could derail any such comparative redirection. What follows is directed to this methodological end.

Initially it is important to clarify our take on the South/North duality, which grounds our comparative analysis, and indeed our arguments for redirection. By concentrating, as we will, on the dialectic of regulatory principles, South and North, contextual characteristics explaining these differences between the two social situations of regulation and the

---

7   Dubash and Morgan (2012).

resultant social arrangements, are revealed. Understanding these differences and how they are exacerbated or modified through regulation, especially under the analytical lens of embeddedness, enables what we later explain as the organic quality of principled regulation to gain policy weight. Once this *model universe* is analytically contained for the purposes of transformative comparative contextual analysis,[8] the chapter progresses to discuss what comparative analysis should entail. From there we explore key challenges in achieving the social anthropology of regulation which the later discussion of social dis-embeddedness requires (see chapters 4, 5 and 6). The objective of this chapter is to address some of the reservations which researchers might harbour concerning the merit of, and method for, achieving such an anthropology.

FROM SOUTH TO NORTH WORLDS

In addressing the complexities of social, political, economic and cultural diversity, even when modelling trans-global comparisons, any dualist approach such as distinguishing the North and South Worlds risks drastic oversimplification. The paradox inherent in applying meta-comparative contexts to understand the empirical specifics of social anthropology creates, at the outset of this comparative enquiry, a tendency that is difficult to avoid and if not confronted will indeed undermine the project by confining the application of our analysis to abstract generalizations. We are not the first to recognize and hopefully inform this challenge. In his later years, Polanyi appreciated this problem when endeavouring to construct and model a *comparative economic history* examining the nature of markets, trade and money in primitive and archaic societies.[9] Polanyi and his collaborators identified a new conceptual logography with entities such themes as 'substantive economy' and 'forms of integration' to support the possibility for a generalized and universal process in managing the various species of economy throughout history to be classified, despite their differences and uniqueness. They did so in a methodological tension between universal themes and culturally and historically related realities.

Immanuel Wallenstein owed much to Polanyi. Agh[10] gave Polanyi credit as the most influential fore-runner of world systems theory analysis although Braudel and Marx would have had legitimate grounds

---

[8] Henham and Findlay (2002).
[9] See Dale (2010), pp. 1–18.
[10] Agh (1990), p. 93.

to dispute that crown. Wallerstein's world systems theory is not satisfied to remain a theoretical conjecture for understanding rather than establishing the progressive influence of global capitalism across global regional diversity.[11] His theory uses the method of comparative modelling at the meta-level of states and their economic interconnectivity. Drawing a clear divide between the North and South Worlds, Wallerstein based his theory on a prioritization of economic measures over other more substantive indicators of maturity or the developed-ness of society. Wallerstein distinguishes North and South Worlds in terms of configurations of global economy. Nation states are situated in distance from the core, constructed by powerful developed economies (on the economic scale) which claim ownership of the primary means of production. The more developed North is characterized by a shift in state economies toward the financial sector as opposed to production of goods, while concurrently maintaining dominion over the means of production exported to lower-wage areas in the South World.[12] The South World would thus be positioned in the periphery of Wallerstein's construct, with transitional states in the semi-periphery.[13] World systems theory is an attempt to calibrate states into concentric circles, each reflecting stages of development depending on where they sit vis-à-vis the core. If, like Wallerstein, our analysis was satisfied with economic (or more correctly capitalist economic) referents then the dissection of the world in this way would be convincing. In fact it has been just such economic calibration which has driven anti-contextually much of the North/South World regulatory distinction.

Wallerstein further identifies exploitation as a symptom of the capitalist world system's impending collapse – with the core exploiting the semi-periphery (transitional states as we see them) and them both exploiting the periphery as the loci of production shifts from the higher-wage periphery to the lower-wage semi-periphery.[14] In some respects the roots of this economic model of international relations lie in structures of dependency (heavily identified in our later case-studies and determined as characteristics of unsustainability). Such dependency can be created or at least exacerbated by the cycles of socio-economic development which fundamentally maintain the distinctions between North and South Worlds, either sponsored through post-colonial aid

---

[11] Wallerstein (2000).
[12] Ibid.
[13] Ibid, p. 254.
[14] Wallerstein (2000).

delivery or the prescriptive intervention of international financial organizations.[15] These dependency relationships are compounded North-to-South through multi-national corporate domination,[16] technological and industrial dependence, capital/debt slavery and other mechanical externalities arising from and perpetuating the imbalance of global economic order.

Wallerstein's analysis for our purposes is both instructive about and flawed by a distinction of North/South Worlds through the lens of capitalist economy. As with an over-emphasis on the state in world-to-world regulatory reflection, another necessary precondition for a more grounded comparative project is to specifically identify, and mark as significant contextual variables, the mechanical externalities imposed North-to-South (such as wage labour or a cash economy dependent on a dislocation between production and capital). By so doing the opportunity emerges for a comparative analysis of regulation that respects anthropological integrity rather than mechanical economic modelling. Adapting the comparative methods used to construct the model which Wallerstein advances, with states as the foundational units within the meta-architecture of global interconnectivity, we zoom down to the state as a regulatory context. Against this focus, we comparatively explore the empirical observations of crucial qualitative conditions influencing the direction of regulatory principle in particular governance contexts. In this way, comparison takes into account the special characteristics that grow out of the socio-cultural (rather than purely politico-economic) contextual dimensions *within states*. From critically interrogating contexts with the artificial political location of state boundaries the comparative endeavour can then add social particularity when reflecting on the North/South duality, providing insight into how principled regulation emerges as the preferred strategy rather than any otherwise unchallenged acceptance of state regulatory authority as legitimate.

What seems like a new social anthropology of global regulation is an endeavour too grand for this chapter, even though it has much merit. To contain the analysis which follows, the discussion of social embeddedness will be restricted to a comparison of market economies which retain some local or regional integrity from those which have become largely removed from cultural or communal social bonds. An example is between markets trading in goods and services with a consumer base which is local and subsistence, and markets in derivative *products* that

---

[15] Findlay (1999).
[16] Cardoso and Faletto (1979).

are inextricably dependent on supranational location.[17] The purpose of this resort to market economies as a comparative referent is to reveal how essential features of social regulation can be more effectively juxtaposed South-against-North, offering a more positive regulatory engagement over what are organic features of difference in regulatory cultures and social bonding.

The North/South duality has an established legitimacy in global development scholarship and policy.[18] Our claim to its analytical utility, however, does not rest on political or even analytical orthodoxy. In fact it might be said that the essence of this legitimacy is in its North/South alignment, one which our analysis is committed to challenge and reverse. Our method is constructed to question any notion of legitimate global governance that relies on and is complicit in the elevated regulatory position of the North. Were regulatory legitimacy to depend on reproducing North World neo-liberalist market economies at the expense of and to subjugate the social priorities of the South to economic or monetary motivations of the North, then we reject that legitimacy as central for the critical purpose of our comparative exercise, beyond critiquing its foundations.

It is not inconsistent to accept the relevance of diametric 'worlds' while at the same time arguing against the manner in which this duality has become politicized. The use of these two 'world' paradigms delimits the way in which we (for the purposes of our larger argument about regulatory principle) conceive of 'worlds': not in some grand economic or social development sense, but much more specifically in terms of the way social bonding through embeddedness distinguishes the social/cultural/economic relationships in these different worlds. Applying a distinction resting on degrees of organic social connection (see chapter 3) essential regulatory pre-conditions like state disaggregation and the consequential absence of features of the regulatory state offer (and are offered) distinctly different interpretations. These can be achieved through an initial consideration of regulatory relationships and regulatory projects in the South as compared with the North.

Despite the limitations inherent in this 'worlds' duality, we employ it in an original fashion by reversing the conventional comparative

---

[17]   Another indication of social dislocation is the contemporary emphasis in share valuation on speculative rather than productive profit expectation. Such qualifications, even if they may seem somewhat model, would make manageable the critical reflection on new ways of seeing mechanical purpose for global regulation.

[18]   Dubash and Morgan (2012).

direction – here, from South to North. In so doing the analysis is broken free of the prevailing socio-economic development dogma, and is open to some fundamental reimagining of regulatory principle and policy. In chapters 5 and 6, for instance, we argue that a distinguishing feature of South World economy is its emphasis on sustainability, which, when compared with North World economic emphasis on individualized wealth creation, suggests profoundly different options for regulatory application. Indeed with even a collapse and reconstruction of the social, political and economic arrangements which currently dominate global governance constructions,[19] and the reshuffling of governance priorities economic to social (touching human social organization, the state, and the market), it would be important to understand the *mentality of change* when thinking about the market and how it relates to society, and its place in state and global governance.

The chapter proposes a wholly different comparative perspective from which the analytical focus is formed, such that the illumination of regulatory principle can consciously achieve and maintain a direction opposite to contemporary regulatory convention – from the South to North Worlds. In addition, the comparative referent is no longer captured by the North World regulatory state. However South and North Worlds are conceived, it is no longer necessary, through accepting the over-whelming dominion of a prevailing global economic model, that global regulation must move North to South.

Accepting for the purposes of this chapter that the 'worlds' duality is useful, or at least not an abstraction that impedes a genuine reconsider-ation of regulatory principle, relationships and outcomes (see chapter 3) then it is necessary to flesh out the comparative methodology which will work the duality to its best effect. But first we need to discuss what has and will stand in the way of that analytical outcome, and why global regulatory discourse has not prioritized any such free-wheeling cultural engagement.

IRREDENTIST REGULATORY SCHOLARSHIP – GIVING THE SOUTH A VOICE

In the prevailing North World regulatory literature there is an analytical alliance between consolidated states, economic and political hegemony, and more recently, influence in networks of multi-national corporate

---

[19]   Findlay (2008).

globalization. In any case, the regulatory state is (in the contemporary literature) the indicia of regulatory development in the North World (along with constitutional or reflexive self-regulation). From a South World perspective, mirrors or semblances of the regulatory state also become a feature of regulatory disenfranchisement under the North/South comparative gaze. While it would be over-simplified, however, to distinguish the South World regulatory character again in terms of *states* or more precisely the relationship between the state and the private sector (as a reflection of the stage of development), in the case of South World with its dysfunctional or disaggregated states, exploitative commercial sectors, and denuded regulatory capacity, this is a comparatively distracting reflection. If states and state relations are to more effectively inform the comparative project within and across both worlds, then defining the South World in terms of shared histories of countries rather than the delimitations of political geography or state functionality enables the acknowledgement of diversity within that *world*,[20] particularly in terms of its engagement with globalization.[21] Also, considering the different *lived* histories of cultures and peoples, rather than only their stages of economic modernization or their geo-political value, breaks the comparison free from North-centric temporal and spatial determinants which may tend to justify rather than explain the current analytical focus of global regulation.

The absence of local voices on regulation beyond the state is not the only methodological difficulty facing analytical repositioning. Because of the degradation of national research capacity and empirical foundations in the South World, their often politicized inaccuracy and the propensity of multi-national commerce to conceal their dealings in de-regulated South World development, it is difficult to get any accurate regulatory picture of non-state regulatory initiatives. Even reports from international agencies such as the World Bank[22] tend to be generic.

Compounding the difficulties in this task of unlocking the South as a regulatory player as well as a misunderstood patient and problem is the additional interest of this chapter in alternative motivations for social bonding. To be creative and comprehensive in this regard, the empirical researcher needs to look well beyond potential regulatory scholarship and into the fundamentals of cultural identity, where ignorance of cultural building blocks makes any observation reliant on the filter of translation.

---

20   Dubash and Morgan (2012), p. 261.
21   Findlay (1999).
22   Estache, Rossi and Ruzzier (2002).

As actions carry different meanings and bring different consequences depending on cultural placement,[23] individuals, their perceptions and the context in which their essential frameworks of meaning exist, social actions can be understood as a process of mutual constitution.[24] The set of ideas and values that justifies action, also essential in constituting their cultural context, will be expressed pervasively in many aspects of social life. From a regulatory perspective, the forms of regulation must be sensitive to this 'meaning' loop, if it is to be influential in forms of social bonding. Such bonds, although the subject of regulation, are themselves regulatory forces in action made more powerful because of their organic nature, returning back and legitimating links to the society.

Future empirical enquiry into the transition of regulatory principle and its impact on social solidarity (and vice versa) needs to redirect the originating regulatory research concern to the South World, not for any benevolent levelling of the scholarly playing field but to pragmatically recognize where global crises lie, and how regulatory irredentism has skewed the theoretical and policy interest in regulating global crisis.[25]

For the purposes of this analysis it is necessary to appreciate that distinctions like North/South, developed/underdeveloped, West/East are transitional, and certainly not culturally *pure*. That said, these distinctions form productive foundations for exploring what are the forces that economic and social transition direct towards regulatory need, and how these influences are affected by difference and development in regulatory principle. As with other generalizations on culturally located regulatory principle, it is difficult to construct an overarching regulatory theory which is culturally sensitive and subjective. The answer to the tension between universal and subjective regulatory understandings, we suggest, could be found, for our purposes, in the limited non-Western regulatory literature, distinct from that which has a South World interest but:

- employs the West as the reference point,
- is written by Western scholars or local scholars using Western comparison,
- confines itself to English language writing about indigenous problems and indigenous solutions,
- is not able to sufficiently engage with the influence of colonialism – with post-colonial thinking, and as a consequence, and/or

---

23 Bruner (1990).
24 Fiske, Kitayama, Markus and Nisbett (1998).
25 Findlay (2013a).

- neglects social/cultural integrity because it is influenced by colonization, particularly in the adoption of the regulatory state referent.

Through the recognized influence of externalities in the local regulatory mix, the difficulty with distilling and adapting localized regulatory readings is in distinguishing cultural and social characteristics when they employ common but originally culturally foreign notions of economy and value, such as money. Perhaps this is unavoidable because regulation as a scholarly enterprise is an off-spring of post-Fordian capitalism. Even so, how can research distil concepts of regulation that precede contemporary economy, and are designed to sustain social bonding over materialist advancement? Any search for these socially embedded regulatory principles, relationships and outcomes will be constantly thwarted by the ever-present regulatory overlay of processes sponsored by the state and externally influenced and measured by a world of functioning states and commercial exploiters.

WHAT METHODOLOGY SHOULD INFORM THE QUALITATIVE ENQUIRY INTO CULTURALLY LOCATED REGULATORY PRINCIPLE AND ASSOCIATED FORCES FOR SOCIAL BONDING?

Recognizing the limitations of qualitative enquiry, but more particularly being wary to reduce complex social relations down to units of measurement, it is our argument that context-specific qualitative analysis provides a richer comparative direction when addressing the North South regulatory divide. In favour of this selection is the need to address the transition of regulatory principle from many dimensions, and in a manner allowing for the identification and deconstruction of normative 'shields' (a brief example of this is our later mention of elder care regulation in Singapore). Another justification for a qualitative approach in our regulatory project is the need to marry method with theorizing which employs ideal types and model *states*. As noted on several occasions thus far, a critical concern for this comparative redirection is to better understand the universal referent of the regulatory state North to South, by attempting to reveal its model position, against the strains that emerge in its contextual application. Recognizing as we do that the North/South dichotomy itself is model, the challenge is to employ modelling within theory building and to struggle with identifying and comparing the characteristics of social relationships within model domains. Paradoxically then, we are relying on modelling, made 'live' through rich context-based comparative analysis to critique the analysis of model regulatory states which does not progress to the contextually comparative stage.

Once we accept the premise that there is no gold standard in regulation against which countries measure their regulatory principles, relationships and outcomes, this enables a more creative engagement both with:

- the model states we wish to critique and the nature and impact of their application, and
- the transformative processes of regulatory principle in the particular social contexts identified for comparison.

Contextual immersion is essential prior to any comparative exercise which aims at digging deeper into issues such as the nature of regulatory principle, and the degree that regulatory relationships and outcomes are socially embedded. For example, to the extent to which the United Kingdom sees its healthcare industry as suitably contained within the confines of domestic regulatory regimes and resultant social bonds, its target user is vastly different from that of Singapore, where the industry relies on a mix of private insurance and compulsory state contributions. The different conditions governing the provision and regulation of health services in either context affect a wider range of personal affairs, family sustainability, and the national taxation and insurance mix. In a normative sense the regulatory contexts range from welfarist state health service universal guarantees, to a combination of individualized insurance responsibility, selective but capped state provision, and cost coverage versus profit motivations for industry participation.

Levi-Faur has identified four types of similarities and variations to build into designing comparative research of regulation: cross-national, cross-sectoral, international regime-wise and temporal.[26] Depending on the type of similarities/variations the research design chooses to examine, one can explain such phenomena by forces operating at the chosen level. For example, variations in the stage of regulatory development across nations could be explained by differences in the political processes and outcomes which in turn affect the regulatory development of these nations. By adopting a technique of compound designs to maximize the explanatory power of variations and similarities, the proposed solution is a regulatory form which takes into account the forces operating depending on the spatial and interconnected focus adopted (nation/sector/

---

[26]   Levi-Faur (2004).

international influence/temporal), offering a stepwise analysis that would arguably achieve a more well-rounded research outcome.[27]

What the Levi-Faur schema tends to underplay, and we wish to confront, is the *model nature* of his distinguishers; the nation, the sector, international, and across time. It might equally well be argued that not to look at these as discreet *steps* in some more dynamic comparative analysis is to unnecessarily contain their essential and constant inter-action. This is more than a concern about research frame. It highlights a deeper consideration of the *process* involved in comparative engagement. Should not the comparative referents however selected be first analyzed in terms of the interaction between these four criteria (or any other) to establish their contextual reality and to suggest the more informative interactions which would reveal much through a later comparison?

Moving beyond analyses for the purposes of explaining differences in existing regulatory situations whether by nation, sector or otherwise, we hope to understand firstly why some societies are constructed with particular institutions, while others are able to do without. In using comparative analysis in this way, we will deepen our understanding of the relationship between institutions, processes and social bonding against the generation and influence of particular regulatory principles. In singling out the identified social factors and bonding relationships for comparison, it is not unhelpful to drill down into national patterns, policies delineated according to sectors, the strength and scope of the international regime which touches the national and the sectoral, and each against historically specific temporal patterns. That said, these four fields of analytical tempor suggest that the resultant analysis is constructed with an inherent bias as these factors are prioritized from a Western viewpoint. Taking Berthoud's criticism of particular perspectives necessarily having their own culturally bounded conceptions[28] in revealing and thus acknowledging such limitations of comparative methodologies, the irredentist trap in such comparison can be reduced by having the process governed by sophisticated theorizing of unity and diversity within and across societies and cultures.

More than explaining the outcome of comparisons, theorizing can be a tool for thinking about regulation as a form of bonding within society. Our argument of regulation as social bonding depends on multitudes of interactions taking place amongst people in society, and regulation may only pick up on a subset of these myriad bonds. As a case in point, in

---

[27]   Ibid.
[28]   Berthoud (1990), p. 172.

Singapore, legal regulation may step in to require the maintenance of aged parents by providing rights to these parents to claim financial support and monetary contribution against their children.[29] Whether these rights are actionable and if indeed will be exercised, depends on a range of factors such as whether the abandoned parent is subject to abuse and thereby the endangering influence of his or her children, whether the children as between themselves have an arrangement for provision of welfare for the parent, and other issues which essentially reflect the internal affairs and relations between persons of the family. These issues are in turn tied up with the question of the role of the state in providing social welfare to the elderly persons in society, and consequentially also questions of taxation and public health insurance. In this way, we see regulation as a mechanical interference into the relations and interactions which grow organically out of persons coming together as a society.

The regulation of elder care identifies an interesting example where reflecting on cultural archetypes is not sufficient for understanding the nature of regulation. Asian values are said to be evidenced in the respect accorded parents and grandparents. The introduction of some legal back-up for this respect bond is not a denial of those values. However, the complexity of regulatory principle and its multi-layered meanings are not at first apparent if enquiry is fascinated by cultural values alone. The true nature of regulatory principle and its hierarchies can depend on market analysis as well as regard for social and cultural bonding. In societies such as Singapore, where the workforce demographic contains a significant reserve of cheap domestic migrant labour, the maid becomes the essential mechanism to make filial piety a household reality. Above elder respect, Singapore is ruled by the prevailing regulatory commitment for economic growth. All other regulatory principles are subservient to this. With the male and female bread-winners engaged in wage labour, their contribution to the economy could not be sustained in the context of a non-welfarist state, were it not for the affordable availability of cheap migrant domestic workers as care-givers for the young and old. Therefore a market analysis of workforce contexts is an essential complement to suggestions of Asian values and filial piety if an understanding of the

---

[29] The Maintenance of Parents Act (Cap. 167B) states that any Singapore resident, 60 years old and above, who is unable to maintain himself adequately, is entitled to claim maintenance from his children, either in a lump-sum payment, or in the form of monthly allowances. Relatives or caregivers may apply for court action on a parent's behalf, with the parent's consent.

principles behind the regulation of elder care is ventured in Singapore. Neither cultural values nor the *Maintenance of Parents Act* alone tells the story.

If we draw a distinction between mechanical and organic types of social bonding (which will be elaborated on in chapter 3), this too is useful for explaining context-specific variants in regulatory principle and associated forces. Regulatory principle here refers to the value supporting a particular scheme of regulation, or the direction that regulation moves society towards. This is similar to the concept of *sitte* used by Hegel in connoting the mores and customs operating in a communicative and productive manner as amongst those within a social unit, quite apart from laws that are seen as a province of the state or moral norms that lie within the minds of individuals (such that consensus becomes a problem for the former instead of the end result).[30] In this light, the unity of universal and individual freedom that is largely unrecognized in the worldview of regulation today acquires a special significance for this book (see in chapters 4 and 7 a deeper discussion of liberty through contexts of mutuality and social responsibility). Public life does not have to be viewed as the outcome of mutual restrictions of personal liberties on the part of each individual within a society, but it could and indeed should be the platform for providing opportunities where the fulfillment of each and every individual's freedom is assured through social responsibility.[31] Similarly, by extrapolating Hegel's reversal of the state-individual relationship, it is our argument that instead of taking socialization to be something that is the outcome of mechanical regulation, underlying regulatory principle should exhibit and understand natural (thereby organic) solidarity as the regulatory force supporting such cohesion. In this way, wider organic social bonding grows from the solidarity of individual actors within that society which, as Hegel argues, exists *a priori*.

Once we acknowledge the desire for social and mutual recognition[32] at the individual level, society can never only, or even primarily, be reducible to relations for the furtherance of simple economic self-interest.[33] By investing regulatory norms with intrinsic social meaning directed for and by solidarity, the inter-subjective struggle for recognition by each individual is given a place at the societal level as is reconciled and resolved through frameworks of mutualizing interests (see chapter 7).

---

[30] Honneth (1995).
[31] Rawls (2008), p. 224.
[32] Rawls (2008), pp. 62–3.
[33] Fukuyama (2011), p. 45.

Without compatible regulatory principles, the regulatory organization of society (economic and beyond) cannot be said to have legitimacy through mutuality given that individuals subject themselves to and abide by the rules merely out of self-interest.

Order through organic solidarity is an ideal and itself has value but this is not enough on which to ground a radical argument for the repositioning of regulatory principle. This book posits much practical justification for this repositioning and provides sociability as a mechanism for its achievement (see chapters 5 and 7).[34]

CRITIQUE OF THE DIFFUSION APPROACH

Once we accept the premise that the conception of regulation derives or at least inherits its meaning, in the form of regulatory principle, from *the regulated*, it becomes a contextual apparatus of its subjects, not essentially of the state. This is the starting point for our critique of the diffusion approach, and in chapters to follow it gives a constituency and a social responsibility to our conceptualization of sustainability.

Diffusion is the notion that the regulatory order, shaped in some dominant countries and sectors, is then transported (not necessarily translated) to the rest of the world, thereby leading to regulatory colonization and expansion.[35] Whether this takes place via the vertical, top-down or bottom-up approaches or is more lateral in its intrusion, diffusion promotes the regulatory state as a transplantable model. Along with this general position comes an attendant growth of regulatory agencies to manifest state regulatory capacity, capturing the worlds, where institutions of state governance can support or at least not subvert such influences, particularly in contexts of transitional development. In terms of global regulatory agendas, this takes place through networks specialised around economic issues and commercial sectors,[36] or where governments subject to strong influence from hegemonic world powers with economic regulatory agendas of their own kick-starting an adoption of the global model as regulatory reform. Regulatory solutions shaped and growing out of North America and Europe are increasingly internationalized and projected globally even in transitional or fragmented

---

[34] Findlay (2013a).
[35] Levi-Faur (2005), p. 24.
[36] Ibid, pp. 26–7.

state settings, despite the challenges and dislocations such developments encounter.[37]

In this process of grafting where consideration of the suitability and sustainability of regulatory reform for the particular social context is not central in the transmigration process, regulatory 'reform' may prove to be little more than an exercise in creating new opportunities for governance dysfunction and external mechanical market exploitation. Take for instance where the regulatory strategy requires transparency for efficacy and legitimacy, or trust and goodwill for collaboration. In disaggregated states with predatory commercial sectors and weak institutions of governance, the absence of these conditions can be turned into opportunities for corruption and exploitation.[38] Conventional networks of productive cultural bonding can also be perverted in such regulatory abstractions when regulatory solutions prescribed by atomistic theories of society which designate the individual as the basic unit for analysis. In more communitarian social contexts, individualist regulatory transplants have little resonance except as creating possibilities to distort conventional social bonds for individual wealth creation in societies where benefit is more commonly mutualized.[39] For neo-liberal regulatory construction, the interests and actions of individuals within the society are thus assumed to have at least some regulatory convergence in such societies, to the extent that social values and institutions become viewed as compatible with individual wealth creation.

Where social solidarity is deeply communitarian, regulation to protect individualized benefit presents a denial of forces that bond society. Furthermore, regulatory principle favouring this atomistic view of society directs its attention to individualized interests (particularly in private property relations as discussed in chapter 4), and in so doing ignores general benefit which in North World settings might be ensured by responsible corporate frameworks, functioning states or a vibrant civil society.

Further, proponents of a diffusion approach towards regulatory development often raise the argument that regulatory mechanisms comprise no more than a simple coordination of human actions through employing the use of incentives (both positive and negative in nature). If this is so then regulatory universalism rises above contextual variance in application. A compatible legalist approach to regulatory principle and frames (such as

---

[37] Ibid, p. 13.
[38] Findlay (2013b).
[39] Orton (1930), p. 636.

justice is ensured through a dogma of equality before the law), considers peoples not as moral beings in complex arrangements of social responsibility,[40] but primarily as *homo economicus* (self-interested individuals merely responding to such incentives without essential consideration of the value behind the rules which protect and exclude self-interest).[41] The individualization of regulatory focus discounts the role that shared moral and cultural beliefs, and that familial and community ties play in personal decision-making and preferencing. Over-individualization of regulatory principle and practice, especially in contexts where communitarian bonding is legitimate and otherwise valued, risks the alienating consequences of a regulatory project dis-embedded from other important solidarity forces.

Any approach to regulatory principle and process which values contextual foundation cannot escape the issue of ethics which inform principle as a critical characteristic of social identity. Such ethics exist often in the form of religion, and as Weber investigates in *The Protestant Ethic,* celebrate the presence of the individual as the focus of human activity and material interest. Particularly as an explanation of why wage labour chimes with an individualist ethic Weber suggests that the values of Protestantism frame a chief human motivation for work as an individualized method for personal wealth creation.[42] Thereby this work ethic regulates the sustainability of individuals and societies in terms of individualist responsibility and reward for its recognition.[43]

The significance of a protestant ethic for the development of capitalism as the currently prevailing global economic paradigm lies in its cognitive legitimation of the acquisition of goods by men through its emphasis on wage labour as a necessary and legitimate means for doing so.[44] To morally confirm individualized wealth creation through this ethic, a combination of the limits placed on consumption and acquisitive human action inevitably resulted in the accumulation of capital through the religious instillation of the compulsion to save. In this otherwise frugal context, a distribution of resources which grows out of the authority of religious beliefs gives the individual a socially dangerous sense of

---

[40] Rawls (2001).

[41] Fukuyama (2011), p. 120.

[42] Fukuyama (2011), p. 162.

[43] As we suggest in our concluding chapter, this becomes an ethic open to discrimination and oppression when labour values vary greatly from market to market and where access to wage labour is mechanically constricted through frames such as structural unemployment.

[44] Weber (1930a).

entitlement to the resources he has amassed and indeed attributes a moral duty to the continued practice of wealth accumulation. This pattern of the regular reproduction of capital through continual investment and reinvestment, the spirit of modern capitalism, is itself foreign to traditional types of enterprise associated with the acquisition of wealth to satisfy subsistence needs and communal benefit, preferring the accumulation of wealth for its own sake.[45] It is also paradoxically opposed to other fundamentals of its own religion such as the prohibition of usury. In this respect the ethic grows to serve the chosen economic order.

Framed in this way, it becomes clear that capitalism and the use of economic rewards and punishment associated with individualized wealth creation and justified by its supporting ethic cannot be the only regulatory framework for understanding and regulating human behaviour, no matter how potent is its legitimating potential. Indeed, other strong ethical and economic alliances successfully preceded capitalism for centuries and co-exist with it in other social frames. The South World, even in transitional states, is predominantly influenced by other ethics and operates, modifies or promotes subsistence economic orders. By singularly preferring an incentive-based approach towards regulation as the sole determinant of economic and social regulatory outcomes, the ethic and its principles are neglecting the very real possibility that the actual workings of any transplant of regulatory design that has yielded some measure of success elsewhere would always be replicable despite profound variations in the social relationships and ethical foundations of the host country. This de-contextualized exportation of principle and practice puts regulation at the forefront of a much more pervasive colonial enterprise North to South.

Acknowledging that material gain is but one factor operating in a menu of positive and negative regulatory options all dependent for their impact on social resonance as much as efficacy in more developed economic and political systems, brings regulatory and social sustainability into focus. This is so, we later demonstrate, particularly now that the capitalist world system and its individualizing ethical legitimacy are being deeply questioned in these terms, as is their market frameworks which have progressively dis-embedded from their social locations and responsibilities.

The diffusion approach sees regulation, which is in our consideration manifest through the management of social rules, in the limited terms of functional utility. As a result, the subjectively experienced coherence of

---

[45]   Weber (1930b), p. xi.

any society is diminished in the analysis of regulatory transmission and its benefits, and an approach towards regulatory design and development based on such a limited understanding of social relevance would be similarly limited. It is our argument that a diffusion approach reflecting even unconsciously some colonial transplant of the global regulatory state model is unsustainable in principle and practice, certainly for those cultures with differing ethical emphasis and social arrangements. For global regulation in the future, with ever-diminishing natural resources, contracting capital bases relative to exploding populations, and slowing economic growth, such an economic model also has passed its utility. The regulatory principles, relationships and outcomes which currently shore up the capitalist model are no longer sustainable nor will ensure sustainable societies. We will make this argument in two stages; first, that the use of legal transplants is inherently problematic when we track the development of the regulatory state as the perceived link between economic growth and any essential unhitching of regulatory functions from political priorities (see chapter 4); second, that the regulatory state framework may not be a natural transition for particular societies. Ultimately, the legitimacy of the governance framework in place in any regulatory context which is socially resonant, derives out of structures that adhere to the social solidarity achieved through active and dynamic social relationships rather than mechanical economic regulation (see chapters 5 and 6).

Failures of a Legal Transplant Approach

The theory of regulatory competition proposes that the major motivation for regulatory reform is to appease and attract capital through a commitment to attractive market environments and a stable regime for investment.[46] This view accepts that delegating regulatory functions to agencies independent from political pressure gives credibility to that country's governance system. Colin Scott expands on this by arguing for independent regulation to be viewed as a form of governance distinct from the state, without need for a dependency on state law.[47] For instance, the injection of capital into a country's economy, particularly where the legal framework protecting consequent property rights remains formative and less well-developed than in consolidated states with sophisticated markets, locates within the four corners of the contract. In the event of

---

[46] Gilardi, Jordana and Levi-Faur (2006), p. 8.
[47] Scott (2004).

failures in the commercial trust relationship, enforcement through court procedures is necessary for contract rights to become actionable and thereby valuable. Because of the need to maintain consistency in the government's approach towards outside investors and direct capital investment sources, together with the worry that expropriation might be politically motivated and personally incentivized, the regulatory argument runs that independence of these decisions is key.

Behind any such assumption, however, is the presumed legitimacy of the contract form, and the actuality of legal frameworks and institutions which will effectively ratify contracts when the form is subverted. In addition, there needs in civil society to be a consciousness that respects or at least fears the contract form making its regulatory significance through general contract compliance rather than the eventual back up of capable and inclined legal institutions. We will argue, concerning the transformation of legal regulation as it presently protects private property rights (see chapter 7), that the failure of contractual *ethics* in current commercial practice means that even if these instruments are enforceable they may not produce sustainable market arrangements (see chapter 5 in which we detail this concerning migrant labour contracting).

With alternative solutions to the less rigorous institutionalization of property rights protection through domestic law and its enforcement, such as the signing of bilateral investment treaties, and the availability of arbitration and other dispute settlement agreements, these regulatory legitimators come with their own set of regulatory complications. Alternative regulatory options may encourage forum selection or present problems with maintaining the consistency and hence predictability of decisions and regulatory outcomes. Again, the legitimacy of what these institutions and processes would be required to enforce, along with the legitimacy of their enforcement decisions, may be critical to a positive regulatory climate in terms of world-to-world economic arrangements. None of this can be assumed in disaggregated states or predatory commercial environments.

The foundational motivations for developing a regulatory state framework ultimately stem from the desire to establish strong rule-based or constitutional regulatory paradigms.[48] From the position primarily of economic regulatory principle the regulatory state framework is intended to assure investors of the state's aversion to the arbitrary expropriation of foreign capital. Once we understand this foundational basis and work from this understanding, the next question arises: does the regulatory

---

[48]   Black (2010).

enterprise, by way of the legal transplantation of a global regulatory state model, in the case of all states and societies serve that purpose of building a strong rule of law or other constitutional regulatory frames? The simple answer in the context of disaggregated states with predatory markets is that the appearance or trappings of these governance characteristics attendant on the regulatory state model could be at best no more than the emperor's new clothes; pretending security of investment and offering not even the cloak of basic protections. Developing global regulatory agendas through diffusion can amount to not more than borrowing the institutions and agencies as governance indicators of a regulatory state framework that prevails in the North World of consolidated states and accountable markets. This policy of mimicking is a pretence which encourages risky capital investment and offers profligate regulatory transparency and transaction.

That is an approach that sees institutional design as a mechanism for altering the relationship between private investors and governments[49] which is, once again, a return to the consolidated North World state referent, neither necessarily useful nor realistic when we consider the disaggregated nature of many South World states and societies.

THE POWER OF CULTURAL CONTEXT

An important starting point for this book is that cultural values lending meaning to human life and ensuring firm social bonds are created by specific processes of social development (see chapter 4).[50] More than monitoring human conduct in economic action, the understanding of a deeper regulatory social meaning is essential to explain human action. Within this, economic life has to be examined in the context (and not as the basis) of the historical development of a culture as a whole. By adopting a diffusion approach to regulatory migration and transformation, the recent phenomenon in the North for the delegation of decision-making authority from the executive branch of government to technocrats and regulatory agencies has meant that developing countries struggle to attempt achieving some form of constitutional regulatory arrangements that might be seen as natural and legitimate in the North.

It is our argument here that the primary failure of the diffusion approach stems from an inadequate appreciation of the place of contextual meaning and essential regulatory social value/principle particularly in

---

[49]   Gilardi, Jordana and Levi-Faur (2006).
[50]   Weber (1930b), p. ix.

situations where the regulatory state is either a modification or even a shadow of its North World form, something which is not simply or accurately explained by the failings of South World regulatory principle (see chapter 3). Without understanding the diminished role that economic action should play in evaluating the conditions for transforming regulatory principle to enhance bonds of social sustainability, and the need to first culturally adapt regulatory migration North to South (such as through more indigenous legal transplants) to the local conditions and particularities, the diffusion approach will not produce sustainable regulation or regulation focused on sustainability as we later define it.

Is the Regulatory State Framework as Universal as we Presume it to Be?

Regulation can be viewed in political, structural terms in the North World, as a transformation from representative democracy to indirect representative, majoritarian democracy. In this sense the delegation of regulatory authority is no longer to elected representatives, but experts supervised by elected representatives with power to formulate and administer policies autonomously.[51] The associated argument for the rise of the regulatory state and its constituent regulatory institutions sees trust as the answer to a diminution of democratic responsibility.

Growing trust in regulatory institutions, principles, relationships and outcomes reduces concerns regarding transparency and accountability, at least in terms of narrower evaluations of regulatory legitimacy.[52] However, in developing countries, the transposition of responsibility for regulatory projects from fundamental organic structures of social bonds in complex civil society, to a negotiation between disaggregated states, predatory commercial arrangements, and an under-resourced and often compromised technocracy is a recipe at least for further society/state disengagement. The consequence is a greater distancing of regulatory accountability from institutions and mechanisms which have the peoples' trust. An example of such disappointment is the case of the electrical industry in Brazil.[53] The Brazilian experience shows that the political economy of the host country can often be an impediment to institutional reform in developing countries. It may be that the regulatory state framework is not as universal and pervasive as it is presumed to be. Because political institutions align with how self-interest is constructed

---

[51] Levi-Faur (2005), p. 13.
[52] Jordana and Levi-Faur (2004), chapter 1.
[53] Prado (2008).

within the disaggregated state,[54] the particular notions of regulated self-interest and recurrent legitimacy to support that framework may not exist such that the political order as an authority for regulation is compromised and de-legitimated in the minds of civil society.

The social expectations for the regulatory state may differ distinctly between South/North. Instead of regulatory principle and practice single-mindedly pursuing bureaucratic independence for investor protection, in disaggregated states such independence impairs the government's ability to control inflation or to protect legitimate consumer interests, or even to intervene in unhealthy synergies between the executive, technocrats and investors to the detriment of social sustainability. Prado argues that sometimes in social circumstances where the executive, the technocrat and the investor are connected through individualized and exclusionist self-interest, governments have legitimate reasons to exercise bureau-cratic power and it could be that governments can contribute in a positive way to the country's development in so doing.[55] Furthermore, where the state still has an effective hand in regulatory matters, regulation can be the outcome of the totality of governance, as opposed to decisions of only regulatory agencies.

In India, for example, the judiciary through its power as a constitu-tional check against the legislature had pushed often-corrupt governments towards a regulatory model characterized by independent regulatory authorities.[56] Further, the judiciary exercised its regulatory authority in relation to state agencies and other policy-making bodies by requiring them to conduct themselves as active trustees for the public goods. In the Indian example, the ultimate regulatory outcome was a product of the actions and authority exercised by a variety of different actors who might or might not be considered part of the state machinery. It is important to remember that despite its disaggregation, elements of the state and the executive have efficient and effective regulatory super-structures. In India, even with the state's disaggregation through corruption and nepo-tism at all levels, the Indian courts and judiciary have, since independ-ence, been largely impartial, interventionist and eager to perform their oversight role in the separation of powers. This balance is just what may be missing in our case-study of migrant labour markets in Singapore (see chapter 5).

---

[54] Fukuyama (2011), p. 7.
[55] Prado (2008).
[56] Thiruvengadam and Joshi (2012).

The transactability of the regulatory state model is not supported, particularly in the South World, by a clear public private divide, which can have a critical influence on the regulatory maintenance of competitive markets. The inherent arbitrariness of determining which side of the state–private divide a particular actor stands means that in social contexts wherein the two sectors are weak or indistinct, the transposition of regulatory state controls as some public private partnership is unrealistic and open to abuse. Nor can the regulatory state model rely on healthy competition between private and public interests to modify regulatory investment and mediate regulatory outcomes.

In disaggregated states (or even in transitional states such as that discussed in chapter 5) the separation of powers model is unclear or certainly unreliable. To what extent can the judiciary be considered part of the state, when some features of its purpose are to serve as a check against the government and legislature? The degree to which we can or cannot say that independent regulatory agencies are separate from the state machinery will in weak states be more a matter of essential social bonding than the governance niceties of the regulatory state. Reasons for this lie in the reality that the regulatory state model is grown from contexts where the regulatory mix is diverse and vigorous, and independence from state, commercial or community interests is possible, sustainable and legitimate even with representative democracies.

Focusing for the purposes of argument on regulation emanating out of the state sphere, the question we are concerned with is whether the state–private dichotomy is useful even if it could be universally applied across the range of cultures and societies. In Fukuyama's example of the transplant of Westminster style government to Melanesian societies, the 'wantok' tribal arrangement, which characterizes traditional Papua New Guinean society, has the leader accountable to his 'wantok' or descent group.[57] As a result, the norms of a Weberian bureaucratic-rational state fail to be cultivated within such societies. The distribution of public resources becomes centred around the tribal arrangement or descent group instead of the much broader sense of people of that nation. To view this reality from a North World regulatory state lens would produce the conclusion that politicians in Papua New Guinea are corrupt and civil society is ungoverned. A view from the South World regulatory lens would emphasize the power of social bonds to adapt sometimes dysfunctional diffused regulatory and governance institutions.

---

[57] Fukuyama (2011), p. 1.

At the supra-national level, we will interrogate whether the use of a state referent when thinking about regional and global regulation is counterproductive. The United States and Europe are two powerful global hegemonies which exercise regulation as a form of global political influence to advance the interests of their own constituencies in the global arena.[58] By reinforcing the state referent at the supranational level without qualifying this context with considerations of hegemony and power imbalance, the self-interest of each state is likely to take precedence over the mutualized regulatory interests of both worlds. A counterbalance to this is the construction of regulatory interests around a global issue, irrespective of the hegemonic location of the community affected by those issues, and apart from the use of state-drawn boundaries, in order to encourage a more inclusive and hence sustainable global response as regulatory principle and practice.[59] It is interesting that in microcosm we will explore the power imbalance which prevails in contracting party relationships where law enforces private property rights often inequitably within and without the contract's domain (see chapter 5). This mirrors the regulatory distortions out of hegemonic interests propagated as international relations and we suggest central to the problematic diffusion of the regulatory state model North to South.

For the purposes of evaluating regulatory efficiency or legitimacy, if the comparison remains with a North World regulatory state, it is not surprising that there is a poor fit in these disaggregated state contexts between the existing normative order and the regulatory principles that belie that social order, and the social structure and the kinds of institutions transposed from the Western model. For instance, the delegation of decision-making authority to an independent regulatory agency necessarily involves the introduction of a large amount of discretion for decision-making, and the regulatory state model therefore depends upon large-scale administrative reform, concentrating primarily on the decentralization of authority to the lower levels of the bureaucracy. In disaggregated states these administrative levels are rarely democratically responsible or accountable to even fragile institutions of governance oversight (critical for Polanyi in determining social responsibility). Such a project of reform requires as a precondition a competent, compliant and corruption-averse civil service to establish a baseline of responsible and capable but principled administrative decision-making at all levels.[60]

---

58 Levi-Faur (2005), pp. 13–14.
59 Findlay (2013a).
60 Schick (1998).

Without ensuring that such a condition precedent has been satisfied, the bureaucracy would be a vulnerable weak-link in the oversight necessity, and the granting of more discretion to more autonomous one-to-one decision sites will simply open the discretionary chain to greater politicization. This has been precisely the experience of developing states, which are more often than not overrun by administrative inefficiencies and corrupt governments. The answer therefore is not in some contextually strained reproduction of North World regulatory state machinery, but rather realistic investment in contextually appropriate oversight of life-structure and processes.

Even with capacity building aid and administrative support from external donors, whether in the form of an international aid organization or programmes initiated by stronger state neighbours,[61] developing countries struggle with the need for regulatory competencies without technical knowledge about public administration and the specific requirements for particular industries. Donor-supported state building projects often trigger questions about indigenous derivations of the rule of law and associated administrative independence amongst those within that society. Aid dependencies, especially when it comes to critical governance frames, can do little more than offer a regulatory overlay which is unlikely to socially embed and thereby gain the local legitimacy necessary for its success and sustainability. In fact these dependencies can stifle organic and resilient developments of regulatory hybrids to counter domestic governance challenges and thereby neuter civil society as a change agent and an owner of its regulatory destiny.

The critical issue to be drawn from regulatory transplantation is one of scope (once social relevance has been addressed) – which reforms are ones that can be (successfully) promoted by international donors, and which are those that *must* be undertaken by political actors within the given society. The scope for donor-driven action is much smaller than that for indigenously grown reform projects. Projects initiated by external donors often begin with an involvement in the public sector, and demonstrating less of a tendency for the intervener to engage with the private sector.[62] However, in many cases, donors have a much stronger desire to bring about particular reforms (for their own internationalist agendas) than do many local societal actors. External donors need to be

---

[61] See for example the Australia's Enhanced Cooperation Program and the Regional Assistance Mission to the Solomon Islands.

[62] Fukuyama (2007), p. 7.

realistic about their potential leverage when contemplating the transplantation of regulatory reform, and this requires at the very least recognizing the positive and negative potentials of the existing socio-political system.

In the private sector both North and South, local and international, we see the emerging preference for voluntary regulatory norms, as opposed to those that find their source in the state, created by societal actors often in response to perceived failures of state action. Such regulatory dimensions have a bottom-up effect in terms of the shift in awareness of regulatory principles, relationships and outcomes. Private actors are often *repeat players* in the regulatory coordination game who understand the dynamics which operate within that particular industry or sector, and can manipulate regulatory projects to particular commercial interests. The bottom-up evolution of regulatory projects, specifically out of socially embedded market contexts, can be especially valuable for developing countries characterized by weak state capacity to promulgate and enforce regulation,[63] and when market players and civil society are actually more aware of the workings of the market than those at the top or from outside. In addition, bottom-up regulatory evolution is likely to consequentially generate more rooted social legitimacy and associated oversight reiteration without external resistance.

Cultural Relativity without Relativism

Where the source of a particular regulatory norm locates in the state, and reform is initiated at that level, the process involves the projection of enforcement power throughout society. Notwithstanding the authority of the state, the strength of the society and its ability to resist such penetration is the counteraction to top-down regulatory imposition. This social reactivity and its impact depends on a variety of factors most of which go toward the legitimacy of the state action, or of external commercial/administrative intervention. It is often that socio-economic modernization will be unable to break down the social structures already in place without locating regulatory principle in the hands of the legitimate elements within civil society. The regulatory empowerment of civil society through the decentralization of regulatory authority moves in two directions: the first is the more noticeable mobilization of resistance against the consolidated state/commercial authority which can grow to acquire its own socio-political revolutionary potential, and the other less acknowledged ingredient is the strength of the state/commerce nexus to

---

[63] Braithwaite (2006).

take action and indeed, to effect desired changes, when necessary, even against popular resistance.[64]

By way of illustration, consider a change in employment structure particularly when introduced in a drastic manner, for example – the withdrawal of massive amounts of investment from the labour-intensive manufacturing industries in the developed North World consequent on the opening up of cheap labour manufacturing opportunities in the developing South. Without a state/society regulatory alliance that can manage such a shift in demand for human employment, and provide relief in periods of unemployment, the fractured social structures which pre-existed that workforce change cannot simply be replaced by the restructuring rigours of modernization when the displacement of manual labour by a technologized workforce does not provide material and social benefits across the social frame. Further, more difficult is the renegotiation of essential trust relationships between private actors and the state, if the private sector is left to face and manage the rancour of a displaced workforce. The sharing of regulatory principle and regulatory responsibility is critical if the austerity/restructuring medicine is to be taken by all for more than the benefit of the few.

The strength of state authority is often the missing connection when we think about governance through government, with strength here directly influencing legitimacy, and not one based on mere formal rationality.[65] Such conditions can be frequently observed in the less-developed South, where poor governance is a deep-rooted problem. In such circumstances, Krasner has explored the viability of a model of shared sovereignty for development projects instigated by international organizations. His model envisages external actors (most of which come from a North World background) playing the role of trustees or guarantors.[66] These can be specifically directed towards managing the use of the revenues from development projects, such that they would be funnelled towards similar aims or infrastructural needs, instead of potentially corrupt ends.

Corruption, we argue, can thus be constructed as a form of social order (or more precisely, disorder) that exists in the environment where modernization plans are hatched. By ignoring the stake that people have in their country's development direction and approaching and then dealing only with the state which robs the people of their community

---

[64] Balbus (1973), pp. 2–4; Fukuyama (2011), p. 431.
[65] Balbus (1973), pp. 7–15.
[66] Krasner (2004).

security and value frameworks, the regulatory strategies designed to lift South World societies out of poverty through maximizing their resources (human and otherwise) often fail to demolish the problematic social relations that in fact inhibit growth beyond the economic sense, that is, sustainable growth.

Where-to Contextual Relativism?

In seeking to avoid the myopia of cultural relativism when endeavouring to answer the myopia of mono-cultural imperialism, we advance the use of a comparative contextual approach facilitated primarily by case-studies and a qualitative analytical method (see chapters 5 and 6). Deep contextual *drilling* prior to any comparative endeavour enables the researcher to recognize the image of the South as the impotent recipient of an imperialist development trajectory, and to see the creative solutions that enable regulatory coordination in forms that have been marginalized from the North because of the subordination of social relations to the dominant economic system.[67]

As we elaborate on later, looking at cultural relativity and specifically global economic divisions in any model form has its dangers. Further-more, regulatory development is broader than the sense in which it is often used, that is, referring simply to economic modernization. Taking regulation to be the intervention and construction of social bonding, cultures and peoples necessarily become a greater part of the regulatory project than wealth creation, and we represent this below through our discussion of embeddedness.

COMPARATIVE CONTEXTUAL APPROACH – FOCUSING ON THE FOUNDATIONAL IDEOLOGIES FROM WHICH ORGANIC REGULATORY MODELS GROW – LINKING BETWEEN CONTEXT AND REGULATION

Organic regulation that fosters and is fostered by social bonding itself is subject to the core social principles to which any particular society subscribes. These principles form the bonding contexts, and here such contexts are explained in summary to draw the connection between context, and the manner in which regulation is rationalized. The method

---

[67]   Polanyi (1944), p. xxv.

thus moves beyond regulatory scholarship to engage important cultural languages which explain social bonding and suggest locations for qualitative enquiry.

Qualitative Enquiry into Social Bonding as Regulation

To invigorate our assertion concerning the value of cognitive investigation we look briefly at an external regulatory oversight option popular in the developed North World – audit. The essence of *audit* for the North World regulatory state is a useful example of the tensions between mechanical and organic regulation measured as a reflection of social bonding, and in terms of regulatory capacity to seek and establish legitimacy through socially accepted oversight. North World regulatory states are said to have created an audit society, that is, 'a collection of systematic tendencies... the extreme case of checking gone wild, of ritualized practices of verification whose technical efficacy is less significant than their role in the production of organizational legitimacy'.[68]

The audit regulatory strategy approaches trust and accountability by forcing oversight beyond internal compliance or social emancipation, presuming that trust relationships, if they remain, have become a mechanism of concealment or at the very least require external verification for their legitimacy. While audit has a medium-term potential to return legitimacy through the revelation of trust, corrupted or other deviant forms of mutuality conceal inappropriate self-interest. In the short term external oversight risks annihilating fragile trust bonds and often misunderstanding strong social bonds which in part require the safety of intimate social location. In addition, performed inadequately, audit only offers another quasi legitimating process whereby regulatory malpractice is concealed.

Alternate to the oversight of external audit, the strategy in more primitive societies may be to seek instead the cultivation and nurturing of trust through maintaining symmetry and centricity within society. By ensuring reciprocity and redistribution as the goals of behaviour, trust makes for the dutiful discharge of obligations because each person's interest is in the health and continued existence of their community. In a simpler sense, trust enables each self-interested person to appreciate giving as receiving, because of their vested interest in the shared growth of their economy/society as a common good.

---

[68]   Levi-Faur (2005), p. 21.

Similar to the pros and cons of external audit as an oversight legitimator is the North World governance characteristic of *political liberty*. Notwithstanding the desired results of political liberty as a check and balance over autonomous and non-accountable governance, the institutions and structures set up to generate a tension between the state and its subjects as a regulatory balance, and preserving the difficult coexistence of the two has led to political instability in the North World, and even more common violent insurgency in fragmented South World state arrangements.[69] We examine the natural nexus between social liberty and social responsibility in chapters to follow (see chapters 3 and 4).

When looking at the options of more complicated, externalized, socially dis-embedded and force-based or individualized oversight regimes in order to ensure regulatory purchase and legitimacy, regulatory growth and transplantation may neither provide answers to the problem of political irresponsibility or to the concealment of economic risk. The search for oversight mechanisms which can consolidate the broadest social legitimacy where states are weak and commerce is predatory, needs to be located at the deeper social level. Here demands for legitimacy in an atmosphere of well-placed trust are revealed, as socially sustainable regulatory policy entwines with broader organic social bonding. Our method is a pathway to this exposing and appreciating this nexus.

CONCLUSION

The next two chapters argue North World regulatory principle operates within consolidated state frameworks, dislocated market societies, and reflects socially dis-embedded productivity relationships. The same could be said for dominant economic regulatory scholarship. More recent efforts to develop critical analysis of South World regulatory problems and answers have consistently remained connected to the referent of the regulatory state. This chapter has questioned the direction and utility of such analysis that does not sufficiently engage with South World regulatory environments, being largely subject to North World state interests and multi-national opportunism fostered by disaggregated, often dysfunctional, domestic states. The methodology we have just encountered is a

---

[69] Dobransky (2012).

call to break free of the regulatory state referent and to engage in a comparative exercise on more organic terms world-to-world.

If, as in many South World contexts, the state is dysfunctional or destructive in translating regulatory principle, then is it instructive or indeed balanced to pose the world-to-world regulatory comparison through a prism of the regulatory state? The chapter suggests that such a comparative preference may be the product of researches into transitional states where North World influence and regulatory aspirations are evident in their regulatory hybrids and limited indigenous success stories. For the vast terrain outside transition, where disaggregated states become the easy targets for critical comparative research, can an alternative research focus be suggested which recognizes new measures for regulatory enterprise? The chapters to follow propose socially embedded market conditions (rather than failed state frameworks), and a different view of market economies, as analytical contenders for a revised comparative location. In this respect the book as a whole challenges comparative researchers to critique North from South particularly when it comes to market economies as a context for distinguishing the regulatory challenges within and across worlds.

3. Social embeddedness and market economies

INTRODUCTION

As discussed in the preceding chapter, a focus of this book is to develop and employ empirical and theoretical research in relation to South World regulatory arrangements, in order to propose alternative regulatory strategies that can, we argue, resolve problems with global regulation which have revealed themselves over the last decade. Having established in this chapter the nexus between social embeddedness and the organic regulatory form that we see as imbuing principle within socially sustainable regulatory actions, we further explore the concept of embeddedness as it applies in particular to the market societies. We do this as a precursor to a more focused consideration of law's function in regulating private property relations which underpin North World market economies, and while currently aggravating social dis-embeddedness as we see it, if influenced by repositioned regulatory principle may act as agents for social bonding (see chapters 4 and 7).

We begin this chapter with an examination of the recent global financial meltdown, and more specifically the numerous incidences of crisis that followed. With the subprime mortgage crisis, the Lehman Brothers collapse in 2008, and the Eurozone sovereign debt implode in 2009, it could now be convincingly argued that the *market society*, which Karl Polanyi identified as emerging along with Western industrialization,[1] is crumbling. While other scholars continue to focus on arguments centred around assertions of unnatural *market failure* due to factors such as imperfect information or impaired competition, more often than not alleged to be brought about by over-regulation, we share and contemporize Polanyi's different view. It has now become clear to us that any remedy to the boom and bust, or bubble and burst cycles reflective of such crises would not be found through interrogating failures *within* the market but in the failure *of* the market, and in the risks associated with

---

[1] As discussed in Somers (1990).

the Washington consensus-style dogma that market regulation is the problem not the solution.[2]

Building on our argument for sustainable principled regulation that is derived organically adds to Polanyi's convictions regarding social dis-embedding and fictional markets. This chapter employs the social and political thinking of Polanyi, in the context of his criticisms of market-ization and its effects on society, to argue for the need to shift our principled regulatory focus from:

- the market as having sufficient regulatory capacity for designing and maintaining a self regulatory regime, to
- a regulatory framework which requires state action paramount over any premise that market regulation is adequate or indeed desirable, to
- a more socially engaged regulatory consortium with sustainability as its principle and which draws its authority from the people and its social location.

The second step referred to above may be skipped in situations where the state is fragmented or disaggregated. In these circumstances, and where the commercial sector is often predatory and excessively self-interested, the regulatory state will not take root, and the capacity for functioning state-centred regulatory pre-eminence is just not there.

Such a progression can only make sense if we accept the premise that any form of regulation needs to be built upon principle, with such principle differing depending on the context and intention to influence social relationships and outcomes. It is through individualized wealth and growth principles and the regulatory protection of an increasingly dis-embedded and dis-embedding market economy in contexts of fictitious commodification and exchange that regulation contributes to the erosion of social bonding and the necessity of Polanyi's *double movement*. Later in the chapter we consider double movement welfarism as less crucial to maintain social order against market disordering, if first the redirection of regulatory principle towards social sustainability can be achieved.

Take for example the regulation of labour-force conditions such as the imposition of a minimum wage, without committing to over-arching regulatory principles such as fairness in employment conditions and

---

2 We concede that there may be some truth in this assertion not to be addressed by removing regulation but by redirecting efforts to protect fictional commodities and exchange towards repositioning markets within relevant essential social bonding.

off-setting improvements in productivity; any attempt to regulate would run the risk of further social dis-embedding the market either through reactive unemployment or structural relocation and arbitrage. Issues such as these will be interrogated in more detail when the analysis in later chapters focuses on market sustainability and the empirical examples of migrant work-force exploitation, as against eco friendly tourism (see chapters 5 and 6). These examples will be treated as practical applications of much that is said concerning market economies and regulatory features ensuring or endangering social bonding.

Through a closer analysis of the market/society dialectic, revealed in Polanyi's earlier analysis, the congruent de-regulation/regulation tension which pre-existed and postdated the recent global financial meltdown reveals the assumed strain between protective state regulatory policy and market imperatives. Understanding the 2009 economic collapse as more than idiosyncratic market failure requires interpreting not just the potency of regulatory action, but also the recurring and routine contextual considerations necessitating the resuscitation of failed market conditions. In this respect the chapter is not so much about market failure but the features of social dislocation which inevitably lead to failed markets, if sustainability is conceded as an important regulatory social principle.

Polanyi's position on markets and failure was that the subordination of society and essential social locations and bonds to the necessities of capitalist market economies in strong states produces massive social dislocation, in these and their *client* market economies, and the consequent social protectionism that follows. Capitalist market economies, particularly markets in fictional commodities and exchange, tend to dislocate from essential social fabric. It is this fundamental dis-embedding which leads both to the destruction of market relevance socially (sustainability as we see it) and to the market's destructive force against wider social bonding. With economy and politics conceived as separate in the regulation of such market economies, more organic social order is a casualty.

For Polanyi, the utopian nature of self-regulating markets (SRMs) gave rise to a spontaneous counter-measure even among those few enjoying increased material prosperity. Unrestrained free markets in economic contexts exchanging fictional commodities were said to cause social dislocation and generate externalities which not only inhibited laissez faire market evolution, but confounded its possibility, thereby critically challenging the core economic model for which narrow econo-centric regulatory principle is directed. In SRMs Polanyi identified land, labour and money as fictional commodities, centrally complicit in enabling the laws of the market to replace essential social bonds, and in valuing these crucial market conditions. Market societies resting on fictitious commodities were in Polanyi's view inconsistent with sustainable society, and did not reflect the natural state of human affairs. In such societies, the market moves from being an auxiliary tool to becoming the paramount framework for goods exchange and pricing, while the organization for production and distribution continues to be deeply grounded in social relationships.

The wealth and opportunity imbalances which undeniably emerge from market societies, necessitate a social *double movement* of redistributive and reciprocative economic and political intervention which has largely evaporated in the neo-conservative, post-Fordist shift towards global mega-capitalism and micro-state.

Put at its simplest the analysis to follow seeks to use the social dislocation of contemporary financial markets and the misdirection of regulatory capacity to control the social disorder they produce, rather than the risk on which they rely, as a more useful application of market theorizing than has emerged from generations of interest in regulating market failure. Where we benefit but diverge from Polanyi's analysis is in exploring the contemporary market conditions of global SRMs and to suggest that his differentiation of fictional from socially sustained (embedded) market relationships[3] holds a key to understanding the inadequacies of current market exchange regulation. Further, this market distinction suggests why fictional markets relying on the under-regulated transaction of fictitious financial commodities may be beyond conventional market regulation as currently available in the prevailing international economic model.

In this chapter, we advance the analytical value in disentangling fictional from embedded markets and rationalizing regulatory resources on the latter while exposing the risks to healthy social relationships of proliferating the former. Any such regulatory repositioning, we argue here and later, depends on a conscious rehabilitation of regulatory principle back to social sustainability.

The chapter then concludes by affirming Polanyi's determination that socially dis-embedded markets are failing society and not the other way around. If this is so, then the global economic regulatory mission must instead be interpreted as reconstituting essential cultural and economic bonding, wherein embedded markets operate for society through sociability, rather than facilitating utopian market societies as ungoverned

---

[3]   For a discussion of this distinction, see Block (2003).

self-regulating exchanges of risk for individualized but socially destructive wealth creation. The contemporary crisis in global financial sustainability is selected as a context in which we will explore this inversion.

To set the scene for the analysis of effective regulatory intervention into market societies we need to review the essential composition of a market society, and the place of embeddedness as a regulatory aspiration.

SUSTAINABILITY AND EMBEDDEDNESS

Before seeking to persuade the reader, as we intend to in the following chapter, that repositioning principle within the legal regulation of private property rights is both possible and positive for achieving more generalized social good, it is necessary to clarify how sustainability is connected to social embeddedness. To attempt this it is first important to clarify what we mean by embeddedness. Much debate has been generated in the field of economic sociology about the use and application of this concept.[4] Gemici says that Polanyi's embeddedness concept, despite standing as his most famous contribution to market analysis, has been a source of enormous confusion. He argues, through a close textual interrogation of Polanyi's writings, that this confusion stems from a central fracture in Polanyi's thought, thereby creating an ostensible contradiction:

- Economies are embedded and enmeshed in institutions.
- Market exchange and market economy are self-regulating and dis-embedded.

Gemici approaches this contradiction by declaring that Polanyi uses embeddedness as an analytical construct to discern the changing place of economy in society throughout human history. In so doing he employs embeddedness to specify the degree to which economy is 'separated' from the rest of society. In such a way, the embeddedness concept becomes a mirror for understanding how economy becomes dislocated from its organic social bonds. As an example, market economy is regarded by Polanyi as the first *dis-embedded* economic system in history. If we accept this analysis as restricted to the institutional comparison of market systems to other economic systems then embeddedness is simply a methodological principle positing that economy and society can only be analysed through a holistic approach.

---

[4] See the debate summarized in Krippner et al (2004).

While we agree with the conclusion regarding holism, we do not accept the need to limit the utility of embeddedness to comparisons of markets with economies. In fact, if we view organic social bonding as a complex web, one crucial area of which is economic relations wherein the market is a key institution, then embeddedness can have analytical application to many other situations of social bonding, private property relations being an additional field for evaluation in terms of social location. In our analysis we wish to return embeddedness to its simple meaning of social location, recognizing however within this simplicity resides the question, what do we mean by *social*? It is for us the interactive product of sustainable human and communitarian *bonding*.

While we appreciate Gemici's position that embeddedness is not necessarily a variable or a characteristic of economic systems, we say it is that which can determine the sustainability of those systems in terms of their social location. Polanyi viewed markets and economies as both capable of social location and thereby socially beneficial. Therefore embeddedness requires that whether it is markets or economies we are reviewing against this measure (or any other frame of social bonding)[5] the evaluation must be holistic against a range of forces, which work towards or against bonding. Consistent with this position Polanyi proposes a thesis about the impossibility of separating economy from society because all economic systems are embedded in social relations and institutions. 'While the economy inhabits a separate and autonomous sphere under capitalism, it is enmeshed in society under pre-modern economies in such a manner that studying the economy apart from "the tissue of relationships" that constitutes "the reality of society" would be erroneous'.[6] In chapter 5, we use migrant workforce relations as an example of how the legal regulation of unbalanced and exploitative private property interests, which advance capitalist economies, presents a force for dis-embedding these economies from society. If this is so, and if it can be concluded that organic social bonding provides conditions for social sustainability, then dis-embeddedness undermines sustainability and the forces which work to dis-embed are themselves socially unsustainable, along with the interests they protect.

That Polanyi envisions the market economy as separate from social institutions, functioning according to its own rules (being more mechanical social arrangements) only goes further to confirm our argument that

---

[5] As economic actions within the market are just one category of a wide range of social interactions; see Perry-Kessaris (2011).

[6] Gemici (2008), p. 8.

dis-embedding social processes from their social bonds tends to create in these processes a dependency on externalities such as an artificial division of labour for their essential functioning. We also favour Gemici's interpretation of embeddedness arising as a gradational concept; and that the totally dis-embedded economy is not possible, but some economic arrangements are more absorbed in social institutions and relations than others. It is with this dynamic in mind that we proffer legal regulation principled by the aim of social sustainability as a candidate to assist in returning markets to a more socially embedded location and thereby making them more sustainable, and more able to contribute to social bonding in a general sense, argued more fully in the chapter to come.

In Polanyi's arguments, there exists an almost unidirectional and relentless assumption of the market moving away from the social. Again, while recognizing that such a dynamic at least is likely to be effected by push/pull factors which influence market development and transformation, we are satisfied with observing stages and states at which market societies and social dis-embedding are empirically undeniable. We also consider that, relative to particular market form and social needs the drift to dis-embedding will have differing rates and even peaks and troughs. As Ebner identifies, Polanyi advanced a twofold consideration of embeddedness; as a representation of the connection of markets to the moral fabric of society, and as a political term that refers to social reform and the regulation of markets (in particular regarding fictitious commodities).[7] As has been observed in the recent near collapse of the global financial industry, the reform process as a move toward market re-moralizing cannot be left to the vagaries, even treacheries of self-interested self-regulation. In the case of regulating labour markets closer to this social moral fabric, law can act for social protection through a fairer regulation of the competitive ordering of the market. Along with this, new applications of the law can promote the embeddedness of the labour market through non-market forms of social integration, such as creative citizenship and its potential for expanding legal coverage. As we will indicate later, law is effective in embedding specific values and norms in a labour market that supports rule compliance and trust.

---

[7]   Ebner (2010).

FICTIONAL MARKETS – RE-REGULATION AND THE RESPONSIBILITY OF THE STATE

In employing the fictional market conceit, we recognize that Polanyi conceived of fictional markets[8] at a time when frameworks of commodification and the societal context were vastly different from ours today. Instead we use this idea to explore the manner in which the fictional market conceit provides a contemporary setting for the social disconnection of markets and skews the regulatory mission away from re-embedding market activity, towards protecting market arrangements from the social disorder they generate. In this respect market failure remains interpreted as the failure of supporting market conditions, even when fictitious markets themselves rely on risks which escape external regulation (through misguided trust in self-regulation). Once this misapplication of the regulatory project is identified, the failure of current regulatory agendas sponsored by the state particularly in the form of law, supporting market-based self-regulation, would require more attention.[9]

In Polanyi's argument, the market society focused on regulation wholly depending on market forces that are demanded by a market economy would entail effectively subordinating other significant social bonding frames to the laws of the market.[10] This was carried through in Polanyi's time with the market organization of labour, land and money, and the imposition of the fiction of commodity description for each.[11] Acknowledging the role of regulation to respond to and support the now dis-embedded social contexts invites a consideration of the role of law and in particular these interests served by a system of private property rights. This recognition challenges the function of law in fabricating and perpetuating market societies built on fictitious commodities and

---

[8]   Contemporary trading in a range of what have been revealed as risky financial instruments is represented in global financing as the natural evolution of a new transaction and payment system in a world where money no longer retains any of the significance it did for Polanyi and his analysis of pre-Fordist global payment systems and exchange pricing. Whether this is an accurate understanding of modern payment structures matters little because the value of the trade is contingent and by no means as tangible as was gold or money, and thereby in a way much more fictional than Polanyi conceived markets could be.

[9]   We see the injection of a legal studies perspective into the regulatory and political economy literature as extremely useful to critique the failure of state-sponsored law to regulate the socially destructive consequences of fictional markets.

[10]   Polanyi (1944).

[11]   Ibid, pp. 75–6, 79.

exchange: why has the law been selectively supporting the discriminative and exclusionist institutions of the market through its facilitation and design of a system of private property rights and relationships which serve the interest of wealth accumulation by those with the means to do so? We argue that through the perpetuation of the system of private property rights, the law has indeed relegated the whole organization of society to the control of the economic system by the market. In this way society becomes adjunct to the market such that instead of economy being embedded in social relations, social relations are embedded in the economic system.[12]

The chapter employs the transnational lens of *global crisis to ordering* when examining the failure not only of half-hearted external regulatory intervention, but also the implication of self-regulation in the generation (rather than regulation) of global economic dysfunction through the dominance of risk-based self-interest over any sustainable social commitment to more equitable global economic health. Central to this analysis will be the paradox that the rising economic cost of global financial market failure is disproportionately borne by the tax-paying general public and those dispossessed of homes and jobs through profligate credit over-extension and serial default. That said, in any tripartist sense, the public presently lacks the capacity to participate meaningfully in the process of regulating market misconduct within increasingly complex and interconnected global financial markets. Even economists now concede more accountable regulatory forms are urgently justified by 'pervasive market misconduct, regulatory incompetence, and conflict of interest in the ... financial sector'.[13] All the more is this so for the South World as all the more it is less likely.[14] This is not to say that the public should essentially be compelled to have some stake in the stability of financial institutions. In constructing a framework of optimal regulation, it is important to recognize how de-regulation can consequently lead to over-regulation in the form of massive bank bail-outs, as a knee jerk reaction to the fear that these mega institutions are 'too big to fail'. A tri-partite system through the opening up of the accountability function of

---

12 Ibid, p. xxv.
13 Omarova (2011), abstract.
14 The hurt caused by financial mismanagement has been global, even affecting disaggregated states benefiting very little from modern financial marketeering. However, the limited independent and accountable regulatory influence over financial market practice, which should be inclusive of all stakeholder interests, remains timid and constrained.

public scrutiny (even as involuntary stakeholders) may moderate regulatory reaction if general mutualized public interest is the essential motivation.

Market repositioning was at the heart of Polanyi's thinking. Prophetically, Polanyi insisted that to avoid the demolition of society, the supply of and demand for fictitious commodities in actual market societies must be managed through the political process – that is, through the state or some other regulatory body established for such purpose. If, as Polanyi asks us to consider, there can be no pure version of a market society, then the market can never function in the uninhibited and naturally corrective way that its neo-liberal proponents claim it does, will and should. Regulating the market would therefore perpetuate or expose and manage the lie at the heart of the free market dogma; the belief that the market set free of externalities will always find its optimal balance.[15] Therefore, it is dangerous and indeed self-defeating for the responsibility of regulation to continue to be passed over to those with deep interests in perpetuating and concealing market fictions, and limiting regulatory reach and rectitude.

'Despite their dismal track record as guardians of public interest, bankers and bureaucrats effectively remain in charge of protecting the public from the next financial meltdown'.[16] In a recent article in the *International Herald Tribune*,[17] the observation was made concerning the conventional financial regulatory struggle:

> ... between bankers trying to preserve their most ludicrous business practices, and regulators trying to defuse a system that, many believe, nearly blew up the world economy ... one lesson that emerges (from the public pressure for financial industry pushback) is that the capacity of the financial industry to lobby for its short term interests is far reaching.

With regard to the identified need for the injection of public stakeholder interest into global financial regulation, Omarova doubts that tripartism alone is enough to overcome the failings of financial self-regulation. While not suggesting that any tri-partite intervention outside the industry or state regulators should have executive or legislative power, Omarova believes it essential that the independent public interest element should possess:

---

[15] Block (2003), p. 281.
[16] Omarova (2011), abstract.
[17] *International Herald Tribune* (2011).

- broad statutory authority to collect information from government agencies and private industry participants;
- power to publicize its findings; and
- the capacity to advise legislators and external regulators to take action on issues of public concern.

With these features it is suggested that the third regulatory arm would counteract, capture and defuse the financial industry's power to control the regulatory agenda by putting both bankers and bureaucrats under constant and intense public scrutiny. Even so, this 'more effective and public-minded model of risk regulation'[18] faces significant implementation and operational challenges, not the least of which involves revisiting the basic tenets of financial regulatory philosophy. The greater the adversarial design of a regulatory strategy, wedged somewhere between aggressive industry interest and compromised external regulatory involvement, the greater the likely reliance on an escalating hierarchy of regulatory enforcement. Such a regulatory framework limits its application to the context of well-functioning state systems in which the enforceability of public obligations and private rights and privileges is consolidated. However, most of the world does not operate in such a situation, politically or commercially. In addition, sharp regulation operating within market frameworks is rarely directed at the structural failings of the market which varying development contexts may exacerbate, but in turn presumes a process of rehabilitation to regain the strained market conditions, no matter how essentially problematic these remain.

If Polanyi is right that market liberals are hell-bent on dis-embedding markets from society, particularly where social cohesion is otherwise a strained through corrupt politics or disingenuous development, then a worthy *double movement* motivation for regulation is to return embeddable markets to their enhanced social context through social and economic market rationalization. In so doing the nature of SRMs would change from if not largely ungoverned or only regulated for self-interest to a form of market self-regulation inextricably attached to social sustainability.[19]

One of the failings of fictional commodity and market analysis however, and something not interrogated convincingly in Polanyi's writing, is the tendentious assumption that the market or commodity reality is a comparative referent against which fiction can be understood and

---

[18] Omarova (2011), p. 623.
[19] Block (2003), p. 294.

evaluated. To convincingly address the reality/fiction duality would require a more detailed interrogation of market analysis than we would endeavour within this book. In any case, it suffices for our argument that this challenge be dealt with in a more simplistic if nonetheless essentialist fashion. For the arguments against market societies and fictitious commodity exchange, we choose to focus on measuring their distance from social origins, through employing the concept of embeddedness.

TRICKLEDOWN OF OTHER CRISES INTO AND OUT OF THE FINANCIAL SECTOR – REGULATION TO BOOM OR BUST

Financial industry strain has crippling effects on many components of market economies; vice versa, crises in other economic fields destabilizes the financial sector, and a cycle of boom and bust will press on. This potential cycle can be anticipated for instance in China's vigorous market economy, where economic stimulus is a consequence of a more than healthy export balances to consumer markets in the West/North. The boost that this gives the domestic Chinese economy then rolls over to skyrocketing real estate prices and consequent construction industry expansion, in turn fuelling demand for credit (consumer and commercial) and a drain on capital. Real estate asset valuation loses touch with broad social expectation and occupancy/ownership through high borrowings creates and feeds a fictional market environment.

One reason why global financial markets are so vulnerable to crises in major national economies is their interconnectedness. Again, using the example of China, the US has been critical of the Chinese refusing to let their currency reach its true market value, through the opacity and *ungovernability* of the Chinese banking structure, because of the suggested negative fallout into its own economy. While denying the former, senior Chinese government officials have recently been wrestling with regulation of their banking industry.[20] With the Chinese financial sector now carrying much of the developed world debt, and financing quasi-colonial economic expansion into the developing world, the health of that sector, its accountability and legitimacy have become global regulatory concerns.

Thinking about this area of regulation, the tensions between wealth creation and regulation securing wealth retention create ambiguity in the

---

[20]   Buckley and Wang (2011).

nature and reach of effective and responsive financial regulation, and the attitude of the investor as to its appropriateness. Here, Braithwaite's 'window of opportunity' for regulation out of crisis[21] is particularly apposite as the post-crisis wash up[22] has worked to destabilize interest group equilibrium and their opposition against the regulatory control of wealth creation. However, this grace period for regulatory stimulation only seems to last as long as investor confidence is shaken, and this temporally limited issue-attention cycle gives reformers an often too brief opportunity to re-regulate before any market reform agenda is side-lined if and when the talk of boom returns.

John Lie has attempted to take market analysis outside specific historical and institutional contexts to theorize about markets in transition. He suggests that too much emphasis might have been invested in the market as the only means for understanding the diversity of economic exchange:

> The assumption of market essentialism forecloses considerations of alternative forms of exchange relationships and structures. Given the historical and comparative diversity of market relations and institutions, there is at least a prima facie reason to consider alternative arrangements … In order to advance theoretical works on markets the assumption of market essentialism should be jettisoned in favour of describing and analysing the empirical diversity of actually existing markets. In addition, power and macro-sociological foundations need to be better theorised.[23]

Taking up Lie's exhortation in respect of global financial markets seen against the push for de-regulation, it is impossible not to consider the recurrent and often reluctant regulation of market failure. However, it should not be overlooked that what first appears as market failure might instead be attributable to how the prevailing market conditions have developed and operated over time and how certain market models may have failed the essential social conditions which stimulated their emergence. Take for instance the situation if the measure of market success or

---

21 Braithwaite (2008), chapter 2.
22 Following the collapse of the Lehman Brothers merchant bank in 2008, there appeared to be a global consensus in banking regulation that things had to change. But powerful resistance from banking industry organizations such as the Washington-based Institute of International Finance (comprising the major banks) saw a prevarication in regulatory will, and the impact of the 2009 financial meltdown was largely lost on regulators.
23 Lie (1997), pp. 353–4.

health is competition. Evaluated against the social efficiency and afford-
ability of services which competition is said to promote and ensure, the
international financial market is characterized by banking oligopolies and
cartel relationships which are featured in the development of that market
as it consolidates, must evidence its failure in competitive terms *and*
measures of social benefit.

An article of faith in market-based financial reform and one of the
most intriguing paradoxes in global meta-capitalism, a distinguishing
feature of modern financial markets, is institutional competitiveness. One
of the reasons why financial markets have been prone to collapse in
cycles is the paucity of genuine institutional competitiveness between
financial institutions. As financial de-regulation globalized, arguments in
favour of demanding competition were practically snuffed out as banks in
particular consolidated and internationalized. Financial industries moved
rapidly beyond their national origins and state-controlled obligations, and
at a time when global monetary policy was burgeoning as the preferred
economic technology of developed nations, the mechanisms through
which that policy was to be exercised were increasingly beyond state
influence. In addition, with retail and investment banking consolidated, it
became increasingly difficult for uniform domestic regulatory policy
(fiscal or monetary) to cover the range and risks of banking services and
products. To make this worse, banking consolidation was accompanied
by the colonization by banks of a vast range of financial products and
services previously not considered the province of responsible banking.
This further undermined the effectiveness of competition as a regulatory
strategy in the financial services market, narrowing supply diversity and
demand choice. Add to this the information deficit of small investors, and
resultant uneducated consumer choice, made consumer preferencing a
minimal regulatory pressure. The financial market was responding to the
opportunities of largely de-regulated trading in progressively fictitious
commodities within a climate that challenged and put at risk the socially
embedded reasons for domestic banking services. Banks and financial
institutions exchanged a wide customer base for a more specialized
wealth creation portfolio and traded each other's risks. In all of this,
banking dis-embedded from the essential social bonds that originally and
conventionally justified its retail growth.

As Bernard and Boucher demonstrate,[24] globalization does not necessarily ensure institutional competitiveness. Such competitiveness is

---

[24] Bernard and Boucher (2007).

dependent on institutional design, and strategic institutional entre-preneurship. In particular, *social investments* can enhance productivity through work-force satisfaction and customer conscience. When, how-ever, social investments are minimized in preference to maximizing the self-interest of the entrepreneur investor, then productivity is measured against skewed wealth creation standards that do not adequately take into account risk generation or its management. Institutional competitiveness is not, in such circumstances, promoted for the benefit of the industry but may be retarded through oligopolistic non-productive self-interests which are in turn risky to the industry.

REGULATING MARKET FAILURE – OTHER WAYS OF DOING BUSINESS?

Successful strategies for regulating global financial markets have recently been challenged by fluctuating credit and liquidity waves, and con-strained by the dual need to manage often-unpredictable credit expansion with the same tools as credit contraction. Further, banks and states seem unable to break free of a qualifying *risk management paradigm* in which, as Lie reiterates, market essentialism prohibits the consideration and actioning of other collaborative forms of exchange management. Polanyi identified market risk as essentially *social*.

> Social history in the nineteenth century was thus the result of a double movement … While on the one hand markets spread all over the face of the globe and the amount of goods involved grew to unbelievable proportions, on the other hand a network of measures and policies was integrated into powerful institutions designed to check the actions of the market relative to labour, land and money … society protected itself against the perils inherent in a self-regulating market system … this was the one comprehensive feature in the history of the age.[25]

Sustainability is crucial for socially responsible market regulation. Even the traditional dichotomy between pricing and cost re-imbursement rules tends to be blown out of any balance if market failure is forever imminent due to resource unpredictability or finality, viewed as market externalities. However, if finite resources are seen not as a fictional market condition, but rather as critical social bonds which determine the reality and social value of the market, then prioritizing sustainability for

---

[25] Polanyi, Arensberg and Pearson (eds) (1957), p. 76.

social reasons rather than exploitation of social risk or market enrichment reasons becomes in turn a natural argument. Measuring market failings in terms of social benefit rather than individual wealth creation becomes consistent with broader regulatory principles focused on sustainability.

Financial instability also questions efficient market theory, even if it is separated from social value and location. In the situation of financial markets and their regulation, high-risk lending strategies have been exposed as being in direct conflict with a capital market commitment to safe returns for investors. Even so, rabid risk-taking in the name of wealth creation has sidelined conventional credit prudence. Investors are seduced by the disproportionate returns as risk increases with the more fictitious trading market environments. The morality of investment becomes distorted as a consequence, in favour of wealth creation and against asset or capital security. The investor is now the gambler and the regulator stands in the way of fast money. The eventual cost is social and borne also by those citizens and communities that prop up the losses from risks not of their own making but rather from the fictional exchange which the market distorts or exploits.

NEW ECONOMICS: DEBATE OF FINANCIAL REGULATION REFORM – INSTITUTIONAL COMPETITIVENESS

Reiterating Lie's invocation to always consider the contextual diversity of actual existing markets, is it not necessary to appreciate the normative conditions in which markets operate as critical variables in predicting regulatory requirements and outcomes? With its emergence in the neo-liberal economic period of the late last century, the ethic of wealth accumulation at any cost predominated, justifying tax havens and money laundering, minimization schemes and arbitrage, all of which evidenced and exacerbated a commercial moral bankruptcy constructed by and productive of *fiscal termites*[26] which not only justified risk and excess, but in terms of market expectation rewarded it until the consequences caught up. Braithwaite indicates that in combination with increased regulatory backbone there is a critical need to re-moralize markets to counter the contagion of tax cheating; a contagion requiring reversal – markets in vice to markets in virtue.[27] These considerations could be seen

---

[26]   Braithwaite (2008).
[27]   Ibid, chapter 6.

as reflecting Polanyi's double movement away from the normative and socially operational dimensions of self-interest self-regulation, towards a regulated re-moralism.[28]

At a functional level, regulatory reform requires more effective monitoring. This is best achieved within a framework of mutuality amongst 'regulatory community' (see chapter 6). Representation of key interests is not denied where sociability is preferred, and the accountability framework compatible with collaborative regulation may include proxy advocates, technical experts, agency monitors, designated consumer representatives, and even ombudsmen.

The protected trading context of global cartel banking has enabled a fundamental transition in the nature of banking from a largely domestic service utility predisposition fostering other commercial endeavours, into a powerful market player trading in even more risky financial products generating staggering shareholder profits. This banking transformation has not been mirrored by a sophisticated regulatory answer to the marketing of risk. Where the regulation of anti-competitive behaviour is seen as necessary for the benefits of free market capitalism to be maximized,[29] paradoxically particularly with regulatory capitalism,

---

[28] Following the recent global financial collapses and facing the imminence of further economic crises in the world of the future, new life is breathed into the debate surrounding financial sector reform. The aspects of reform which have become increasing less problematic include:

- improving the governance of financial regulation;
- ensuring the independence of critical regulatory elements and agencies;
- broadening the regulator's intellectual perspective;
- developing a more pluralistic and inclusive regulatory mix;
- being ever vigilant against regulatory capture;
- introducing extra-financial considerations such as social responsibility into the intended regulatory outcomes; and
- avoiding an over reliance on the extremes of ungoverned self-regulation, or overbearing state intervention.

[29] In terms of the global financial market, the regulatory options for freeing up competition include:

- international conventions;
- judicial adjudication;
- regulatory injunction;
- license conditions;
- private interest enforcement; and
- litigation as an anti-competitive strategy.

However, in light of the supra-national structure of global banks, most of these devices have little practical purchase. Even when confronting a combination of

mega-corporations such as global banks thrive in regulative regimes which tend to protect oligopolistic alliances for preferential market share.[30]

What this summary of the competition paradox in global financial markets reveals is a fundamental regulatory dilemma caused by market disaggregation, rather than externalities which breed failure. It is instructive to examine two characteristics of the dis-embedded market which thwart contemporary regulatory engagement where regulatory principle is the sustainability of social benefit: (a) the mystery of capital; and (b) the sect of secrecy.

(a) Invisible or Indivisible Capital?

In opening his analysis of capital, De Soto quotes Braudel in *The Wheels of Commerce*:[31]

> The key problem is to find out why that sector of society of the past, which I would not hesitate to call capitalist, should have lived as if in a bell jar, cut off from the rest; why was it not able to expand and conquer the whole of society? ... [Why was it that] a significant rate of capital formation was possible only in certain sectors and not in the whole market economy of the time?

The capitalist world is constructed and maintained by variables that may not be explained in purely economic terms, and this realization has a central relevance for the proliferation and prominence of communitarian regulatory strategies outside the fragile frame of the finance industry and its fractured market focus. Among these variables, sociability opposes the individualist and meritocratic motivations for social engagement central to capitalist economics, which (coincidentally) resonate in the discourse around the boardrooms of the global financial institutions.

'(Capitalism) is out of touch with those who should be its largest constituency, and instead of being a cause that promises opportunity for all, capitalism appears increasingly as the leitmotif of a self-serving guild of businessmen and their technocracies'.[32] Capital accumulation, distribution and management do not, however, need to be seen or to be regulated

---

public and private enforcement, anti-competitive banking cartels around product pricing and fees for service have been distinctly resilient.

[30]   Braithwaite (2008).
[31]   Braudel (1979).
[32]   De Soto (2000).

only within such terms. De Soto argues that the mechanisms of capitalism, such as global financial institutions and processes, do not well service under-capitalized states or those states with disaggregated political or commercial frameworks. This disconnect in turn means that the negative impact of global financial crises on such states and communities may be greater due to capital drain, or at least from not being counterbalanced against the years of wealth creation and their benefits which preceded collapse in capitalist western economies. Such under-capitalized economies are not given a seat at the table as well when it comes to globally determining the regulatory responses from crisis to ordering. Capital starvation in this sense leads to regulatory disempowerment and the further disadvantage that may flow from regional undervaluing in geo-political regulatory prioritization.

Even in the case of emergent economies the broader social benefits of capitalism may be short-lived and selective. Back to the example of China, the social costs attendant on rising economic inequality and the prospect of labour retrenchment from prolonged periods of full employment cannot be ignored. The capacity of richer income households and capital income earners to absorb rising living costs will not soften the negative impact on poorer labour income earners. The resultant inequality has led to popular protests and inevitably to eventual political instability and crack-downs to shore up failing authority. This instability poses further strains on economic performance, but more significantly reveals unraveling social bonding. External to China and to other emergent economies, the current account imbalances fueled by selective capitalist development now pose equal risks to their economic future because of the trade dependence on failing external consumer demand, despite vigorous efforts to stimulate domestic consumer activity. Policymakers are running out of regulatory options, at least in the form of conventional fiscal policy.

Kapstein earlier identified crisis and the risk of further crises as catalyzing the interest in regulating international financial markets, but this too has not eventuated to its predicted extent due in part to the forces opposing regulation and favouring fictional market interests and outcomes. The challenge in Kapstein's world was to transform that interest into a regulatory strategy which would not be, as it eventually was, attacked or subverted by a self-interested regulate/regulatory sectors. The failure that eventuated was both with the regulators and the regulated. Weak governments are finding it increasingly difficult to implement international regulatory policy co-ordination to steady financial markets as the world views, goals and interests of advanced economies and emerging markets come into conflict. In 1989, Kapstein projected the international co-ordination of banking regulation as a way of resolving the regulator's dilemma with financial market control.[33] He focused on the role of market forces, consensual knowledge and state power as critical in bringing banking accord to fruition. On the other hand, Braithwaite might suggest that it was both the absence of regulatory accountability and the incapacity of self-regulation which precipitated the demise of financial markets along with risky and indulgent market behaviour.

Both Kapstein and Braithwaite fall short of a market critique which sees the ills of contemporary global financing as inevitable outcomes of market dis-embeddedness but prefer to concentrate on regulatory inactivity, prudential delinquency or institutional fragmentation. However, as unsecured sovereign debt and foreign exchange risk are both products of globalized financial markets, when the risks these investment options project become social reality rather than investment variables, then all states suffer well beyond the home jurisdictions of the banks concerned or their regulatory agencies.

Kapstein's version of collaboration to minimize the fallout of these global risks does not take into account the massive negative influence that global banking crisis can have even on the capital flow necessary for states and economies that manage through micro-financing and localized financial markets. This said, a collaborative strategy which only imagines participation by the mega financial institutions will not accommodate the interests of smaller, disaggregated economies even if due to crisis the playing field of international finance is tipped more in favour of non-bank financial institutions. The major difficulty Kapstein suggests in *banker's club* collaboration is the variability in the enforcement experience of each member in the regulatory environment with which they are most familiar. We would go much further to say that this form of collaborative regulation has the potential to capture itself in its own diverse and member-centred self-interest because it fails to recognize and incorporate the massive victim interests of the small fish who collectively carry great loss from these crises but individually mean little in influencing the client base of a mega bank.

---

[33]   Kapstein (1982).

Sect of Secrecy

In his review of Paul Krugman's unnervingly prophetic book *The Return of Depression Economics and the Crisis of 2008*,[34] William Leith in the *Guardian Newspaper* observed:

> The entire edifice of capitalism is based on capital – which is really just another word for confidence. Wealth is created because people who have capital, or confidence, expose it to risk … If people believe your confidence to be authentic, the risk you take is likely to be small. But as soon as people think you are bluffing they panic – and panic destroys wealth faster than confidence can ever increase it.[35]

If this is so then regulatory intervention into the financial market following a collapse in capital (confidence) should not be directed at merely shoring up wealth creation as a result of restoring confidence. Regulation might require a repositioning of our appreciation of capital and relationships with it so that risk to capital is spread through more fundamental and long lasting re-distributions.

It was a cult of secrecy and self-interest which led to the recent global financial daisy chain of lost control – allowing wild and lucrative risk taking to become more and more distant from the responsibilizing influence of capital creation and management. Playing with other people's money was the foundation of wealth creation particularly in modern corporate banking practice. In addition, consensual knowledge both of the nature and the extent of risk, which Kapstein indicated as essential for effective regulation, was concealed particularly from those who eventually carried the greatest harm and the least benefit.

The financial industry developed not as some exclusive alliance of capital owners or managers but of wealth managers, traders, product marketeers and financial advisors who were not as bound or burdened by the need to create capital or to directly account for its rise and fall. In this market, confidence became unhinged from capital and risks were as such made much more risky. Regulators lost whatever limited control they had over market intermediaries (auditors, analysts), intermediaries over managers, and managers over more aggressive employees. The decision-makers in the financial industry were, through distance from responsibility and realistic evaluations of capital risk, largely able to

---

[34] Krugman (2009).
[35] Leith (27 December 2008).

avoid public and private regulation of tax, accounting standards, investment restrictions, and even government subsidies.

If wealth management in the financial industry has drifted away from an essential link to capital production, then what was marketed through the industry has also changed fundamentally. The industry turned to the marketing of risk for itself. Derivatives became used as counter-regulatory instruments, enabling their purveyors through hedge funds (much the same as bankers did with trusts just prior to the Wall Street crash in 1907) to circumvent national and international rules, rating agencies, self-regulation by boards, regulation by market conditions, or by the audit of traders.

The examples of illusory and indivisible capital and market secrecy seem to suggest that all regulation requires is a firm redirection towards communitarian responsibilization, and the market will rehabilitate accordingly. Such a causal assumption is neither verifiable nor actual where the essential bond of accountability from the market to its context has become dis-embedded as it moves to fictitious exchange.

DOES INDUSTRY COLLABORATION MEAN *SOCIABILITY*?

As the Basel III rules could be interpreted, the core issue for industry collaboration may be the protection of self-interest, and the self-governance of self-interest, rather than any genuine devolution of regulatory power to a broader base of cooperative and mutualized stakeholder interests. In this regard industry collaboration has the double movement characteristics of Polanyi's SRMs, with private interest exerting a growing influence through market expansion and public interest featuring only insofar as it aligns with and protects that private interest.

What was centrally at issue for the Basel consortium of major banking agencies (Basel Committee on Banking Standards) was who should set limits on the retention of capital – the money that banks accumulate though issuing stock and holding onto profits – money they are eventually not required to repay. Through legislative activity particularly in the USA and the United Kingdom and their central banks' direction,[36] state regulators have sought to require banks to finance their operations with more capital and less borrowed money. Operating this way means that banks will appear to be less profitable, thereby affecting bankers'

---

[36]   Wyatt (2011).

productivity bonuses (a bone of public contention in the whole bank bail-out saga) and the attractiveness of banking returns to shareholders, investors and market speculators. In addition, re-emphasizing capital liquidity will necessarily draw banking activity away from the more risky but profitable financial activity in trading fictitious commodities, which was once restricted to the province of investment banks.

The way in which the Basel Committee has managed this issue[37] suggests the flaw in viewing this form of industry collaboration as any genuine experiment in *regulatory sociability*. While agreeing on capital retention measures that force banks to reduce risk, the Committee imposed a long phase-in period for these requirements to bite, a period in which the banking industry lobby worldwide could use to water down the impact of the rules.

The earlier Basel II rules, perhaps worse than no regulation at all, gave the appearance that the major banks were sufficiently cushioned against risk when in fact the banks had seriously under-estimated the malignant potential of their loan holdings. As the US housing market fell away, and the domino effect on bank liquidity took hold, derivatives tied to the US housing market, with top credit ratings, suddenly became near impossible to sell and were effectively worthless, radically endangering the apparent capitalization of over-exposed banks.

Faulty regulation also worsened the European sovereign debt crisis by assigning government bonds almost zero risk when many European governments teetered on insolvency. This encouraged banks to extend billions of dollars in credit to profligate states with no clear capacity to honour these obligations. This set up a dangerous relationship between the solvency of countries and the health of the world's largest multi-national banks.

The old-fashioned regulatory aim, not yet adopted by the Basel committee, was to set a minimum level of capital to be held against gross assets, regardless of estimated risk on investments, in order to restrain the banks' strong incentive to make optimistic assessments and to super-charge leverage. Banks consider this leverage tool as a blunt regulatory instrument, almost an insult to their sophisticated efforts over the past decade to create complex and competing internal risk management systems, as well as a threat to their profits and to payouts for top banking executives. Where the approach to regulation takes the form of govern-ance as opposed to government, with a soft law type approach, it is difficult for the regulatory response to move beyond the *groupthink*

---

[37] *International Herald Tribune* (2011); Ewing (2011).

phenomenon that may have emerged. In this respect, it might be important to ensure that there is a good mix of different types of actors for a regulatory strategy, as we earlier explained.

The Basel rules in any case are only benchmarks and it is up to individual nation states to translate them into domestic laws. Even so, lobby groups such as the Institute of International Finance have published studies indicating that maintaining the Basel rules will force banks to substantially curtail lending and to undercut economic growth, representing the former (which was an aim of the rules where risky lending was involved) as retrograde rather than prudent. In any case, such studies ignore the huge social costs of financial crises for communities with no representation through the banks to the Basel regulatory regime.[38] It is interesting now that due to adverse public opinion towards bank bail-outs and bankers bonuses, legislatures have more courage to challenge the banks' self-regulatory mechanisms and their lobbyists, but the time for this is limited by any return to the boom days of wealth creation. Assisted by the regular revelations of rogue banking practices, it is harder for the banks to argue they have learnt their lesson and should continue to be trusted with the reins of self-regulation.

THE FAILURE OF THE GLOBAL SOCIAL? REDISCOVERING SOCIAL RESPONSIBILITY

Global economic dysfunction is not only an issue of fictional markets and risky exchange. The malaise of modernized economic models, we argue, is a deep dis-embeddedness represented by the imbalance between regulatory concerns for failing Western developed economies (due to vanishing liquidity) and the potential collapse of emerging market economies as a consequence of diminishing consumer demand beyond their shores. Such a degenerating relationship seems to have confounded the modernist development mantra of inevitable economic benefit for all through the de-regulation of financial markets and the aggressive regulation of anti-competitive trading behaviour. This push-me-pull-you regulatory mix has led to the inevitable failure of capitalist market relations, as well as the impotence of bilateral regulatory strategies (between the industry and the regulators). The consequence for emergent, transitional and South World economies has been the devastation of expanding

---

[38]   Berger and Bouwman (2009).

wealth gaps and the social strain which accompanies national economic obsessions with rapidly expanding growth.[39]

More than offering an opportunity for changing the consciousness of bankers from vice to virtue, financial market regulation following a market crash needs to enhance its medium-term influence by addressing the role of this market in helping to grow the global wealth gap. At the World Economic Forum in Davos in 2011, the chief executive of JP Morgan Chase lashed out at what he viewed as being unfair criticism of the world's financial wizards: 'I just think this constant refrain "bankers, bankers, bankers" – is a really unproductive and unfair way of treating people ... people should just stop doing that'.[40]

Ironically this 'defence' preceded the massive regulatory penalization of just this bank for staggering market malpractice. Even as a result of financial crisis, the word 'banker' has become an epithet for the undeserving rich, and inequality once accepted as just a part of economic growth, is increasingly challenged in an economic world where social responsibility is rediscovered. With Bill Gates bringing cassava to Davos in 2012 to highlight the need for a focus on global agriculture to feed the starving, the energies of major financial regulators such as the World Bank cannot be limited to conditions of global economic crisis. Socially responsible economic regulation demands synergies between poverty eradication and financial market well-being. In order to achieve this certain fundamental transactions are foreshadowed.

Profit to Sustainability

As the foregoing brief analysis of financial market collapse and regulatory inhibition reveals, the risky pursuit of short-term profit for individualized gain has not only endangered wider networks of global financial viability, but also the fabric of a laissez-faire capitalist global economic model. Some commentators take a simple view of the regulatory failure/market failure analysis. Shleifer for instance declares that the regulation

---

[39] Here, we are alluding to even more interesting meta questions such as what will be the global regulatory ethic after the demise of material profit as the measure of modernization and imperialist global economic development? Once market societies are rationalized (with or without their cooperation), how will questions of sustainability over profit lead to a fundamental reconsideration of resource distribution, and will the global financial repositioning after crisis usher in new dragons to guard the gulf between the two worlds of resource benefit, unless market embeddedness replaces market exploitation?

[40] Quoted in Pfanner (25 January 2012).

of economic activity globally is ubiquitous. However, standard theories of economics and of regulation continue to be wary of the influence of regulation over healthy economic growth. Shleifer argues that the ubiquity of regulation can be explained not so much by market failure or by asymmetric information about market behaviour, but by a failure on the part of the courts to settle disputes over private legal interests cost effectively, predictably and impartially.[41] This largely legalist argument, however, begs the question what about the failure of law as a regulator. It also presumes an objectivist and essentially responsible motivation for the manner in which law ensures private property relationships. We predict that in fictitious market contexts such assumptions need critical review (see chapter 7). Law's relevance and capacity as a socially beneficial regulator can better be addressed by approaching the following challenges to legalist regulation:

- capture by clients with significant private interests at stake;
- the partiality of private property relations;
- the myth of privity and of parsimony;
- the impossibility of parity;
- the limitations of jurisdiction;
- the fragility of authority based on state sovereignty; and, more recently,
- the preference of the commercial sector when selecting modes of dispute resolution to go anywhere but law.

Shleifer's confidence in legal regulation as a saving mechanism for vulnerable market relations chimes in with De Soto's celebration of private property relations in broadening access to capital and the benefits of capitalism. In the section to follow we introduce our interests in the socially destructive (while individual/protective and exclusionist) function of legal regulation as it currently protects and promotes private property rights and relationships.

It would be fair to say that the debate about transforming global financial arrangements and relationships is not confined to refining one regulatory mode such as law and its protection of property rights. The pursuit of profit, and the generation of economic wealth, are now being questioned internationally both as adequate measures of regulatory motivation or sustainable social outcomes. In the section and the chapter to follow we chose to single out legal regulation for analysis as a

---

[41]   Shleifer (2010).

dis-embedded (and dis-embedding) force within the socio-economic phenomenon that is the market because, among other things:

- private property rights and relationships are crucial for creating and maintaining market economies cut free from their original social origins (if such can even be remembered); and
- much if not most of law's activity as a regulator in North World economic contexts is in the protection of exclusionist private property rights and relationships.

Law for All?

Seen against the greater project of this book in empirically charting the path to market embeddedness, this section introduces some key considerations in understanding and utilizing the tensions that emerge in attempts to resituate legal underpinnings in financial regulation following the financial crisis, and in doing so, to shore up markets that up until recently have not relied on law beyond the protection of private and transactable property rights.[42] Much more analysis should be directed to the transformation of law which is essential as we see it, for property protection to be more inclusive and as such more able to complement sustainable social bonding. In addition, consideration will be given to re-valuing private property in terms of a broadened access portfolio, rather than a destructive and ever-diminishing *price* measure of limited dispossession to enhance only individual wealth creation.

In contemporary North World market economies, private property protection confinement of the role of law in financial relationships is essentially a 'haves/haves-not' application of the facilitative function of the law. Although we do not agree with Margaret Thatcher's advocating of De Soto's argument that the failure of third world and centralist economies is a lack of rule of law that upholds property rights and provides a framework for enterprise,[43] we do concede sense in De Soto's prescription to political and economic leaders in such contexts to 'Do at least three specific things: take the perspective of the poor, co-opt the

---

[42]   The chapter takes as a given that the pressure for wholesale retreat from market regulation as the recipe for market resilience has not survived as the unquestioned political pre-determinant of responsible global market management.

[43]   Quoted in Reed (2001).

elite, and deal with the legal and technical bureaucracies that are the bell jar's current custodians'.[44]

The prescription of law as a device for determining and discriminating access to property and to the means of production is, in our view, an essential explanation as to why law is becoming progressively less relevant as a socially responsible (as opposed to property interest selective) regulator. This is so either for those without such access, or even for those with access but who now, through the collapsing of time and space, are unable to enjoy law as their mechanism of exclusionist rights protection.

The problem for law as a more universalist, inclusive and accessible public benefit regulator, which the regulatory principle of sustainability requires, in contexts of private rights protection and fictitious market exchange, is obviously that for the majority law is *the* mechanism for concealing, disguising, despoiling and disenfranchising those public benefit rights if they are ever in fact actionable in a social context (more on this in chapter 4). De Soto accepts that in the present capitalist age, prosperity follows capitalist economic systems, but these systems have only thrived in the West. He puts the problem down, wrongly in our view, to an inability globally to produce capital. This is a particularly unsustainable conclusion in a world where wealth has heavily located in non-capitalized or capital dependent fictitious markets. De Soto then locates this problem squarely in the court of regulation. The fault as he sees it does not lie with the self-interest of the rich but the incapacity of the poor to access the protection of private property rights.

> Formal property is more than a system for titling, recording and mapping assets – it is an instrument of thought, representing assets in such a way that people's minds can work on them to produce surplus value. That is why formal property must be universally accessible: to bring everyone into one social contract where they can cooperate to raise society's productivity.[45]

The impediments to achieving this outcome are not simply in the narrow consciousness of the poor. To our thinking this resonates Marie Antoinette's apocryphal response to the poor having no bread, 'then let them eat cake'. Any limited appreciation by the disenfranchised of property, property rights and the potential of property surplus is a consequence at least of the secrecy imposed by the wealthy economies about the nature of property, and a fundamental denial of universal access

---

44   De Soto (2000), p. 190.
45   De Soto (2000), p. 218.

to the regulatory protections by more than exclusive individualist interests, which is seen by this limited class of beneficiaries as making property negotiable and valuable. This is a cult of secrecy and self-interest designed to thwart cooperation over the ever-growing global wealth gap. The law is too often employed by the cult to endorse its privilege. At the very limit, law is a device for determining the exclusive boundaries for those who may participate in the protections it provides.

The regulatory rehabilitation of law in the project of market embedding is developed in our next chapter, and while we earlier conceded that law is merely one of the many regulators which could be selected as appropriate for this project, it enables sharp edged engagement with one of the key procedural impediments to the *socialization* of market economies. Contract law in particular, if our aspirations for law as an agent for social change are to be convincing, will need to broaden its contextualizing of legitimate interests and eligible parties. Intellectual property law will need to progress from its role in encasing copyright and entombing patents and trademarks behind some presently porous access shield of legal sanctions and penalties. As progressive intellectual property thinkers have conceded, law's role is shifting to the facilitation of revaluation, expanding licensed access, and managing the negotiation of damages arising from inevitable access liberalization.

It is sufficient to indicate here that to break the law/private property protection nexus in favour of law's expressive capacity to assist stake holders in appreciating the shared value of access which broader property engagement allows would enable property for use, not for wealth.

CONCLUSION: SOCIABILITY BY ANY OTHER NAME

Polanyi enabled market analysis to focus not on what produces market failure but how the social dislocation of capitalist (and particularly fictitious) markets can fail to maintain, and can even destroy, essential social relations. Regulatory focus, therefore, should not be on controlling market-induced social disorder to perpetuate fictitious markets, but to return markets to a socially embedded utility. This preferred outcome can be achieved, we argue, through corporate regulatory sociability.[46] That said, corporate players in the market do not hold the key to market re-embedding. Markets, through a collaborative return to social utility (and this may involve a shift in consumer preferencing along with profit

---

[46] Findlay (2012).

and growth purposes for fictitious markets), will become part of a wider re-embedding of economy into society. All regulatory stakeholders will need to share in this reform. The essential pressures for sustainability will fuel the shift from risk to fate in market principles, relationships and outcomes.

Collaborative regulatory exercises such as those touched on here do not necessarily constitute sociability if their primary purpose is to colonize the regulatory agenda for their own interests. This outcome is revealed above through capture even of genuine tripartite approaches to regulation, or through constructing a self-regulating consortium of self-interest to deflect and diffuse other mechanical regulatory intrusions. While these collaborations can be viewed as emerging organically from within the system to be regulated, they do not satisfy at least one other critical test of sociability, that being the mutualization of interests towards a common good (see chapter 6).

In *The Great Transformation*[47] Karl Polanyi argued that the development of the modern state went hand in hand with the developing modern market economies and that these two changes were historically inexorably linked. Modern state development and the power of its authority, he considered, demanded changes in social structure that allowed for a dream of competitive capitalist economy, and that a capitalist economy required a strong state to mitigate its harsher effects. For Polanyi, these changes implied the destruction of the prevailing pre-capitalist social order. Prophetically it now seems that the great transformation of this social order through twenty-first century neo-liberalism (as with laissez faire self-regulation), and the destruction of communitarian constituents which it requires, would be the eventual challenge to capitalism. Market over-regulation is not the threat to globalized capitalism,[48] the threat is rather the risks inherent in dis-embedded fictitious markets and the misleading utopia of market competitiveness which challenges an insufficiently regulated global political economy.

On the market and methods for its regulation Polanyi speculated that the construction of a SRM necessitated the forced and mechanical separation of society into economic and political realms. Despite producing (selectively that is) 'unheard of material wealth', Polanyi viewed the market, no longer being about *real* land, labour and money but rather fictitious commodities which do not claim an independent rationality in

---

47   Polanyi (1944).
48   Braithwaite (2008).

any truly *marketable* sense and as such *the market in fictitious commodification*, as 'subordinate[ing] the substance of society itself to the laws of the market'.[49]

How does one regulate a fictional market in fictitious commodities? As mentioned at the outset of this chapter, Polanyi considered necessary, consequential and pervasive social dislocation, and spontaneous responses by society to protect itself will come about once the *free* (de-regulated) market attempts to separate itself from the fabric of society, as clearly has been the recent priority of the global financial trade. Socially responsible economics will emerge, as it has, in this reflexive movement obviously as economics is not as a subject closed off from other fields of enquiry.

The resultant risk for regulation in engaging with fictitious commodities in fictional markets is that it too will dislocate from the social and political core realities of civil society. Sociability requires that regulation be essentially embedded as a community construct. For this to be achieved and maintained there would be no room for regulation to assist in the artificialization of commodities or markets. Regulatory sociability could provide a bridge for bringing markets and society closer together and through this process socially responsible economics becomes the framework for a more essential market rehabilitation and reform (see chapter 6).

In an appreciation of the regulatory crisis and its market context in contemporary terms of a *Great Transformation*,[50] has Polanyi proved his predictions that 'after a century of blind "improvement", man is restoring his "habitation"'?[51] Are we facing the reality of market failure or failure of the market as a central regulatory challenge, not so much for regulation to assist market sustainability but rather to facilitate economic transition in a social world?

Central to Polanyi and others of his generation was the idea that progress could only come through conscious human action based on moral principles.[52] This conclusion is emerging from the wreckage of banking anarchy in the last decade, and social responsibility is replacing self-interested individualism as the ethic of economic analysis. Sustainability as a key regulatory principle, we argue through sociability, is the

---

[49] Polanyi (1944), p. 71 and chapter 6.
[50] Interestingly the meta-theme of the World Economic Forum 2012 is just this notion. For a critique see, Elliott (2012).
[51] Polanyi (1944), p. 257.
[52] Block and Somers (1984).

appropriate way forward in returning markets to some semblance of social connection.

In his book *The Communitarian Persuasion*, Selznick (2002), after listing the dangerous temptations attendant on short-term economic gain, says this about market failure:

> Society needs new ways of doing what was previously done by (conventional mechanisms of profit regulation). We need to do by public policy and institutional design what earlier was done less consciously by family pride, or the psychic rewards of a modestly successful business based on a vocation or craft. (After a preference for an expansion of non-profit organisations for critical service delivery he continues). In this work, moral idealism is combined with economic realism. Resources must be mobilised, investments monitored, costs controlled. These activities are not untouched by market forces. But the so called 'non-profits' can resist the market's indifference to culture and morality. If social policy encourages these associations and activities, it will acknowledge the worth and redeem the promise of civil society.[53]

Regulation has its place in transformation as much as it does in resuscitation. If Selznick's aspiration for civil society engagement over profit as a measure of market viability is to be tested, then the task for regulation is to take a form in which civil society has a place and for which investment becomes the *people's business* rather than the plaything of risky business.

The following chapter seeks to reconsider legal regulation and private property revaluation and access as a challenging test for the transformational imperatives explored in this chapter. As law's association with private property transcends to inclusion and accessibility, where general interests are legitimate and communities of shared interest made eligible, then the capacity of law to complement sustainable regulatory principle is unleashed and returned to its social location.

---

[53]   Selznick (2002).

4. Legal regulation, private property protection and the sustainability project

If I were asked to answer the following question: *What is slavery?* and I should answer in one word, *It is murder!*, my meaning would be understood at once. No extended argument would be required ... Why, then, to this other question: *What is property?* may I not likewise answer, *It is robbery!*, without the certainty of being misunderstood; the second proposition being no other than a transformation of the first?[2]

INTRODUCTION

In his anarchist critique of property, Proudhon rests his argument on two considerations of inequality which should challenge rather than attract law's complicity. Firstly, property allows the owner to exploit its user. Secondly, that property creates authoritarian social relationships between the two; property as theft and as despotism. The interconnectedness of these two indictments of property relies on a view which sees the oppression that property creates as ensuring exploitation. For Proudhon, and millions since, the appropriation of our common heritage (such as access to or possession of property) by a few through mechanisms which declare the process as *legal* (such as through contracts or title deeds), gives the rest of society little alternative but to agree to such domination and let the property owner appropriate the fruits of the labouring dispossessed.

On the other hand, rather than having to be theft or always requiring oppressive relationships, Proudhon confronted the assertion that property is in fact an agent of liberty if it can be opened up to wider, more equitable arrangements of possession and enjoyment – 'If the liberty of

---

[1] Proudhon (1866).
[2] Proudhon (1890); Guérin (2005), pp. 55–6.

man is sacred, it is equally sacred in all individuals; that, if it needs property for its objective action, that is, for its life, the appropriation of material is equally necessary for all'.[3]

The paradox of theft now, freedom and liberty in the future is what inspires our consideration of repositioning the principles underpinning law's regulation of private property relations. Useful for what follows in this chapter, Proudhon distinguished property from possession, the latter providing wide benefits of use and the former enabling the *exploitation of man by man,* under the protection of laws which endorse and are in turn endorsed by authoritarian, exclusionist social relationships.

> Property, acting by exclusion and encroachment, while population was increasing, has been the life-principle and definitive cause of all revolutions. Religious wars, and wars of conquest, when they have stopped short of the extermination of races, have been only accidental disturbances, soon repaired by the mathematical progression of the life of nations. The downfall and death of societies are due to the power of accumulation possessed by property.[4]

In the previous chapters, we have surfaced the weaknesses of the North World regulatory state model as the dominant global frame for developing regulatory principle, and in so doing, suggested the value of a shift in thinking about regulatory principle, relationships and outcomes, assisted by a deeper consideration of South World approaches to sustainability and social bonding. A redirection away from the North World and its primary regulatory state referent enables a critical comparative analysis of transformations in regulatory principle (or their incapacity) primarily in the economic realm. In chapter 1, we traced the forces and interests which promote or prevent a shift in regulatory principle, with particular focus on the emerging transition away from individual wealth maximization and economic growth at the nation state level, towards recognizing socially located sustainability as the dominant purpose for economic imperatives within social regulation.

This chapter has three conceptual directions. The first is to locate law as a regulatory force which currently works against generalized social bonding as a consequence of its role in the protection of exclusionist private property rights. The second analytical focus is on the ways in which, through a relocation of the regulatory principle which the law presently advances in its protection of private property rights and relationships, legal regulation might also be repositioned:

---

[3] Proudhon (2011), p. 96.
[4] Proudhon (1866).

- from a force for the exclusion of parties and interests, to a mechanism ensuring and enabling the inclusion of wider legitimate interests and more eligible parties within contractual protections; along with
- a redirecting of legal protections from the alienation and disposition of private property, to increased accessibility of the benefits provided by law (reinterpreted away from individualized benefit as an inevitable legal regulatory priority).

The final analytical consideration of this chapter is to construct a matrix for thinking about socio-economic sustainability, in terms of regulatory principles, relationships and outcomes which promote or retard social bonding. This matrix will then enable a comparative analytical frame for the two case-studies which make up the remaining body of this text.

The chapter commences by interrogating the sustainability of law as a regulatory project, through the possible repositioning of legal regulatory principle to ensure the sustainability of social bonds rather than the securing of individualized wealth creation as its primary focus. Next we explore briefly why the regulatory anthropology of legal regulation over private property rights is as it is. The chapter then plots law's regulatory relationship with private property and how it currently undermines the potential for socially embedding private property markets. From this understanding we offer practical suggestions regarding how a redirection of law's regulatory principle can change the prospect of law as an agent for social responsibility and social ordering. The chapter approaches this transition as an opportunity to employ the law/private property rights and relationship nexus in governance and political ordering which recognizes and adapts the value of socially embedded markets. In such settings legal regulation works for social justice and welfare, social responsibility and collective liberty; characteristics, we argue, of socially embedded market relationships. The chapter concludes by reiterating how and why sustainability should be a new or a renewed imperative for law and its positioning of property rights within embedded market economies. In achieving this aim, we suggest, law will become more sustainable as a regulatory agent through protecting social as well as individual wealth creation, and general benefit.

LAW'S SUSTAINABILITY?

We begin with an enquiry into law's role and its relevance in regulating human behavioural patterns[5] and creating and maintaining sustainable economic, political and social outcomes, especially through the protection of private property rights and relationships. Law, we consider, particularly in North World regulatory contexts, has become essential in the construction of propertied society and the nature of its dichotomous social bonding (inclusive/exclusive, weak/strong, sustainable/commodifiable). Law and legal regulation enhance some bonds and undermine others by prioritizing and advancing particular regulatory principles (and therefore rejecting others) whether tacitly or explicitly. At the same time, law has failed in both expressing and facilitating[6] a regulatory environment within which the challenges to economic and social sustainability (in terms of general interest) can be seen for what they are, that individualized wealth creation requires an exponential economic growth eventually incompatible with general social 'good'.

Against this dualist understanding of law as a change agent, sustainability therefore has to be recognized as a *dynamic* rather than temporal or spatial outcome of regulatory preferencing. Socio-economic sustainability is an evolving state, pitched against the challenges of present day global economic regulatory principle and its celebration of individual wealth creation and exponential economic growth in markets of finite and diminishing resources. As the recent global financial crisis well established, there are forces that work towards or against market sustainability.[7] Once appreciated as a moral question (determined against broad considerations of social responsibility for the sake of sustainability), the nature of the market as a socio-economic context reveals pre-existing tensions between individual and collective benefit which sustainable regulation must resolve.[8] For law to adapt to these new market conditions, its protective dimension needs to value core principles such as parity, equity and liberty in a context of social responsibility. Proudhon viewed individuality inextricably located in the collective consciousness. The existence of the individual and of any liberty they claim depend on collective social embeddedness. Social responsibility therefore is the organic atmosphere in which individual freedom is enjoyed. When directed to the possession and use of property the general good is what

---

5   Black (2002), pp 4–5.
6   Morgan and Yeung (2007), pp. 5–6.
7   Omarova (2011).
8   Rodrigues (2013).

gives value to individualized freedoms arising from mutualized property relationships. The attainment of general good gives legitimacy to the system of property rights and ensures its social sustainability within the arrangements of mutual benefit which can be facilitated through regulatory mediums such as law.

In contemporary North and South Worlds, it is becoming increasingly obvious that economic interests are no longer aligned with the general social good, if they ever were so in practice. The idea of the general social good is important here not merely because of the legitimacy it accords to regulatory purpose in a social context, but more substantially as a tangible benchmark for the justification of political and social institutions in the daily lives of each and every citizen.[9]

In terms of sustainability, general interest offers an alternative to individualized wealth creation, one which enables, through the identification both of sustainability's regulatory features and its essence as a regulatory outcome (see chapter 6), a convincing evaluative comparative framework for considering the relevance of regulatory principle. When sustainability is raised it is not just a 'for what' question, but also 'for who'. We prefer in this text to talk in broad terms of social sustainability where individualized wealth creation and exponential economic growth exist within, and are conditional on, wider considerations of the general good. Accepting that social location is important in determining the nature and future of sustainability (particularly for market economies) it is relevant to investigate the relationships of mutual benefit which might counter and contain the subversion of sustainability through individualized wealth priorities. This dimension of analysis is consistent with our earlier work on mutualized interests and regulatory sociability as the preferred global response to significant contemporary crises.[10]

Legal regulation can be measured in terms of its broad social legitimacy, against its influence on sustainability and its capacity to transform private property access and transactability away from its contemporary exclusionist focus on individualized and state-centred concepts of wealth and economic growth. In this chapter, we have selected the institution of private property rights and their protection as a context for questioning the place of law as a social bonding agent. In the literature which interrogates the ownership of the means of production, in terms of those responsible for production,[11] as well as the writings on economic

---

[9]   Rawls (2008), p. 13.
[10] Findlay (2013a); see also Proudhon (1927), pp. 118–19.
[11] Marx and Engels (1867), chapter 32.

redistribution,[12] exclusive private property rights and relations may rest on neither just nor equitable foundations, and as such may not prioritize either general good or social sustainability. From the regulatory frames of disaggregated states in the South World right through to the vagaries of global social ordering, the relevance of law for issues of governance and the construction and maintenance of political order, liberal or otherwise, is crucial. Specifically for the interests of this chapter, there needs to be a greater link between law's regulatory relevance, beyond the institutional and procedural dis-aggregations in fragmented states. This repositioning of law's regulatory role without the state in the South World where states are often the problem and not the solution, can be viewed in a similar fashion to what challenges law's regulatory relevance in the North World with its diminishing recognition and engagement of law in more pluralist regulatory relationships. North World neo-liberal legalities do tend to, as is the case with the protection of private property rights and relationships, undervalue pluralistic ordering or holism in governance and to that degree can represent a powerful force in repressing organic and more diverse social bonding. Law in this sense tends to shut down and close out the possibilities of accessing, possessing and enjoying property as a more mutualized, and thereby socially sustainable, general good.

According to Rawls, 'If all societies were required to be liberal, the idea of political liberalism would fail to express due toleration for other acceptable ways (if such there are as I assume) of ordering society'.[13]

We make this argument more strongly below by bringing into focus our criticisms of the existing role to which law sees itself circumscribed, particularly where its expressive and facilitative functions are wedded to a framework of individualist neo-liberal rights and responsibilities, to the detriment of a more social justice focus in the perpetuation of property and its equitable (and sustainable, we would assert) possession. Specifically in charting a way forward for legal regulation and sustainable property possession the chapter advocates the development of a model role for the law through employing the three M's – markets, moralities and mutualities – as a matrix.

The extent to which distributive justice should therefore feature in each society's own determination and definition of sustainable social justice depends on the unique equilibrium to be found in the regulatory principles upon which society is built. In the push for principled regulation to pervade governance policies and decision-making, it is

---

[12]   Rawls (1971).
[13]   Rawls (1999), p. 59.

necessary to enquire who we expect to locate the legitimacy of law as representing and enforcing the foundational social justice principles upon which regulation for sustainability relies.

As an aside, due to the limits of the text, we cannot explore in any sufficient detail whether sustainability in the North or South World, proved through the achievement of general good, relies on the sometimes ubiquitous assumption that mutual interests ultimately can be reached, and against what measure. Because of the differing interests that exist amongst citizens, in making a political decision for a sustainable outcome measured through the attainment of a general good, a latent enquiry in our research is whether our concept of *social beings* amounts to free and equal persons each prioritizing political justice and the common good, or whether people simply bargain their own economic and class interests, tainted by their religious or ethnic antagonisms.[14] This in turn impacts on our idea of mutuality which is essential for the functioning of regulatory sociability, and the accommodation of the concept of community in regulation seen through social bonding. In our work on sociability we suggest that mutuality does not necessarily grow out of common or even compatible interests. In fact it can be the fear generated in risk societies which compels diverse interests to, sometimes painfully, seek out the common good, turning risk to fate.

Law can have a role to play in orchestrating the general good through the mutualizing of individual interests, for the purpose of regulating to sustainable social bonding. This can be achieved by providing a normative framework and a facilitating process to negotiate difference in favour of mutuality. In *The Law of Peoples*, Rawls moves his consideration of the relationship between law and justice away from individualist notions of responsibility, through seeing individuals as ethically significant units. Law can have a key role to play in the re-conceptualization and the broader framing of social responsibility. Where private property relations are concerned, if driven by sustainability as its regulatory principle, law can open up access and diversify the means and outcomes of enjoyment for individuals engaged in the delivery of the common good. In addition, if through a redirection of regulatory principle, law returns to an ethical framing, then its role in supporting the individual as ethically significant units of social bonding becomes organic rather than mechanical. Law, therefore, can act as an organic bond where it is socially embedded rather than a mechanical force sustaining fictional assets such as inequitable access to property benefits.

---

[14]   Rawls (2008), p. 5.

As we develop later in the book (see chapter 7), principles of liberalism and liberty can be seen as based on two fundamental precepts:

(a)   the maximization of individual interests, limited only to permit (but not necessarily to participation in or ensuring) equivalent liberty for all persons; or
(b)   distributive justice which advances those who have less, through some constraint of liberty.

Rawls sees individuals rather than communities as being the primary units of moral concern and therefore the consideration of liberty at its most basic level is a general good and a mutualized consideration. Rawls stops short of requiring law as a regulator to see that this is so. He does acknowledge however in his later writings such as *The Law of Peoples* (and we concur) that the idea of responsibility has little meaning in a modern world outside its social context.[15]

In repositioning law's role as regulating in favour of social sustainability, we consider law's function as a *responsibilizing* agent to be central. Here we appreciate the need for law to move beyond its conventional connection with responsibility; where legal consequences flow from the exercise of rational choice and free will, problematic as these notions are in legal practice. For the purposes of this text we are more concerned that law ensures a degree of *fidelity*[16] between individuals, their motivations, their behaviours and consequences as forms of social transaction. In this respect law becomes the social arbiter in different stages of human agency with the purpose of ensuring that, through whatever essential rights and relationships it protects, critical social bonding is sustainable (chapter 5 charts the failure of this process).

LAW'S REGULATORY ANTHROPOLOGY

The anthropological direction of the research to follow (see chapters 5 and 6) will reflect from the perspective of societies (preferentially South World societies) which remain still less comprehensively dependent on mechanical features of modernization that prioritize individual wealth creation, to examine the nature of their social bonding, existing as it does without necessarily and recurrently individualized and legalized applications of concepts of private property rights. Social bonding here may

---

15   Rawls (1999).
16   Ashworth (2000).

take the form of community-based action/intervention or family units reflecting a shared interest in the determination of each individual's action. In their communitarian form and subsistence priorities, organic social bonds coalesce societies often seen as 'without the law', or law as the North World knows it. Property is conceived as a common good which belongs to the family, the community, the tribe or to society as a whole, and it is in these 'anti-individualist' terms that we developed our view of law as social bonding (for both sides of this assertion see chapters 5 and 6).[17] Collective interests and community as they identify property benefit become the priority, now unfamiliar when considering North World normative and commercial applications of law as a mechanism for social exclusion and regulatory transaction. Employing these 'anthropologies' of comparative property relations, the purpose of the law in North/South World regulatory contexts should suggest how, through a repositioning of regulatory principle towards sustainability, market economies in the North World and their social connection, can be re-embedded for the benefit of a more general economic and social good.

In chapter 6, we assert that the contemporary role of the law in maintaining private property rights and relationships is in part a story of law's failure as a regulator measured against the advancement of public or general interest. In the context of correcting or avoiding future global financial crises, as an example of such regulatory failure (see chapter 3), if law is to provide a more effective regulatory function it will need to re-evaluate the concepts of value (or 'wealth') which it promotes, as well as endorse something beyond an often exclusionist preference for the protection of individual wealth creation. In this regard a mutuality of interests,[18] and at least the recognition of a contestable place for more universalist public interests as legitimate contenders for legal protection, arises as a challenge to present day exclusionist legal protections of private property rights.[19]

At this point we should briefly digress as to why individualized wealth creation and state-fuelled exponential economic growth are unsustainable. There is no need to establish this if the reader accepts our

---

[17]   This is a view with which Proudhon and other mutualists would not be comfortable unless we make space for the liberty of the individual within the common good, or as Rawls would require, that the common good does not automatically disadvantage the needs of the individual. In our later discussion of communitarian sustainability we will try and reflect and reconcile these conditions.

[18]   Findlay (2013a), chapter 11.

[19]   Perez (2002).

associated premises; first that individual wealth creation is a feature of dis-embedded market economies, and that such dis-embedded economies are socially unsustainable. If these assertions are not accepted then we must turn to several other justifications.

There is now substantial literature which connects individualist wealth creation and exponential economic growth with the expanding income gap in emerging economies and establishes this as a significant threat to their economic sustainability (see chapter 7).[20] If this correlation is correct then wealth maximization and economic growth which favours the few at the expense of the many is practically unsustainable for orderly economic development. It also fails the test of utility; the greatest happiness for the greatest number. From a more theoretical perspective, we agree with Posner's clarification that economics and utilitarianism are not one and the same.[21] Accepting that utilitarianism is a persuasive justification (and outcome) for legal regulation, and we don't say this is essential, then the moral worth of such action is judged by its effect in promoting happiness. Economic analysis limits these effects to wealth maximization; happiness through wealth for the individual provided that the 'community' of the wealthy is not so narrow as to degrade the happiness of a sufficient number to satisfy the conditions of utility. Sustainability analysis broadens out the consequences of happiness as a range of influences for social bonding. Economic analysis of law (its distinctly western/North World perspectives) works from a free market model which requires that through merit or other individualized opportunities to access wealth, wealth maximization might be ethically, as well as practically, advanced as the utilitarian happiness measure. People are happy because they are wealthy in a material sense, or getting wealthier. Despite the fragility of this argument, if one impugns the preferred economic model (and we see vast and recurrent evidence of that happening today) we attack the irredentist assumption of wealth creation as a realistic option for individuals (and even societies) in the South World where access to capital and participation in private property privileges are critically class determined and finite.

---

[20] Findlay (forthcoming), concerning sustainability and income inequality.

[21] That said, we would hold that economics also has to have a principle it values above all others. In the sustainability context such a principle does not have to be valued in terms of the dollar sense, or restricted to being quantifiable into dollars and cents. Economics as a regulator of principle has the capacity to have a broader reach than law once broken free of material wealth valuation. A wider economic principle can promote a wider utilitarian measure of success through generating the greatest happiness for the greatest number.

Furthermore, if we approach from a contemporary South World context the wealth effects of rights assignments (posited by Dworkin),[22] such as whether a universal 'right' to internet access is too costly in monetary terms to achieve, the precondition of flexible wealth distribution requirements against which right's transactions can be evaluated in economic wealth terms does not hold. The 'value' of such a universal right is measured through access to knowledge, and not its financial cost. The reason for this is that such economic/rights theorizing says little if anything about the reality of inequitable wealth assignment or the discriminatory allocation of resources. What makes this theoretical paradigm more abstract and distracted from the inequities of wealth maximization in the South World is its dual assertions as to being both ethical and practical. It suffers in our view from similar problems that arise through the application of individual preferencing to social conditions where such preferencing is either not available or not carried out in an individualized paradigm. As with the critique of utilitarianism at large, if wealth maximization and economic growth are to be achieved by making vast populations in the South World miserably poor then the moral and social unsustainability of the profit aspiration, in terms of a general good, is clearly, we argue, also economically unsustainable when economy is a global and not merely a hegemonic consideration. If law and legal regulation have a part in this outcome, we say that they share in the critique concerning sustainability.

In our work to follow we do not require that legal regulation produce income equality or that in some ways it ensures justice only through the collective decisions of individuals in the 'original position'.[23] Rather, we will argue that legal regulation, repositioned through principles for sustainability, is compatible with the individual's incentive to be productive, but for the purpose of social responsibility above individual wealth creation.

In moving law into this new engagement it is useful to propose a global economic anthropology which is a development on from the failing free-market model. When we think about the current operation of post-Fordist capitalism and how a capitalist world order has grown out of particular institutions and regulatory actions, we should reflect on how law's regulatory role has evolved, constrained within capitalist ideologies, and the rights frameworks which complement these. Borrowing from Sen's distinction between *niti* and *nyaya* – that is, organizational

---

[22]   Dworkin (1997).
[23]   Rawls (1971), p. 27

propriety and correctness mainly concerned with the task of defining rules and institutions (*niti*) and the focus on a comprehensive idea of realized justice (*nyaya*)[24] – we can see how law, although restricting its role in the capitalist world order to a facilitative one, has had tremendous impact on and consequences for the way societies bond, and individuals within them live their lives.

Through the analysis of the system of private property rights and relationships (in specific commercial and developmental contexts) offered next, we are able to argue that law carries within it normative values complementing a deeply individualized property focus (committed to restricted access and a disposition to maximize value in a material way) and does more than merely facilitate in any neutral sense daily inter-actions between persons with interests in individualized wealth creation. The legitimating normative framework for law in a social sense, interest-ingly, goes way beyond its individualized focus and would have law stand as an institution for improving the quality of lives of those whom it serves (observed in terms of the society). Stripped to their core functions, regulatory paradigms (through law) are about social bonding and should have as their central purpose (if social legitimacy is to be sought), generalization of the benefits of property relations.

LAW'S REGULATORY RELATIONSHIP WITH PRIVATE PROPERTY

Turning now to the specifics of repositioning law's regulatory relation-ship with private property, and its capacity to enhance rather than endanger the social embeddedness of the markets it serves, this chapter will look at these issues in turn:

1. What is the relevance of law when considering questions of governance and political order, resting in social bonds beyond individualized wealth creation?
2. What are the liberties and freedoms emancipated by the capitalist world order through the generation and protection of exclusive private property relations?
3. Are the notions of social justice and welfare necessarily at odds and therefore in tension with market societies where private property relations tend to dis-embed the market from general social bonding?

---

[24] Sen (2009), p. 20.

4. Employing the use of the three M's – markets, moralities and mutualities – are we proposing in this chapter a viable model role for law, through critique and theorizing?
5. Can the concept of community be accommodated within a capitalist world order if, through theories such as sociability, property is protected by the law for attaining and maintaining the general good, and enlivening individual freedoms through the recognition of collective social responsibility?
6. How does law as it is currently framed by society construct and support the system of private property rights, so as to defer or defeat a mutuality of interests that would make more available access to property and capital and thereby expand mutualized benefit (and economic social responsibility) through the lens of the South World?

We have made the point before, and here below it will be specified, that the central hypothesis regarding legal regulation, private property protection and social embedding/dis-embedding has two parts. Both work from the assumption that as a consequence of the conditions surrounding the recent global economic crisis,[25] economic regulatory principle is moving from individual wealth maximization and exponential economic growth, to more fundamental considerations of market sustainability and social embeddedness.[26] The corollary of this assumption is that as markets shift away from their essential social location, they are experiencing and at the same time stimulating the regulatory disengagement which has produced profound market failure.[27]

The first limb of the hypothesis argues that if socio-economic sustainability will become the new regulatory principle for a more socially embedded global economic order, then sustainability can be understood in terms of markets, moralities and mutualities. These three variables have been selected because markets are essential contexts for contemporary economic regulation and will remain so even as regulatory relationships and outcomes shift from the wealth creation emphasis towards concerns for market sustainability.[28] *Mutualities* can be taken to mean, in a specific consideration of sustainability in the context of socio-economic bonding, the relationships which comprise market interconnectedness that maintains a wider social benefit from market outcomes. Moralities

---

25 Findlay (2013a), chapter 7.
26 Krugman (2009); Krugman (2011).
27 Findlay (forthcoming).
28 Laffont (1994); Leith (2008) and Lie (1997).

are critical in considering where the wealth creation regulatory focus has failed society, and how a 'remoralization' of market relationships will help to ensure more sustainable outcomes. As Marx observed, economic struggles invite moral struggles and '(political economy) is – for all its worldly and debauched appearance – a truly moral science'.[29]

In this limb sustainability should be understood as a dynamic rather than a temporal or spatial outcome, as we elaborated on earlier in chapter 3. Therefore in looking at these three features of regulatory principle we need to consider the forces which work for or against sustainability.

The second limb of the hypothesis is that as legal regulation (or its absence) appears to have been at the centre of the recent financial crisis, and eventually became a regulatory contender for its rehabilitation,[30] law can offer a specific regulatory frame through which markets, mutualities and moralities can be evaluated in crises and in transition. To sharpen the analysis further it is intended to concentrate on private property relations created and maintained by law to understand how regulation has assisted in the recent market crises and can otherwise be turned to advance socio-economic sustainability.[31] In particular, the research will focus on how law's regulatory function, in selectively and exclusively advancing particular property interests and ignoring others, has participated in markets becoming socially dis-embedded and how through reconsidering law's function, markets, mutualities and moralities can be reinforced and returned to more socio-economically sustainable outcomes.

The method we suggested in chapter 2, when applied to this specific regulatory context and the empirical case-studies to follow will also have two phases. Initially it will identify factors which influence markets, moralities and mutualities towards or away from socio-economic sustainability. This matrix will essentially be interactive in that if sustainability requires definition then it can be achieved through looking at markets, moralities and mutualities (and their interdependence). In order to achieve a convincing and analytically useful definition we expect it will be necessary to understand what it is in the 'three M's' that supports or subverts sustainable socio-economic outcomes, initially determined against their social location and relevance as a 'general good'.

---

[29] Marx (2005 edn), p. 361. For an interesting exchange on the relationship between morality and the recent financial crisis see (2013) 'Discussion Forum'.

[30] Shleifer (2010), pp. 27–43.

[31] Perez suggests this particularly by utilizing an expansion in the parties covered by standard form construction contracts in order that community interests can contest within the contract relationship the narrower self-interests of owners and developers. Perez (2002).

Once the matrix has been devised then it is intended to apply to understanding two socio-economic phenomena, one which is clearly socially dis-embedded, and the other which can claim social connection and relevance. For the purposes of this empirical phase the project will consider migrant labour (as unsustainable private property relations) in Singapore (dis-embedded) and eco-tourism (as sustainable market economy) in the elephant parks of Northern Thailand (embedded). Returning to the analytical focus on legal regulation the project will specifically explore the private property relationships and outcomes (in terms of the 'three M's') which assist in dis-embedding in one context and embedding in the other.

Prior to advancing these analytical pathways, it is important to say a little more about the broader conventions of law's role in governance and ordering. In capitalist market economies it is nigh on impossible to ignore the importance of private property rights in the wealth and resource *ordering* from which capitalist market economies are governed and in turn govern.

REPOSITIONING LAW'S PRINCIPLED REGULATORY RELATIONSHIP WITH PRIVATE PROPERTY

If as we intend, law is a key to the embedding of market economies back to sustainable social bonds, then the law's role in regulating relationships with private property requires transformation. It is incumbent on us to present some brief reflections on how we view these relationships in their contemporary North World context. Of necessity these reflections may be unsatisfyingly general. However, here we intend at least to focus on the features essential for transformation.

So far we have identified that these relationships tend to be:

- Exclusionist so as to create value by limiting those who can divest property; and
- Focused on transactionability rather than possession/use.

In these ways, property relationships, if they are to reflect wider social bonding, will require transformation to include broader interests, and embrace values more centred on property as a social rather than an individualized benefit. Any such transformation could take one of two routes:

- a fundamental reworking of the concept of property; or
- a reconsideration of property as it connects to other critical social values.

For reasons which are largely pragmatic, as they are more likely to require a less radical shift in the role of law as a regulator, we will advance the 'property plus' transformative approach. To be clear, it is law's role in regulating private property relations which is our current concern. However, it is the nature of that role in its North World individualist predisposition which we see as a challenge to sustainability and it is that which we identify for reform. At the heart of such a transformation will lie a commitment to the social sustainability of these relationships and their regulatory outcomes. To achieve sustainability, and to avert many of the more socially negative aspects of law's engagement with private property, the repositioned regulatory principles governing these relationships should be:

- Reciprocity – where law ensures just interactions between often contesting stakeholders and promotes the move to mutualizing interests in an atmosphere of social responsibility;
- Revaluation – where law enables markets in private property to fundamentally change the meaning of goods, and thereby to open up the possibility of 'pricing' goods in manners which prioritize social bonding, rather than individualized wealth creation; and
- Fidelity – where law ensures the nature of the relationships between individuals as socially responsible and thereby sustainable.

Associated with these fundamental principles (and influenced by the analysis in *The Theory of Property*) the social bonds which are possible through a new cognition of law's regulatory role over private property can be grounded on certain approximations:

- of the equality of faculties;
- of the equality of fortunes; and
- of the equalizing potential of redistribution.

Along with what Proudhon refers to as 'the infinite progress in science, law, liberty, honor, justice' (all viable contestants for a repositioned regulatory principle), there seems, in our argument, to be no reason beyond an inflexible ascription to a failing economic model, why if a repositioning of regulatory principle is advanced and achieved, property relations cannot be regulated for liberty (collectively understood) rather than for oppression (resisted through the general good). In order to achieve this it is important to confront (as does Proudhon in *The System of Economic Contradictions*) the essentially *contradictory* nature of property, depending on its relationship with law. For instance, property can be the right of occupancy and the right of exclusion, at the same time it can be labours' reward and the denial of its fruit, society's spontaneous work and society's dissolution, an institution of justice while at the same time being theft.[32] Law needs to reconcile these contradictions with the objective of social sustainability as its focus.

Nominating property as *private* fundamentally imbues it with distinction and degrees of exclusivity. It is private as a consequence of its domain, and through the ownership rather than the origins of its productivity. For private property to co-exist in a broad context of social bonding the challenge is for legal regulation to ensure that private property and its privileges become a *natural* (organic) rather than a *fictional* (mechanical) *right*. Where the benefits of access to and enjoyment of private property arise out of mutualized, moral and market embedded relationships law has an organic (internal) rather than mechanical (external) regulatory force. In that respect legal regulation is not limited to the protection of private property but extends to the protection of access to it, collectively and individually.

If the legal regulation of private property rights has a unique potential for endorsing collective liberty, social responsibility, and inclusion and access to proprietary benefits of possession and enjoyment then this has in a regulatory sense, important consequences for how we envisage social governance.

THE RELEVANCE OF LAW IN GOVERNANCE AND POLITICAL ORDER

This section commences with identifying the often less-noted governance tensions between modern economy and society, and in so doing uses critical legal theory and regulatory anthropology as tools of analysis to question and interrogate the role of law in endorsing and maintaining mechanisms and institutions (such as the system of private property rights) in ways which dis-embed economic imperatives from essential social bonds. What belies Adam Smith's claim in favour of the invisible hand of the market and its almost supernatural regulation and governance

---

[32]   Godwin (1986), pp. 125–6.

aura, is an assumption that the free market economy would allocate resources in a manner superior to government direction. There are therefore two dimensions to this argument, an economic and a political. As law negotiates these two dimensions, we remember Rousseau's words – 'Does it follow that it [inequality] must not at least be regulated? It is precisely because the force of things always tends to destroy equality that *the force of legislation should always tend to maintain it*'.[33]

This observation provokes questions concerning who the law should look to as its constituency and for whom it should exist to protect. Given that the role of law is often seen as creating a collectively rational civil society which enables the conditions for maximizing production as a means of commodious living,[34] then when the law as an institution delineates the rules for property ownership and exchange in market contexts silently governed by scarce natural resources, inequalities emerge through providing the security of property ownership and lawful industry which progresses the present economic model.[35] Such a role for law moves liberty from a collective concept to a purely individualist context, at the expense of endorsing responsibilities for sustainability which are intensely social.

Social cooperation as we envisaged in our earlier developments of regulatory sociability enables the coordination of social activity for the mutualized interests of (rational) citizens engaged in collective regulation which is fair and justifiable to each individual interest (reasonable). Therefore, the law (or legal regulation) as a manifestation of such coordination (i.e. social bonding) has to meet the dual requirements of rationality and reasonableness. Rationality and reasonableness through legal regulation, therefore, should underpin individual and social contexts for regulatory choice as we see it, even when people come together motivated by fear and with distinctly separate interests which require mutualizing. In such regulatory environments law can provide a reflexive and responsive framework where fear eventually progresses to trust and mutual interests for a general good, not subjugated to individual interests where they lose much social value.

As it stands, the law in its support for and perpetuation of an individualist and exclusionist system of private property rights is, as we argue, likely often to compromise or override its responsibilities to provide a mechanism for the rational and reasonable mutualizing of

---

[33] Rousseau (1766), chapter 2. See also Rawls (2008), p. 234.
[34] Rawls (2008), p. 45.
[35] Hobbes (1983), pp. 26–7.

individual interests, benefitting a common good. In the contemporary global economic context, the mechanics of how capitalism conceals features of domination and exploitation are detailed below, through a summary of Marx's labour theory.[36]

Progressing beyond individualized wealth creation as a motivation for social coordination, we advance mutuality as a solution to the regulatory paradox of social cooperation within a competitive framework heavily reliant on problematic regulatory assumptions such as self-regulation and peer surveillance. Through the mutualizing of interests we hold that internalized and often self-interested regulatory frames which have sometimes been essential to promote or maintain cooperation and collaboration, are rarely sufficient safeguards for the values of sustainable market economies. We will later detail the need to give mutual interests greater form and function if social sustainability is to proliferate through a repositioned legal regulation. In particular, as Perez suggests with the widening of interests included under standard form construction con-tracts, mutualities can gain greater market location through an expansion of legal protections and inclusion within legal actionability.[37] Such a transformation will require argument in political, economic and ethical terms (expanded on in chapters 5 and 6).[38]

Essential for each of these analytical paradigms is a reformulation (or perhaps a socio-historical rediscovery) of what we argue is law's essen-tial purpose measured against social sustainability: the creation and maintenance of *binding agreements to cooperate*. Within this notion, *agreements* have a meaning which is both legal (contractual) and mutual (collaborative). Envisaged in this way, law can be seen as the glue that *enforces* sociability. Law can be both the principled frame and the medium for negotiating the recognition and reconciliation of competing interests within a wider construction of mutual benefit. Law is a device for moving communities of risk to communities of fate. Law takes on a

---

[36] It is impossible in such a sketchy review to do justice to the original theorizing or subsequent critical treatment. Here we do no more than advance the themes of labour value to later assert the transaction of labour as an unbalanced private property relationship endorsed by law or allowed through its absence or partial intrusion.

[37] Perez (2002).

[38] Similarly, in Hobbes' view (in the context of the Social Contract as the means through which the emergence of civil society looking to a sovereign to maintain the conditions of such harmonious co-existence), social institutions, education and culture each have a bearing on the identification of the principles which serve as the foundation for law/regulation.

capacity, through a fundamental revision of its role in private property protection to ensure that individual interests are not irreconcilable with wider concerns for sustainability.

LEGAL REGULATION IN THE POST-FORDIST CAPITALIST WORLD ORDER

In today's economic world order, many of the arguments canvassed in discussions of governance are premised on the need for a system which protects private property rights for individuals and private actors so as to enable and ensure the conditions of capitalist coexistence. If one maintains that property rights in a market economy should be resistant to redistribution and hence insulated by law against distributive justice,[39] preferring to rely on the location of individual property rights within the market to enable efficient allocations of scarce resources, then what of the aspirations of fairness (reasonableness) for law which recognize more than private property rights?

Through the individualization and the diversification of wealth forms and productivity capacities, economic freedom in the form of freedom to contract and the legal protection of ownership rights over personal and real property reveals law as being less interested in communitarian values like equality of opportunity and social justice, despite these being aligned with the normative values of social justice which can legitimate law's authority and the liberty it endorses. Where liberty is inextricably tied to individualist and exclusive economic freedom, and competition is advanced as the moderator of free market economies, legal regulation has led to a system delineated according to positioning in a propertied class, exhibiting and advancing ownership of the means of production and paradoxically the power to moderate competition in the interests of the individual and not always that of the market. Through this system, law operates as the champion of individualized and exclusionist property interests which seem to evolve further and further away from any original social utility or commonality of interest and sharing of responsibility. The system fails to recognize, or is indeed blind to other stakeholders in property possession, besides *owners, licensed occupiers and transactors*, as defined by law.

Interestingly, and perhaps counter-intuitively to the manner in which we prefer to use it in transforming regulatory principle, sustainability has

---

[39]   Nozick (1974).

an arguable relevance as a justification for the exclusionist nature of property rights. In these terms property rules (such as ownership and defeasibility) are designed to manage the problem of resource scarcity. However, relating this for example to intellectual property, the law protecting copyright, trademarks and patents might not essentially prioritize the issue of scarcity, but rather through restrictions on access and the use of scarce knowledge, *manufacture and maintain* scarcities for the sake of ensuring property pricing and value. In this example law protects private property as a scarce resource and to maintain inflated pricing as a consequence of its limited accessibility. As with the mass violation of these property rights through piracy which is a feature of emergent economies in the South World, the law is flouted because of its role in excluding access to what is viewed from the perspective of these economies as a sustainable rather than a transactable property relationship.

The discussion of markets below, and our developed critique of the current idealized conceptualization of market economies as free and competitive and thereby essentially self-regulating, raises bigger questions for capitalism as a regulatory world economic order. Thinking about social coordination through law, finding the common interests the attainment of which require social conditions (such as law) for the common good, necessitates identifying and investigating forces for mutualizing interests across peoples and cultures, which then will support regulatory principles promoting be governed sustainably.[40]

In order to shift our regulatory thinking beyond an amorphous sense of 'good' primarily equating with individualized wealth creation, a starting point should be envisaging the system of private property rights and its history within the development of the prevailing global economic model and its consequences for South World social development. Parenthetically, a North World economic predisposition in the literature has failed to enable a general critical appreciation of the role of law in governance (and legal regulation in dis-embedding market economies) where the protection and perpetuation of exclusive private property rights is a basis of the dominant economic model.

---

[40]   Rawls (2008), p. 225.

SOCIAL JUSTICE AND WELFARE

The implications of thinking about law as a scheme of social bonding for the furtherance of the social conditions necessary to maximize social sustainability is a tall order.[41] Having established the narrow purposes of property rules that are predominantly focused on using self-gain or self-interest as regulatory principles, and measures of the efficient allocation of resources within a market economy, we ask whether ideas of social justice and welfare are necessarily at odds, and therefore in tension, with market societies where private property relations tend to dis-embed the market from general social bonding?

An interesting example to test social consensus regarding the tension between individual liberty and social welfare where property rights are concerned is in procedures for state confiscation of privately owned land, more commonly known as the concept of eminent domain or compulsory acquisition.

The Fifth Amendment to the United States Constitution states that '… (nor shall) private property be taken for public use, without just compensation'.[42]

Article 8 of the European Convention on Human Rights provides that:

> Everyone has the right to respect for his private and family life, his home, and his correspondence and prohibits interference with this right by the state, unless the interference is in accordance with law and necessary in the interests of national security, public safety, economic well-being of the country, prevention of disorder or crime, protection of health or morals, or protection of the rights and freedoms of others.[43]

Public use carries with it some form of societal agreement/acquiescence or some degree of common good sieved through the majoritarian consensus of executive decision-making, measured by principles upon which common good is formed and valued. However, there is a struggle contextualizing compulsory acquisition between state-determined communitarian needs which take precedence over the sometimes less actionable interests of the individual and communities through the mediating solution of just compensation, the determination of which is up to judicial decision-making.

---

41   Ibid, p. 301.
42   Fifth Amendment to the United States Constitution.
43   Article 8 of the European Convention on Human Rights.

An interesting example of this is Singapore, being a unique commercial property environment in which the prioritizing of a market oriented approach to social problems is said to be the driver for property transaction and wealth creation through economic growth. Much of Singapore's personal wealth vests in real estate and much of the state's capacity to generate revenue is through the management of private real estate property relations, particularly by acquisition or compulsory conversion. Enabling this state incursion into private real estate rights, in Singapore, the Land Titles (Strata) Act provides for the collective sales of individual real property units even when an owner is against the sale. What was initially conceived as the subjugation of individual private needs to the welfare of the public has developed in Singapore, through the free market state, into a mechanism to allow the majoritarian (private) interests of those who live and own real property within the same estate to overrule the decisions of those in the minority, a process which the state facilitates and benefits from.[44]

In another example, Japan, which does not recognize eminent domain powers, deals with the acquisition of land for redevelopment in a similar fashion: for instance when Roppongi Hills was slated for redevelopment, the compulsory acquisition offered was a revaluation of private property rights providing disproportionately large amounts of financial inducement to the landowners prompting their agreement to the sale.

Through the two examples discussed above, individualized wealth creation interests in property protection can be seen as eclipsed in preference for a conditional notion of societal or shared interests, which in fact benefit the state or other corporatized parties. Private property contractual interests are mediated by the regulatory state in tampering with the market for state benefit. The law is a tool in this sense for income redistribution but under the guise of market capitalism.

LAW AS SHAPED BY ITS RIGHTFUL 'CONSTITUENCY' – A LABOUR THEORY OF VALUE

The separation of property from labour has become the necessary consequence of a law that apparently originated in their identity.[45]

In making sense of what Marx sought to express above, we look at the process through which exploitation within a capitalist framework takes

---

[44]   Part VA of the Land Titles (Strata) Act (Cap. 158) (Rev. Ed. 2009).
[45]   Marx and Engels (1867), p. 584. See also Rawls (2008), p. 344.

the form of an application of laws which protect individualist property ownership and exchange – laws which frame the right of capitalists to appropriate the dispossessed and under-valued labour of others, or the product of that labour. To take this observation to its logical conclusion relies on law enabling the systematic appropriation of property from those who produce labour, an important if fictional component of production and exchange. And in Polanyi's view, this is relevant when considering the justice of economic institutions that endorse such arrangements.[46]

If we look at property from the perspective of those who produce and reproduce, rather than those who possess through the limitations of ownership or licence and transact it, an argument can be made that this system has failed even the people who enable its expansion (such as pension fund contributors, and real estate mortgagees) as illustrated by the numerous contemporary instances of massive institutionally-based financial fraud, and the failure of international investment value structures. In such situations of systemic failure, where is the law's interest directed, or its reluctant engagement delimited? In the recent restitution of the global financial collapse, it was taxpayers who carried the brunt of the greed, ungoverned risk taking and irresponsible mismanagement by those acting on behalf of the wealthy minority who played the investment racket for individual wealth maximization at staggering levels of short-term return. It remains these taxpayers who see no personal or communal gain from their compulsory investment as the state now chooses to privatize resuscitated banks back into the hands of the same investors whose imprudent thirst for wealth motivated the risk that led to the institutional and process collapse.

In both North and South Worlds the dependence of labour on the means of production to unlock its wealth potential remains unresolved, at least in terms of who benefits from the market economies with artificial divisions of labour and productivity exchange. In order to exercise and apply their labour power, which is in the South World too commonly the only factor of production over which the workers can claim ownership or possession, workers need legalized access to, and opportunities for sharing possession of the means of production, currently owned beyond their reach. In the capital starved and employment repressed South World market economies, a more generalized access to productive capacity may be deemed unproductive when measured against the current economic growth drivers where workforces are paid little and working conditions

---

[46]   Rawls (2008), p. 351.

are largely unregulated.[47] This is where law may be necessary to prioritize social over economic growth measures (see chapter 5).

It is only when exchanges in labour and production are revalued against social sustainability rather than individualized wealth creation that the consequences of freeing up access to, and possession/ownership of private property might be considered socially responsible rather than economically disadvantageous. For such a reconsideration of the value of labour and production, and a reconfiguration of parties benefiting from private property in exploited workforce economies, the distributive role that the law (as a wider regulatory frame that incorporates notions of social justice) cannot be avoided.

Mill, as a defender of laissez-faire capitalism, never envisaged rules relating to private property rights (including those dictating the manner of holding property such as the outcome of inheritance and bequest) to be aimed at equalizing property access and benefit. Instead he, as a founding father of the economic model that currently prevails in the North World and for global economic ordering, viewed the legal protections of private property having as their purpose the amelioration of the consequences of large concentrations of wealth in the hands of few. The resulting unequal spread of property ownership and possession thereby creating fragmented propertied classes over time was a natural byproduct (perhaps unintended and regrettable) of such wealth maintenance strategies.[48] Although based on utilitarian considerations, Mill saw these private property exclusionist rules as subject to and indeed demanding considerations of distributive justice in order to be practically workable. Limited distribution was necessary to maintain the conditions of social order which enabled the perpetuation of class-based property exploitation.

Wherein exists such massive and apparent inequality *world-to-world*, it is now not possible for the wealthy to turn away blindly from the structural causes of poverty that have eventuated from the unsustainable exploitation of resources, endangering global order and even the economic regulatory model that made wealth for the few.[49] In matters of social and political equality that often arise within a liberal democratic framework for governance, there always has to be underlying normative values according to which official state decisions are made, thereby shaping the law.[50] If these take the form of regulatory principles then it is

47   Rawls (2008), p. 325.
48   Ibid, p. 316.
49   Pfanner (2012).
50   MacKenzie (2005), p. 14.

now for the survival of the haves *and* the have-nots that the shift to sustainability is as pressing as it is inevitable.

We are proposing a regulatory role for law beyond simply just a mechanism that facilitates the conduct of social relations of any kind. The plurality of societies North and South demands both diversity and specificity in principle which recognizes cultural histories and unique social contextualization, along with a more socially responsible private property dimension. As with our critique of the transferability of the regulatory state model, a one-size-fits-all approach to sustainability principles does not provide a socially embedded solution.[51] Even when we see justice as fairness, what remains unresolved is the fact that impartiality within fairness can take many different forms and have quite distinct manifestations. Such diversity then needs a comparative envisaging across and between worlds.

Comparative contextual analysis requires the determination of justice in context before some comparative crafting of new private property legal relations which will have relevance within and across worlds. That said, we have suggested some universal 'wrongs' with the system of legal/ economic regulation as it is and it is also possible to present very broad themes for the repositioning of principle which can be nuanced to particular social conditions. Without a given set of principles of justice that together identify and distinguish the institutions needed for the basic structure of a sustainable socially bonding society, any universalized call that law should make private property a force for social bonding by reflecting procedures of 'justice as fairness', as developed in Rawls's classic theory, remains an uneasy aspiration difficult to translate into regulatory practice.

DEVELOPMENT OF A MODEL ROLE FOR LAW IN GOOD GLOBAL GOVERNANCE

Reflecting from the analysis above and focusing on the idea of law as social bonding, we now need to consider the features of South World societies (examined in chapters 5 and 6) and the forces that work for and against regulatory bonding.

Forces for social bonding have specific social and cultural relevance and are contextualized in particular dynamic social patterns and relationships. Notions of property, practices of possession and legal rules for

---

[51]   Sen (2009), p. 57.

protection must be mindful of these conditions. By rethinking concepts of private property protections against broader considerations of social sustainability in varying contexts of social bonding, we set out our matrix below which takes a three-pronged approach towards measuring the effectiveness of law as a social bonding agent advancing public or general interest or broad-based social good.

Reviewing the matrix in terms of the three M's, markets, moralities and mutualities, we are given a clearer idea of how law should sit within social contexts where bonding is embedded. We expand on each of these requirements below, and by understanding sustainability in terms of markets, moralities and mutualities, we thereby determine three contexts for measuring the outcomes of a sustainability project through developing first a model role for law. In so doing we advance on Polanyi's conditional interpretations of individualized to mutualized interests.

Markets

Markets are the essential contexts for contemporary economic regulation and have been argued to endure in this way even as regulatory relationships and outcomes shift from wealth creation as a fundamental objective towards concerns for market sustainability.[52] The resilience of the market as an idea, a place, a framework of exchange and a mechanism of interest enhancement depend on the social and economic interconnectedness of human beings from which exchange relationships grow whether for primitive subsistence, or as the recent global financial collapse has shown, for greed (undertaking of excessive amounts of risk to gain what is perceived as 'free money'[53]). Property rights in turn enter the picture because they enable the standardization of the form of products for market exchange (both tangible and intangible), being adapted for diverse, massive and frequent transaction.[54] This purpose of private property rights within the marketplace is even clearer when we consider the fictional instruments of exchange such as cheques, share certificates, promissory notes, bonds, contracts, receipts and chattel papers. With the delineation of ownership and entitlement provided by private property rights, the transfer of resources to their highest valued use (artificial as this may be) is the professed solution to scarcity. Earlier in chapter 3, we explained how specialization and the division of labour cut across organic social bonding such that capitalist/labour relations become intensely

---

[52] Laffont (1994), p. 533.
[53] Leith (2008).
[54] De Soto (1993), p. 3.

distorted. Law steps in to regulate such situations back to order for the benefit of private property value and exclusivity. In the context of private property, we can imagine how a similar transformation takes place as the categories of property multiply where market players try to distinguish a new and more valuable product innovation from that which already exists in market exchange. This is a destructive trend for social bonding as market relationships and interactions lose connection with crucial and essential social backgrounds and contexts, where sustainability is their primary value.

Any convincing attack on dis-embedded market economies and their proclivities will first address the neo-liberalist conflation of the market's function as an analytical tool with its associated normative ideal (distorted by unquestioning acceptance of variables such as competition and unregulated currency exchange).[55] Even if we seek to constrain law's role to facilitating the efficient allocation of scarce resources, it does not follow that the resultant market analysis has to be actualized into material benefit for those who profit from resources which are much more renewable (such as all resources with a focus on the productivity of labour power rather than raw materials).[56] By the retention of markets as the mechanism for determining who has the greatest need or who is able to produce the most value, it does not follow that land owners and owners of the means of production, as protected by the existing scheme of private property rights, should receive as their personal income monetary equivalents offset by the market's evaluation of labour power product, which do not return in proportionate wealth allocations to the workers. Rather, the prices arrived at through the operation of the market can retain their function as economic indicators used to derive a scheme of economic activities based on allocation efficiency determined consistently against features of social sustainability which value other things besides money and exchange. While the prices paid as income for labour power can be quantified in terms of the actual cost of the renewal of such resources, the prices imputed to consumption and production, unlike labour power, may have no distributive role because consumption in particular is both fragmented and sometimes indifferent to resource renewability. In the capitalist world order, the distributive role for these inputs of productivity other than labour still exist, and it is the appropriate regulatory role for law to ensure the efficient distribution of resources, and prevent a resultant downward spiral denying income

---

[55]   Boettke (1994), p. 272.
[56]   Rawls (2008), p. 350.

equity, maintained by a system of private property rights, which risks market sustainability through the selfish exploitation of resources. Legal regulation towards sustainability can distinguish between the use of the market to organize economic activities efficiently, and to endorse a system of private property relations in which the worth of resources is only measured through the personal income of the owners by virtue of what are often coincidental rights of ownership.

Moralities

The belief that moralities are significant as a social bonding context stems from more than recognizing the need for a 'human face' beyond the inhumanity of economic despotism. Sustainability implies equity and that necessitates at least a consideration of social responsibility which is built on mutualized moralities. The move from individual to mutual interest is both motivated by fearful necessity and mutualized morality.[57] Where the wealth creation regulatory focus for motivating regulatory principle has time and again failed society, it is only through a remoralization of market relationships that sustainable outcomes can be ensured. The morality argument for private property rights as it stands is limited in scope, and we see it mainly as providing these conditions:[58]

1. Legal certainty which encourages investment;
2. Motivation for responsible decision-making on the part of the owners of that property;
3. A background for social experimentation which spurs progress; and
4. A basis for economic calculation by expanding the context within which price and profit and loss signals can reasonably guide resource use.

We wish to challenge the proposition that clearly defined property rules are necessary for a political economy to emerge in our friction-ridden world. From our research (elaborated on in chapters 5 and 6), we have identified trust as a major player in the regulatory game within South World contexts. This means that social bonding relies on trust as a regulator in such contexts, thereby enabling society to bond and be sustainable even without the interference of law as constructed by and for the essential pre-conditions for economic order (the problems of which we have identified earlier).

---

[57]   Michnik (1990), p. 24.
[58]   Boettke (1994), p. 274.

Taking first the words 'free and responsible agents' often used to describe individuals and corporate personalities interacting within the market, we argue against the moralities (or lack thereof) in a system where individualized ownership is supported by private property rights.[59] Earlier we disputed the moral and actual freedom in marketing labour under capitalist conditions. Even at this basic level, there cannot be said to be any personal independence guaranteed by the freedom of contract where participation is not equal and parity is only really normative. Because of the surplus value assumed for labour where it is in abundant or non-discriminating supply, the value produced by surplus labour (taking the form of property owners' personal income) can eventually dispossess workers from the essential commodity necessary to sustain and maintain their labour power. This outcome results from exchange/ price disempowerment experienced by workers who have no actionable way to anticipate or influence how much labour power they have to invest to gain returns from in order to purchase commodities for their own subsistence, when price and cost are determined by markets in which they have no moral or practical standing.[60] The price of commodities and the cost of labour power are geared to property owner's income rather than being predictable variables dependent on the true value of labour power.

To the point of being *responsible agents*, workers and owners need to enter into and respect binding agreements which ensure compliance with orderly and amicable price and cost frameworks, ensured by the certainty that the cost of breaching such agreements outweighs the benefits of doing so.[61] The power imbalances exhibited through contemporary private property arrangements, such as the notion of *caveat emptor*, that is, 'let the buyer beware', challenge the redistributive impact and social viability of such binding agreements. In circumstances where buyers do not (or could not) have the knowledge or access to that knowledge-base from which to make an educated decision, or where the seller employs the use of deception, then the transaction which flows is based on expectations of trust, and the difficulty in enabling purchaser action where they realistically develop or anticipate a lack of trust. In these circumstances the essence of trust which underpins binding agreements and their functionality cannot be legitimated or confirmed to the benefit

---

[59] Rawls (2008), p. 324.
[60] Ibid, pp. 326–7.
[61] Birmingham (1970), p. 284. See also Goetz and Scott (1977).

of all parties and for the system of commercial transaction through trust-based contracting.

Mutualities

Mutualities is used here in the sense of bonds which comprise market relationships, that in turn should sustain wider social relationships in a nexus which ensures the essential social benefit of market outcomes. Mutuality of interests can be determined and engineered by law through the establishment and maintenance of binding social agreements.

How does law defer or deny the mutuality of interests that would make more available access to property and capital and thereby expand mutualized benefit (and economic social responsibility)? Looking at South World societies, where more equal access to the means of production and finite natural resources exist, suggests that the legitimacy of social bonding (even through more organic forms of law) rests in generalized rather than individualized property arrangements.[62]

The mutualized benefit of more accessible property arrangements has to be first identified and then acknowledged enabling a universalized recognition of the benefits that more distributive justice can bring, in terms of social sustainability, and in particular the sustainability of both legal regulation and the property relations it endorses. Therefore, with social sustainability as a core regulatory outcome, mutualities become the focus of law as social bonding.[63]

Having established our argument regarding the need for a commitment to distributive justice and other foundations of inclusiveness and shared progress – all of which fall squarely within the terms of general social good – the procedures or mechanisms to facilitate such shared outcomes require more concentrated analysis. To this end we offer a brief consideration of ways other than individualized rights protection and wealth generation, whereby law's command of private property can advance common good.

So what of common good? In the context of a response to attacks by Mises on his interpretations of Guild Socialism,[64] Polanyi raises three rebuttals which we find uniquely applicable to the role of law in protecting mutualized interests. We have classified these rebuttals into our analytical frame for understanding the forces towards and away from sustainability:

---

[62] Rawls (2008), p. 352.
[63] Ibid, p. 351.
[64] Mises (1928).

1. *Markets:* Property should not be equated alone with the rights of disposition, at the expense of the protection through rights of appropriation. We believe that the current role of law as it endorses private property is to concentrate on exclusivity, in terms of the right to exclude others (even those with greater need) and the right to exclude society as a whole, through narrowing the field of those who can benefit through disposition.[65] If law is focused on more inclusive arrangements where property can be more sustainably acquired (and used), then property can be emphasised as a thing of value (which can be expressed in different ways such as use or aesthetic appreciation) rather than as a means for production. Common property as well as collective property rules, are explored further below. Such a repositioning of emphasis also has the potential to re-distribute property interests in flexible and relevant ways rather than crude fiscal mechanisms such as regressive taxation.[66] More diversified rights to appropriation need not be vested in the same hands as those of disposition. Instead, law can represent a more pluralist social agenda in terms of the utility of private property for public good.

2. *Moralities:* It is distracting to see law as the institution of regulatory power when it comes to private property, trumping all other social bonds. Constitutional legality, and its regulatory model of the separation of powers, while subjecting contesting paradigms to the dominance of the legislature under the rule of law, does not deny the critical influence of other power forms. This is equally the case when appreciating the transaction of private property within market settings. While the law may introduce safeguards such as penalizing multiple property ownership (through some form of taxation), more often than not these legal safeguards are not able to withstand the influences of market incentives such as short-term profit gains

---

[65] Where dispositions of real property are invariably the realm of individual decision-making, how land as a resource is allocated becomes less susceptible to social interest of the collective. For example, if a garden or a park is privately owned, then the value that it has to those who use it becomes completely overlooked in a decision to redevelop the land as a more profitable enterprise.

[66] Examples include the nationalization of property and an indirect redistribution through progressive taxation schemes which enable the state to tax the rich and use such taxes for the benefit of all (such as inheritance tax). Also, there may be regulations that order some owners to make available their property to the public benefit.

crystallized by the frequent trading in real property without reflecting on the greater good or general benefit. Trust mechanisms, where property is possessed and worked through intermediaries, are legal devices more often than not designed to conceal and defeat regulation against the accumulation of wealth through say the speculative trading of social necessities, or fictional products in critical social markets. And as a result, derivative forms of concepts of ownership evolve out of such practices, which further punish those who are deprived of the opportunity to understand such thinking and appreciating commercialized market practices. If law is to bind agreements to co-operate then it must also manage the power imbalances that characterize engagement between different interests in contractual environments.

3. *Mutualities:* Law can and should represent a variety of interests and even those in contest. Within the circumscribed space we possess for using self-interest as a motivator, if we can enable mutualized interests to be identified, then sustainable outcomes can be worked for because it is no longer one's own self-interest that stands alone mandating one uncompromised outcome. For instance, note the shift in the discourse of automobile manufacturers from contesting with environmental lobbyists regarding the consequences of fossil fuel motors, and the depletion of the resources on which they rely, to seeing the benefits of cooperation and collaboration around the arguments of resource and market sustainability. This normative and pragmatic transition is leading to developing hybrid automobiles which for different reasons satisfy the medium-term aspirations of both interests. This example demonstrates how different interests can be vibrantly managed, and if we see law as social bonding, then should not law's role be to advance similar types of mutualities across different contexts so as to ensure sustainable outcomes? Law regularly finds its purchase in managing and resolving critical institutional conflicts at the heart of which private property is at issue. Law can and should ensure that these conflicts are neither fundamental nor irreconcilable.

ALTERNATIVES? LAW, COMMUNITY AND THE GENERAL GOOD

With law at the centre of this regulatory redirection (general good and sustainability, as opposed to individualized wealth creation), we compare different theoretical views about law, and the purpose of legal regulation, in order to see what influences the construction of political and legal systems which are more compatible with general good and its sustainability. Depending on any particular philosophical view of law, the consequent process of rule-making and institution building will be determined. For instance, where law governs questions of personal liberty it will also evidence an active regulatory capacity to affect areas of personal life, even those governed by religion and spirituality. Insofar as governance structures are mechanisms to facilitate decisions based on a broad agreement among citizens, law can be instrumental in achieving what ought to be, as much as ensuring the continuation of what is, and what is not sustainable. Through sociability, law can become a reflexive framework for advancing mutualized interests rather than an exclusionist technology preventing an appreciation of shared risk (revealed through unsustainable property arrangements) and impeding progress to shared fate (more generalized access for the purposes of a general good).

Instead, capitalism commonly seeks to place the interests of the individual at the centre of property arrangements, with the collective interests residing in the authority and activity of the state. Not only does a system which focuses only on the individual-state relationship neglect an entire spectrum of community ties and collective relationships that could exist for citizens and communities comprising that state, but also in analysis and policy-making, individual and community interests compete for recognition within state sovereignty and dominion. In these terms the market model which supports the individualist wealth creation framework, despite being a social creation, sees corporate actors as businesses profiting through the support of the state, which paradoxically derives its authority from its citizens, many of whom are excluded from its favour. This being the case, and law being a crucial tool in directing the state's selective benefit, we cannot continue to see law's role as simply providing objective rules assisting the market to function as a natural equilibrium, performing the role of redistribution which should originally in our view be the realm of law. Contradicting market equilibrium we often see the state injecting public funds into failing corporations, rejecting the free market dogma that it should be market correction rather than state intervention which determines the future of wealth and growth.

Through appreciating the contradictory relationship between the state and the market in shoring up dysfunctional property arrangements, it is possible to draw the regulatory focus away from the disaggregated state with interests often opposing those of the individual within their communities. To correct this regulatory direction law can stimulate individuals coming together and pressing for their interests to be aligned, changing the way communities see law and its role. More than this, at the global level, law can play a part in distilling a common conscience amongst mutualized or mutually disposed nation states, and shift the dominant economic hegemony toward sustainable principles, relationships and outcomes.

One way we consider the law to be facilitating mutuality is through a focus on lives and livelihoods; activist (or organic) law being built, as Hayek has argued, upon 'the customary practices of the people'.[67] Legislatively enacted law (as determined by elected representatives in a majoritarian democracy, and thereby external and mechanical law), on the other hand, emerges from outside the everyday life of individuals within their communities, and as such presents a difficult epistemic problem which challenges the conventions of representative democracy as the sponsor of legal authority. Recognizing this, we advocate sustainable social change based on and finding its location within customary practices of social bonding augmented and encouraged by legislative frames.

Similarly, organic social solidarity (of which law can be a part) emerging out of and true to customary practices, challenges the fragile and inequitable mechanical bonds of the North World. Naishul sees organic institutions as those which arise to accommodate daily life in law and economics.[68] It is these which we highlight and emphasize when we look at South World economies, as evidenced in embedded markets. Much more of this appears in our later consideration of communitarian social bonding and mutualized, moralized market conditions.

REPOSITIONING PRINCIPLE – LAW AND SUSTAINABILITY

Inherent in our argument for a repositioning of the role of law in the protection of private property are our wider concerns about communitarian society (see chapter 6) and individual freedom within social responsibility (see chapter 5). At this juncture it is enough to rehearse law's role within a more communitarian conceptualization of freedom: where interest mutuality leads communities of shared risk to shared fate. Rather than the individualized and exclusive freedom of the libertarian, law in this regulatory model ensures a wider and more inclusive social freedom. The mechanics of this, which we later develop with the assistance of

---

[67]   Boettke (1994), pp. 282–3.
[68]   Ibid, p. 283.

Polanyi's thoughts on *overview* or *oversight*, rest on law's claims to regulatory legitimacy through its function in requiring transparency (see chapter 3). This commitment would be radically inconsistent with the contemporary role of law in guaranteeing the privacy, say of exclusive contractual interests. In answer to this, we argue for guaranteeing a more socially responsible place for private property in legally binding agreements to cooperate, open to the gaze of a wider public interest.

On the strength of the arguments cemented in this chapter, the research case-studies to follow are intended to:

- Critically consider the meaning of socio-economic sustainability;
- Couch this definition in terms of markets, moralities and mutualities (and their interconnection) so that these fields, which are apparent in the contemporary strain on global economic modelling and socio-economic ordering, can be turned toward outcomes which produce or encourage social benefit rather than individual wealth creation;
- Apply the understandings in two economic contexts selected either because they demonstrate social embeddedness or social disembeddedness; and to
- Specifically examine how law and legal regulation, through private property rights, influence the 'three M's' in either of these two contexts towards or away from social location and beneficial social outcomes.[69]

Having achieved this, the analysis will be able to meaningfully contribute to empirically grounded understandings of what makes up sustainability in a socio-economic sense. This will have important ramifications for the wider appreciation of how regulation (and its principles), and how law as a regulatory paradigm in particular, sustains or subverts socio-economic outcomes which are socially beneficial and maintainable.

This book tackles these important issues of global regulatory significance, and argues for the policy relevance of critical analysis to qualify their relevance:

- What are the contemporary socio-economic conditions precipitating change in regulatory principle?
- What is the direction of any such change?

---

[69] For a discussion of regulation for social benefit see Block and Somers (1984).

- How does a shift in regulatory principle reflect a recognition that economy needs to have social location and produce social benefit?
- To what extent is sustainability a feature of any shift in regulatory principle?
- Can sustainability be viewed as a dynamic rather than a steady state in which there are prevailing socio-economic forces towards and away from sustainable outcomes?
- If so, adopting markets, moralities and mutualities, can we better understand the workings of these forces?
- Will sustainable markets better reflect outcomes of social benefit?
- Can a remoralization of market economics better reflect social benefit?
- What are the mutual interests which generate and maintain social benefit?
- Looking at a workforce relying on migrant labour, how does a 'three M' analysis reveal its unsustainability through social dislocation?
- Looking at eco-tourism ventures, how does a 'three M' analysis explain sustainability (and its fragility) through mutual benefit?
- Taking legal regulation as a force for and against sustainability, how in terms of these two examples has law's protection of private property rights influenced markets, moralities and mutualities?

As stated earlier, this is an initial stage in a much bigger investigation into socio-economic sustainability and regulatory principle. This project is a crucial precursor to a much wider social anthropology of embeddedness, in that it will create and 'road-test' a limited matrix for sustainability, which underpins the need for embeddedness and is the consequential outcome of embedded market economies. With that in place the analysis to follow will pilot an empirical evaluation of the matrix in either a socially embedded or dis-embedded economic context. Specifically, the legal regulation of private property rights will be focused on supporting or subverting sustainability. The policy importance of this exercise is to allow for detailing socio-economic sustainability and testing what works for and against it. This is particularly relevant for contemporary market economies if, as we speculate, they will now be regulated under a different regime of principle.

CONCLUSION

Beginning from the natural and arguable presumption that justice is a value which the law upholds and indeed should protect, we see just legal regulation in the maintenance and protection of private property interests as necessarily reflecting principles of social responsibility and equity, which *fairness and fidelity* demand.[70] In trying to achieve a measure of fairness in the determination of principles for regulating social order, Rawls projects his ideal of an *original position* where people, living their capacity *qua* citizens within the democratic process, make political/social decisions under a *veil of ignorance* (where their personal interests and conceptions as to the desirability of particular social arrangements do not come into play).[71] It is Rawls' view that this state of devised ignorance enables unanimous decisions about the principles for justice and thereby governance to be reached. Putting aside Sen's criticism concerning the possibility of impartiality manifesting itself even in the unbiased minds of those kept under the veil of ignorance (and thereby the un-workability of Rawls' mechanism for the emergence of principles to govern society),[72] we believe it possible to advance Rawls' project of 'justice as fairness' at least in terms of depersonalizing and reformulating the nature and purpose of private property relationships. Where we digress from his ideal types is by interrogating rather than decontextualizing a traditional domain of exclusion and subjugation – private property – and testing the conditions under which legal regulation can act as a critical mechanism in promoting social cohesion rather than individualist exclusion. This particular critique grows from questioning how people cooperate with each other in society in spite of subscribing to 'deeply opposed though reasonable comprehensive doctrines'[73] such as law and property. In answering this question, Rawls focuses on finding a shared reasonable political conception of justice.[74] We take this further by seeking to understand how the economic and the social, through a repositioning of principles behind law's regulation of property relations, can return to a state where sustainability trumps individualized wealth creation and economic growth. This revolution will be essential in moving North and South World governance to more mutualized appreciations of justice in terms of social responsibility.

---

[70] Sen (2009), p. 53.
[71] Rawls (1971), p. 587.
[72] Sen (2009), p. 57.
[73] Rawls (1971), p. xviii.
[74] Ibid, pp. xx–xxi.

Therefore, in order to develop a matrix for socio-economic sustainability, we have exposed the forces of *markets, mutuality and morality* to the private property frame wherein up until now law has colluded to promote the individual over the collective interest, the individualist over the moral, and thereby dis-embedding the market from the social. In the chapters to come, through delving into embedded and dis-embedded market case-studies, we challenge legal regulation to face the unsustainable future of this progress.

5. Law's place in regulating migrant labour markets

INTRODUCTION

The intention of this chapter is to employ the dis-embedded migrant labour market in Singapore to ground the theorizing advanced in the preceding chapter. Specifically, this and the next chapter will juxtapose market conditions which tend to strengthen or strain sustainable social bonding (see chapter 1), focusing on the matrix of markets, morality and the mutualizing of crucial interests such as private property rights and obligations. In the case of dysfunctional labour relations, the chapter examines how exclusionist private property arrangements have led to:

(a) the rights and responsibilities set out in employment legislation and specified in labour contracts failing in their higher order regulatory purposes;[1] and

(b) the law in principle, relationships and outcomes colluding in the exclusionist private property arrangements which characterize a dis-embedded employment market in which labour power is diminished in its constructive role in social ordering.

It is important for the reader to approach the two contexts of migrant labour exploitation in the following case-study by concentrating on the ways in which the commodification of labour power has both dis-embedded migrant (and coincidently unskilled domestic) labour and in so doing threatens to dangerously destabilize the market economy in the medium term (see chapter 3).

---

[1] By this we mean purposes consistent with the normative framework of law aligned with general good and with social bonding. This distinction recognizes, in fact, that the regulatory purpose of law's current endorsement of private property relationships in the labour market case-study chosen may well be discriminatory in its reflection of individualized interests.

The chapter will conclude with a brief but compelling account of a conflict which reveals the tragic consequences of dis-embedding, when the tensions underlying labour market inequities override the prevailing mechanical controls over unsustainable market ordering.

SINGAPORE'S MIGRANT LABOUR MARKET ECONOMY

Despite the persistence and dominance of mainstream Hayekian perspectives on the economics of wealth and growth, we see mirrored in the pricing and value structure of the migrant labour market worldwide an erosion of the central assumptions of self-regulated market viability, such as competition and productivity appreciation.[2] Migrant or domestic, particularly at the unskilled and semi-skilled ends, the labour-market system is becoming increasingly pliant to discriminatory and flexible employment practices. The re-balancing influence of organized labour has been considerably weakened in recent decades leaving workers with little security to sustain long-term commitments to their family or wider community. The commercialization and industrialization of traditional subsistence labour domains such as the agricultural sector has displaced communities and working populations whose livelihoods depended on retaining control over the value of their labour and its productivity (see chapter 6). Unregulated capital flows have aligned with consumer driven economic development, which has produced armies of dispossessed wage labourers and rendered states impotent to provide universal subsistence environments for their working communities.

The commodification of human knowledge designed principally to service largely self-regulating market economies has produced an insatiable demand for the exploitation of cheap labour, and a robust trade in migrant workers otherwise enslaved in the poverty of their domestic labour opportunities. Not since the fictitious labour commodification in the industrial revolution has the world witnessed such an unsustainable dependency between wealth creation, economic growth, and labour exploitation. Asian dragon economies such as Singapore best demonstrate the conditions and consequences of unsustainable labour market arrangements (see chapter 7).

---

[2]   Bugra (2007).

Guest worker[3] labour markets proliferate an illusion of embeddedness through suggesting a regime of mutual benefit: the migrant worker has access to a better salary which if repatriated can alleviate the poverty in less robust economies, and the host employer has the economic advantage offered by a cheaper labour alternative. In reality, such labour market conditions perpetuate the wage labour subservience of an undervalued labour force, and deflect efforts to ensure more sustainable productivity frameworks in the host economy. And this is just the economic dimension. The wider social ramifications associated with dislocated families and communities, and class structures which normalize discrimination are becoming clear in states such as Singapore, being economically dependent on low-cost labour and yet socially rejecting the value that such workers contribute to Singaporean society.

A WORLD OF UNDERVALUED, UNREGULATED LABOUR POWER

To this point our analysis has developed a theoretical framework that can apply a Polanyian lens to thinking about socially, fundamental and economically significant occasions of dis-embeddedness, such as commodified labour power, in contemporary market economies. We have suggested that in societies where social bonding is such as to align economic with social interests then the destructive ramifications of dis-embedded market economies may be less evident. With labour force, however, this may not be such a straightforward conclusion. The commodification of labour in developing economies over the last century has benefitted the labour requirements of the industrialized North World. This has produced populations on the move, as in China, from rural to urban work opportunities, and from Indonesia, the Philippines and Bangladesh to economies such as Singapore in the hope of a better life. Unfortunately, these transmigrations have not come along either with efforts to regulate the structural failings of the labour markets which stimulated the shift, or sufficiently in the market economies which gain the commercial benefit of cheap labour.

---

[3]   We use this term critically. The euphemism of 'guest' workers implies that the status in terms of residency standing and state protection are at the discretion of the employer and the state. The worker exists in Singapore courtesy of those offering the privilege of employment. Such circumstances are inconsistent with the provision of actionable employment rights and at best offer a dependency arrangement controlled only by courtesy or indulgence.

In this chapter, the setting of migrant labour in Singapore reveals unique layers of dis-embedding:

(a) In market terms, migrant labour is exploited in conditions which challenge the universal rights of workers, and which builds a market reliance on low cost, low skilled, and arguably underproductive labour power. The state has chosen to minimize its regulatory stamp on the market because of the perceived economic benefits in self-regulatory arrangements and in the understanding that under-regulation benefits the state by absolving it of regulatory costs and consequences.[4] Also, where the informal sector of migrant employment (such as with sex workers and unregistered service labour) has become the norm this adds to a more systematic rolling back of the rights of the labour force.

(b) When considering the moral foundations of migrant labour reliance, the link between employment and the associated security for sustaining familial and community commitments has grown even more tenuous.[5] Migrant workers can repatriate salary but in all other respects their economic and social contribution to their home economies is marginalized. This can be particularly costly to home states if, as in Singapore, semi-skilled and highly-skilled migrant workers provide a significant proportion of hospital labour resources. Another wider moral concern is the perpetuation of a wealth-based class consciousness in the host society where, as with Singapore, migrants do the jobs that locals reject, and do the work under conditions which local workers (and the employers of local workers) would not tolerate.

(c) In the negotiation of mutualized interests, migrant workers are so disempowered that the fundamental conditions of private property arrangements, such as agency representation and enterprise bargaining, have no reality for one side of the bargain.

It is not just regulatory failure or regulatory evacuation against which this chapter employs the migrant labour case-study. If our earlier assertions regarding the value of embedded social arrangements as a regulatory tool survive transportation into self-regulating market economies, then we

---

[4] In the case of domestic workers there are flow-on benefits for the state where this labour force offers economically attractive child and elder-care services, and frees up both parents to participate more fully in other aspects of wage labour.

[5] Bienefeld (2007).

need to evaluate the significance of alternative regulatory arrangements particularly prevalent in South World states where market forces remain sufficiently embedded, even if largely due to their subsistence motivations.

At this level, we return to one of the meta considerations for this book; that in the context of individual integrity, if in terms of market location, morality and mutualized interests, human beings are reduced to only their devalued labour then the economic and social conditions responsible for this degeneration need to be a focus of more sustainable regulatory principles, relationships and outcomes.

In the recent years, however, there has been evidence both in their state and societal transformation as part of global economic development strategies, and through their interface with North World economic agendas, of weakening social bonds which embed regulation and its capacities within South World states. Particularly in transitional and emerging economies such as Singapore, as a result of the dominant influence that international capital exerts over employment markets, law and related regulatory policies have become captured by the priorities of self-regulating market economies, rather than retaining the place of economic interests subsumed in the social. For example, in an Organisation for Economic Co-operation and Development (OECD) report written on South Korea shortly after its accession to the OECD,[6] policies such as the high level of real wages and protection against arbitrary dismissal were considered to be irresponsible and profit-inhibiting. The pressure exerted on socially embedded economies to comply with the North World economic model and the discriminatory labour commodification of markets on which it depends, makes any project which seeks to benefit from socially embedded market experience an urgent endeavour. More than aspiring to preserve such South World embedded regulatory studies in some abstract or pastoral sense, our analysis not only advances the potential for both economic and social sustainability in embedding markets, but it identifies, through the following case-studies, the influences stacked against any such outcome often driven by transitional economies for North World benefit.

The case-study of the migrant labour workforce in Singapore provides an insight into how dis-embedded market forces can operate at their worst from a South World context (the disaggregated and impoverished home society) to a transitional economy with relatively less regulatory arrangements than anticipated in a North World regulatory state context.

---

[6]   Jones and Tsutsumi (2009).

As with the absence of the regulatory state, transitional economies are light on regulation commonly imposed from the top down with the state and the employers accepting only certain minimum legal regulatory conditions. The South World migrant labour force suffers the worst of both worlds.

In Singapore, migrant workers comprise an unsustainable 37 per cent of the workforce.[7] These migrant workers mostly travel to Singapore to take up jobs in low- or semi-skilled sectors[8] which have these workers very much in demand, because of the limited pool of local labour willing to take up jobs in industries such as the construction, shipping or maritime industries, or providing live-in household domestic help.[9] Despite the essential services provided by this labour force and its short-term economic benefit, migrant workers especially in Singapore are not paid relative to the value of the essential labour power which they provide. A drawing force for the dis-embedding of this labour market both in its internal conditions, and in the manner in which external valuation is constructed, is the dislocation between productivity contribution and market value, enabled through a massive imbalance of market mutualities, and a gross failure of market morality. This dis-embedding cycle is further compounded by the wage slavery in markets from which the worker migrated. The costs of labour originating from South Asian

---

[7] In 2012, the total labour force in Singapore was 3,361,800 persons out of which 1,268,300 were foreigners. See the Ministry of Manpower website, Labour Force Satistical Information doi: http://stats.mom.gov.sg/Pages/Labour-Force-Summary-Table.aspx (accessed 12 November 2013) and the Ministry of Manpower website, Foreign Workforce Numbers doi: http://www.mom.gov.sg/statistics-publications/others/statistics/Pages/ForeignWorkforceNumbers.aspx (accessed 12 November 2013).

[8] As at end June 2013, the number of Non-Residents in Singapore was 1.55 million and the total population in Singapore was 5.5 million. Also, the breakdown of Non-Resident Population in Singapore was: Employment Pass Holders – 11%; S Pass Holders – 10%; Work Permit Holders (excluding Foreign Domestic Workers) – 46%; Foreign Domestic Workers – 11%; Foreign Students – 5%; and Dependents of Singapore Citizens, Permanent Residents and Work Pass Holders – 15%, Singapore Parliamentary Reports, Tan Chuan-Jin (2013) Daily Average of Non-Residents in Singapore over the Past 12 Months. Col 34 (Vol 90 Sitting 23). We determine this as demographically unsustainable in a socio-political context where progression to permanent residency status for migrant workers is largely barred and where general public opinion is adverse to any recognition of rights of residency for migrant workers within any level of Singapore society. These workers are a shadow population and often receive treatment which would align with a 'bonded' class.

[9] Mizanur (2006).

countries around Singapore are often depressed downwards by several factors including the relatively lower wages paid within their home countries in general,[10] and unemployment or the associated difficulties with finding income-generating employment of even the most menial and transient kind. This is exacerbated by the relentless decimation of subsistence economy alternatives to constrained wage labour options among their South World neighbours. In this sense, the role of poverty and then relative impoverishment form a pincer movement where the worker is dis-embedded in his market of origin (through the depression of labour in commodity production exploitation), and then is further dis-embedded in his host market through the undervaluing of his labour power and his powerless place at the bargaining table. The dis-embedded migrant labour market in transitional economies preys on the dis-embedding social and economic conditions in South World states and exacerbates these.

It would be fair to ask why, in a 'rule of law' claiming state such as Singapore, boasting a strong economy in all sectors and arguing its governance leadership in the region, would not the legal regulation of employment rights and responsibilities redress this tension of dis-embeddedness? The answer lies in the voracious market economy model which is complicit in the impoverishment of the South World and in the unsustainable market dependencies in transitional economies.

STATUTORY RIGHTS

Although rights such as maximum working hours a day, a weekly recreational day off, adequate notice about termination of the employment contract, mandated annual leave, medical leave, maternity leave and overtime pay are legislated for under the Employment Act in Singapore, these statutory rights are not extended to foreign domestic workers who are excluded from the Employment Act provisions. The government maintains that this is so because foreign domestic workers work in private households,[11] which makes enforcement difficult, and thereby

---

[10]　In Indonesia, Jakarta has the highest monthly minimum wage at Rp 2.44 million (US$211). See *The Jakarta Post* (2013).

[11]　This deference to the sanctity of domestic space in Singapore, along with the euphemism that domestic workers are guests in the home, has led to allegations of violence requiring particular penalties for abusive employers, and explaining the dreadful reactions of maids through suicide, child destruction and physical attacks on members of the family.

justifying inapplicability. This argument is specious not simply because many rights do not depend on actionability (preemptory rights never do so), but also because the state and the employers are aware that through regulatory cooperation and a creative application of agency intervention, the supervision of labour rights in private households and building sites should be no more difficult than in any other closed environment. In any case there is no separate legislation which provides the same protection to these workers, even taking into account their different employment circumstances. Similarly, this group of foreign domestic workers is also excluded from the protection of the Work Injury Compensation Act for the same problematic reasons.

Legislated employment protections which date back to the factories acts of the industrial revolution recognize the vulnerable bargaining position of workers in contract negotiations, and the responsibility of states and employers to ensure that their preferential private property interests come along with requirements for basic working conditions. How much more does this need to be the case for transient migrant workers who do not even benefit from the watchful oversight of a compassionate civil society? In terms of their vulnerability in the workplace and their uncertain exposure to random repatriation, work-place conditions determine the quality of life for the migrant workers and their dependents. Having identified these differential legal regulatory conditions exposing their failed endeavours to ensure actionability, this only represents a first step in demonstrating law's complicity in the market exploitation of workers as commodities. In Singapore, law's regulatory reluctance goes beyond negligence. Underpinning law's critical role in the exploitative protection of employer/state private property arrangements determining the migrant labour market are two critical observations:

(a) Actionability/Non-enforcement Should Never Deny Rights

In any context, whether we are looking at regulation at the domestic or global level, problems of enforceability largely depend on the commitment, preferencing, resources and gravamen of the regulator. Yet rights and protections to ensure the benefits of rights are both normative and practical outcomes of the often-skewed social relationships that evolve consequentially out of the power (im)balances on which such relationships rest. The responsible regulatory state either needs to redress such unbalanced labour-force relationships, or at the very least endorse and enforce rights protections directed against the unfair, and often dangerous results of such imbalance. Why in Singapore is the state reluctant to engage with either option, or are employers active in denying rights and concealing the results of their violation? It is explained by the diffidence of the regulatory state and the discounting of regulatory fidelity against the demands of dis-embedded market economies.

(b)   Questioning the Extent of Unenforceability

Beyond saying that foreign domestic workers work in private households, there has been little justification by the state for why situations of worker abuse and exploitation should remain under-policed and largely un-enforceable.[12] The Ministry of Manpower in Singapore conducts mon-itoring and surveillance through random checks on employment status and interviews workers and employers to test licence and contract compliance within other ordinary workspaces, so why should it be argued that respecting the privacy and private property rights in domestic households is a convincing reason for not preferring or respecting the daily employment conditions and safety of maids? Inspections and random surveys/interviews of the employers of foreign domestic help are conducted by the state to ensure against unlicensed employment so why is it not possible to employ the same energy to protect workers' conditions as are currently directed to the protection of state revenue from employment levies?

LIVING CONDITIONS

Excepting foreign domestic workers who provide live-in help,[13] the majority of the migrant workers stay in dormitories or hostel-equivalents, while 21 per cent live in public housing and 15 per cent in private housing.[14] Although there exists regulations requiring employers to

---

[12]   This issue was debated recently in Malaysia where the courts took five years to try a husband and wife for murdering their maid through starvation and violence. Calls have come for establishing a special court to expedite such cases of worker abuse.

[13]   Even here, however, there are no minimum conditions for the provision of living space and subsistence. Many maids do not have a room of their own and sleep in kitchens or with the children they supervise. Some are required to purchase their own food and other staples, or receive the leftovers from the family table. Because many maids provide 24-hour care duties, their working hours can be indeterminate.

[14]   Based on the declared place of residence of the workers, 21% of work pass holders reside in Housing & Development Board (HDB) flats, 15% in private

provide accommodation for foreign domestic workers, legally binding minimum *standards* of such accommodation do not yet exist.[15]

Workers in the construction or maritime industry often have to come to terms with cramped, unhygienic and poorly ventilated living quarters, or are even arranged to occupy unlicensed or illegal accommodation. The government recognizes this as a problem,[16] but has not taken proactive steps to cater for proper living conditions whether by way of direct intervention or legislation.

It is not difficult to understand the economic motivations in primarily self-regulated labour market situations of mega international corporations (particularly those in the construction industry) to import large numbers of workers especially during periods of economic and property boom, and where the local labour market is confined by more than wage expectations.[17] Conversely it is difficult to accept the reluctance of employers (backed up by the casual involvement of the regulatory state) to acknowledge and address the fundamental social responsibilities arising from their policies of investment profitability on the back of deprived working conditions. The involvement of workers who are willing to take on employment at such low wages and minimal sustainability expenses has been key to the flourishing of the building industry and the real estate market which has become the principal repository of individual and commercial wealth in the country, and of manning the maritime industry on which Singapore's economy essentially rests. For the state and for the family unit, child care, aged care, nursing and domestic management provided through domestic and health workers, has artificially minimized welfare, health and education costs, allowing for both parents to work, and for the state to eschew state-sponsored welfare policy.

Similarly, whether domestic, corporate or state sector, these same employers prefer to reduce their operating costs in the form of their obligation to provide decent accommodation for these workers. The *cost*

---

housing, with the remaining 64% living in dormitories and hostel-equivalents. See Singapore Parliamentary Reports, Tan Chuan-Jin (12 November 2012) Non-Resident Population in Singapore. Col 28 (Vol 89 Sitting No. 10).

[15]   Fourth Schedule: Conditions of Work Permit/ Visit Pass for Foreign Worker, Employment, point 4.

[16]   In 2008, the government said that 80 000 to 100 000 migrant workers did not have proper accommodation, or were living in illegal quarters; see Sim (2008).

[17]   The local population rejects certain kinds of work because it is heavy labour, or because it is now (and conventionally) done by subservient workers.

above care approach starts from the moment the contract is signed, and the migrant worker is burdened with the lion's share in repaying the fees of job placement. Domestic workers, for example, may be required to forego their first two months' salary in repayment of fees, and in many households they are expected to feed, clothe and maintain themselves at their own expense, while providing a 24-hour, week long, on-call labour resource for all the family's needs, at the same time that they live with no salary.[18]

Considering chronic under-investment in the natural welfare of this crucial labour market, the exponential dis-embedding of labour force value is an inevitable byproduct of market expansion as these conditions go un-regulated. The need for individual and collective social inclusion in a market where the basic elements of survival are externalized as market costs or profit margins makes the fictitious operation of wage labour in return for productivity so disturbing.

On the issue of productivity, which seems in the migrant labour market to be off-set by low wages and large workforce numbers, all the conventional conditions for its maximization, even those relating to industrial health and safety, have become hostage to short-sighted profit imperatives where the value of the labour commodity is essentially expendable and perpetually replaceable. Recognizing the endemic poverty in surrounding labour pools, and the starvation wage labour base from which workers will compare the conditions on offer in Singapore, the view of the agent/employer/state property relationship beneficiary regarding labour supply is that there is *more where they came from*. Yet, as the civil unrest described at the end of this chapter reveals, exploitation has its limits when it infringes the most basic conditions of human integrity. The workers will risk caning, imprisonment, deportation and the sacrifice of critical salary repatriation, if their treatment denies their dignity as humans.

Were the state to do a little more to regulate the living conditions of migrant workers and foreign domestic workers by publishing the basic requirements which accommodation has to meet, this would create a resultant requirement for some form of oversight. This inspectorate function could not in fairness be required in the building site and denied in the domestic household. Currently the state largely divests the commercial/industrial inspectorate to employers who have a clear conflict

---

[18]   What can make this situation all the more psychologically straining is the reality that many of these women have left their own children in order to care for the employer's children who all too often learn devaluing and disrespectful habits concerning maid servitude from their parents.

of interest, and denies the function to domestic workers arguing that private households present difficulties for enforcement due to the merging of both living and working environments. Not only is this distinction unsustainable, and the derogation by the state of its oversight function in such a dis-embedded market irresponsible, but it is the recognition that just such living/working conditions in which employee rights become confused, and employer responsibilities forgotten, which poses unsustainable dangers for the market. We mention later that the instances of domestic worker abuse by employers have forced the state to particularize criminal sanctions in these circumstances.[19] No less indicative of market un-sustainability are the tragic cases of maids injuring the children they are charged to care for, assaulting their employers, and taking their own lives as a consequence of psychologically destructive working/living conditions.

Another example of unsustainable market arrangements preconditioned by *wealth above welfare* is that as a consequence of the requirement for employers to bear the cost of repatriating workers who fall ill or become pregnant, employers regularly prevent their maids from leaving the house or enjoying normal social engagement. If this condition of virtual imprisonment was to be identified as a regulatory gap meriting government responsibility, then there would organically emerge feedback mechanisms through which the state could receive and consider, and evaluate the extent of the problem and the quality of its regulatory efforts, and the cone of domestic silence would be pierced in a less intrusive fashion than mandatory inspection.[20] If on the other hand the state continues to refuse to include foreign domestic workers in conventional regulatory protections by reason of their living/working environment, it could rightly be accused of complicity through alienating worker victims because of their domestic duties and protecting employer abusers through non-intervention on the irrational distinction of public/private divide. As the policing of worker contract violations shows, the state is not ill-disposed

---

[19]   Section 73 of the Penal Code (Cap. 224, Rev. Ed. 2008) sets out enhanced penalties in cases of offences against domestic workers. This is read with the more common offences perpetrated against domestic workers, namely, voluntarily causing hurt (section 321 with the punishment set out in section 323), voluntarily causing grievous hurt (section 322 with the punishment set out in section 325), and voluntarily causing hurt by dangerous weapons or means (section 324 with the punishment set out in section 326).

[20]   This could take the form of a system of anonymous tips or empowering workers to make reports in situations of non-compliance, following which investigations can proceed.

to exercising its legal regulatory powers where its property interests are at stake rather than extending such a policy if it is the rights of migrant workers that are so exposed.

WORKPLACE SAFETY

Concerns about workplace safety plague migrant workers. Their capacity to earn and their tenuous employment residency status are crucially dependent on able bodies. In the construction industry,[21] despite the workplace propaganda broadcasting shared responsibility regarding safety, employers consciously adopt dangerous work practices exemplified by the transportation of migrant workers in the open decks of lorries often driven by unlicensed drivers.[22] Again the state mandates seat belt security for domestic and taxi transportation, while offering no such concern for migrant labourers who are in no position to demand this equal safety assurance.

Even by reviewing the official statistics of deaths and injuries in the workplace (which are influenced by significant under-reporting),[23] the extent of the problem is concealed through the assertions of a safe workplace, and normative commitments to worker/employer safety compacts.[24] While the Singapore government has set up a Workplace Safety and Health Institute which controls the publication of data relating to workplace safety and health for developing best practices and standards on safety for workers, the simple example of the transportation of workers using open-deck lorries is proof that such efforts remain inadequate. More than this, employers often pressure workers to defer medical reporting and to take time off rather than bear the costs derived from insurance claims and medical treatment. The workers are complicit in this under-reporting for fear that disability may lead to job termination or the assertion of safety and health demands will simply brand them as trouble-makers. The ultimate irony is that if the worker contributed to the

---

[21] In 2009, 31 workers lost their life in construction accidents; see Chin (2010).

[22] Four workers a week are harmed in transport on their way to work.

[23] Motivations for under-reporting come from employers who want to avoid investigation or increased insurance premiums and workers who are willing to avoid medical treatment or to accept paltry financial settlements, other than risk salary penalties or repatriation.

[24] Under-reporting conceals the truth in the statistics and the broadcasting of workplace safety ignores the story that the statistics reveal.

injury and machinery was damaged in the accident or working days were lost then the employer can claim financial compensation through docking their already meagre salaries.

Some forms of worker safety and welfare are almost totally ignored to the point of tragedy. The cases of domestic worker suicide, and of employer/maid assault are far too prevalent to deny a critical need for counselling and mental health services to be provided as a central regulatory plank in health and safety initiatives.

Notwithstanding the news and media coverage about these and other hard issues of migrant worker health, the state seems to have taken the stance that this social responsibility of ensuring workers' safety belongs with the employers and employees in consort, whether this be in the domestic or commercial setting. With the public attitude largely apathetic or even antipathetic when it comes to migrant worker welfare, and therefore with civil society not demanding a solution from their government, against a government criticized for manipulating public perception through an anti-foreigners slant, civic initiatives for the workers' benefit remain scant.

As revealed through the concealment of the injury problem and the undervaluing of its human consequences it is fair to remark that markets cannot function in a vacuum but require external, independent and professional intervention premised on normative rather than profit foundations. This contextualization will enable responsible social bonds to develop in return for economic efficiency. A core principle behind the sustainability of market embeddedness is valuing wider social bonding such as the prioritizing of workers' health and safety over the financial advantage of the employer.

Regarding domestic workers employed and living in the homes of their employers, the figures for deaths and accidents have also become a source of serious concern for the few that care.[25] It appears that their employers are posing rather than guarding against threats of physical abuse, food deprivation, verbal abuse, and even sexual exploitation. Living within such closed environments where these workers simply cannot escape their workplace subjugation, isolation and insecurity, they are as if enslaved by their employers' demands and dominion. Often in simple labour force terms, their obligations of employment far exceed the wage remuneration they receive in return. These demands regularly

---

[25] 'Between 1999 and 2005, at least 147 migrant domestic workers have died from workplace accidents or suicide, most by jumping or falling from residential buildings'; see Human Rights Watch (2005).

require young women to undertake unjustified risks to themselves, whether knowingly or unknowingly. Given the scarcity of land in Singapore, many of these foreign domestic labourers work in high-rise apartments and falling from windows which they are cleaning un-harnessed and untrained is one of the many risks that they take. Since 2000, 75 of these women have fallen to their deaths while working.[26] Despite the alarming figures of deaths and injuries in these circum-stances, the government has been reluctant to adopt changes in guidelines or to ban employers from requiring of their domestic help such danger-ous duties.[27]

HEALTHCARE

The Singapore government does not give any healthcare subsidies to foreigners, and this includes migrant workers and foreign domestic workers. While the Ministry of Manpower requires their employers to bear the cost of their medical treatment by mandating a minimum medical insurance coverage, such requirements imposed on the formal employment sector can have the knock-on effect of making legitimate labour recruitment less attractive and thereby fuelling the exploitation of workers within the informal sector. It is to be remembered that while the chapter has focused primarily on the licensed and contracted labour force there is a significant pool of unskilled and low-skilled workers who could be said to be trafficked into Singapore either to service illegitimate markets or to supplement areas of work more normally the province of contracted workers.

The provision of healthcare as part of the trend towards welfare for the workforce and labour recommodification has its roots in Fordist capital-ism. The decommodification of worker healthcare emancipation in fact serves to exacerbate the labour force's dependence on their labour status and thereby becoming more vulnerable to unfair employment relation-ships.[28] If wages are barely subsistence and the employer offers basic services such as healthcare then the worker is further dependent on the labour market relationship for individual rather than social sustainability. Because of the hazardous nature of their jobs, it is not uncommon to find workers who incur large hospitalization bills that greatly exceed the minimum insurance coverage.

---

[26] Neisloss (2012).
[27] Instead, the state should consider offering more safety training and discuss rules imposing penalties on employers for unsafe work practices.
[28] Standing (2007).

With a continuous dependency on their employers for subsistence insurance provision, meagre wages and living arrangements, these migrant workers live without security. For migrant workers dependency and disempowerment are characteristic of their market placement, with contract termination and indiscriminate repatriation being the ever-present fear. The dependency problem here is consciously magnified and maintained through the state abrogating its welfare responsibility to employers, who are primarily motivated by or concerned with their profit/cost determinants. As argued above, the state in condoning and consolidating discriminatory and exclusion private property arrangements in the labour market, which can be made to benefit the employers on all fronts, has an obligation to ensure what the unequal bargaining power in the employment contract cannot.

A part solution for the dependency/provision conundrum would be to retain the insurance obligation with the employers but involve the state as the administrator through its regulatory function, thereby having a more collaborative tri-partite relationship model. Employers can be required to pay contributions to their workers' healthcare fund into a centralized pool managed by the state. In default of this the state otherwise would suffer through loss of reputation (as amongst other countries, particularly the home countries of these migrant workers) and the social cost of a large number of workers being without medical attention once their maximum insurance payout (legislated for) expires.

The tripartite solution here also reveals the conflict of interest paradox. Through economic partiality and regulatory neglect the state has enabled the market power imbalance eventually to suit its own revenue purposes. The state requires at the engagement of foreign workers that employers must pay a state levy. In this way the foreign labour market becomes a taxation revenue market. As such the state has a financial interest in maintaining and expanding dis-embedded market arrangements if it is not more willed to independently bear the regulatory costs attendant on the market economy. While the imposition of a workers' levy has required payment by all employers to the state, there has been little clarity about where this money goes, and the state has merely issued a statement that 'similar to other sources of government revenue, the foreign worker levies are not ring-fenced for any specific purposes'.[29]

---

[29] Written Answer by Mr Tan Chuan-Jin, Acting Minister for Manpower & Senior Minister of State, National Development, to Parliamentary Question on Foreign Worker Levies Collection, Notice Paper No. 369 Of 2012 For The Sitting On 12 Nov 2012 doi: http://www.mom.gov.sg/newsroom/Pages/PQ RepliesDetails.aspx?listid=64.

DEPORTATION AND FORCED REPATRIATION OF WORK PERMIT HOLDERS

Reasons for the cancellation of employment status and the deportation of migrant workers from Singapore reflect the crude commodification of labour in this market. Reasons relating to health and childbirth are measured against reduced capacity to work and citizenship claims rather than in terms of their human and social impact. Work permit holders are deported should they be found to be pregnant or diagnosed with infectious diseases such as HIV/AIDS. Around 100 pregnant maids are sent home a year,[30] and a consequence of this has been a trend among workers to favour termination of pregnancies through legalized abortion or self-administered, dangerous abortion drugs (because of the prohibitive costs of abortion and the fear of authorities coming across such knowledge). The psychological impact on many of these women of strict religious traditions can hardly be imagined.

No reason for differentiating between those migrant workers providing domestic help and women working in any other industry has been given by the state in justifying such intensely discriminatory employment practices. From any humanitarian standpoint, and particularly in a country which highly values the family, as with any other women who look after the cleaning of the house and manage the needs of their husbands and children, these domestic workers should be entitled to decide for themselves whether they wish to keep their baby. If homemakers, or any employed women for that matter, are able to continue their work during their pregnancy (and may even be protected by employment regulations to do so) then the same should be said for foreign domestic workers. Notwithstanding the contractual nature of their employment relationship, it would be fair to expect these terms of employment, just like those which apply to any other job and industry, not to compromise the worker's right to have a child.

Along with restricting access to basic medical care when mandatory medical insurance does not cover non-employment related injury, migrant workers diagnosed with infectious diseases are without the benefit of social support and counselling, facing immediate and automatic deportation to countries where health services are much inferior to those in Singapore.

Where workers suffer employment-related abuse, they are also fundamentally disadvantaged in producing evidence of such abuse. This is

---

[30]   Liew (2010).

especially so in situations where their employers (often the abusers) are in total control of employment records such as contracts, salary slips and time cards, and are given preferred status in asserting the nature and conditions of the employment situation to the satisfaction of state agencies. Furthermore, employers are in a position to unilaterally cancel a work permit and repatriate the worker when such disputes are raised, thereby neutralizing the threat they pose in any possible abuse prosecution.

Such migrant workers are vulnerable to forced, and often violent, removal by repatriation companies or employment agencies.[31] These repatriation firms each send back around 2000 workers annually,[32] and they are said to be able to do so because work permits are tied to the employment relationship which the migrant worker has with his/her employer. Therefore, the employer terminates the contract and has the obligation from the state to secure the repatriation of workers. Should the employer terminate the employment relationship, the work permits are automatically terminated and repatriation firms operate to extradite these workers back to their home countries, acting in practice for the employers and the state.

Remarkable is the manner in which again the state divests its original responsibilities to employers who in many instances have no interests in the workers experiencing a safe and orderly repatriation, and in fact are principally motivated by issues of cost and convenience. If it is left to the employer to manage the deportation there will be no opportunity for the worker to effectively seek any arbitration of this action or precipitating dispute and the reasons for it. In other immigration situations if an individual has benefit of residency through a range of permits, and these permits lapse or are withdrawn, and the person refuses to leave the jurisdiction, the state needs to issue a deportation order and to ensure the safe and orderly removal of the over-stayer. In Singapore, the common response of the state to migrant worker over-stayers is to prosecute them and to imprison them routinely for three months and administer three strokes of the cane before they are ejected. So even if the state intervenes in the deportation it does so in brutal and punitive terms.

---

[31]   That such enterprises are registered by law and allowed a mandate that often constitutes activities which would otherwise satisfy assault and false imprisonment, is an alarming example of where state agencies entertain discriminatory physical and psychological abuse often of defenseless women, powers which otherwise would not be afforded untrained security personnel.

[32]   AsiaOne (6 August 2011).

The disempowerment through employer-initiated repatriation, in circumstances where the state refuses to adjudicate this exercise of largely-ungoverned discretion, demonstrates more than the absence of a social safety net. In fact, what meagre protections are available to the worker are again extremely conditional and in no way amount to actionable rights expected in conventional immigration disputes. Even when the work permit is removed from a worker and replaced with a special pass (in some situations of disputes), workers become dis-embedded from their maintenance society, in that they no longer have a salary or the basic living conditions and support of their fellow workers which sustained their existence prior to the permit removal.[33]

FOREIGN DOMESTIC WORKERS LIVING AMONG SINGAPOREAN FAMILIES

For foreign domestic workers who are actually live-in domestic help, their access to basic necessities such as food, shelter, communication, medical facilities and the right to private space and time are all determined at the discretion of their employers. Very often, these workers are viewed with suspicion and treated with disrespect by most members of the family with whom they live. They are essentially tolerated outsiders, looked down upon for doing the menial tasks that Singaporeans would never take on as paid work, and yet are expected to conform with the rules of the household, no matter how discriminatory these might be applied.

One area over which employers often keep tight control is the domestic workers' time off from work. In Singapore, the requirement for a mandatory weekly day off for domestic workers was brought into effect on 1 January 2013.[34] However, this new measure is not without its problems: first, this protection is not offered to those whose contracts were signed before 2013. Second, this new regulation allows employers to come to a mutual agreement with a worker as to giving up some or all rest days each month, provided that compensation of at least one day's wage on top of their monthly salary is offered in return. Given the imbalance in power of the negotiation and conclusion of these employment contracts, this begs the question why the regulatory state is limited

---

[33]   Interview with Alex Au, the Vice President of Transient Workers Count Too (TWC2) on 12 September 2013.
[34]   Transient Workers Count Too (TWC2) (26 July 2013).

to conditionally creating an employment requirement, while at the same time offering no real means for the worker to action this privilege.

The explanation why the state has again deferred the implementation (and the cost) of this market condition can be gleaned from the many comments in Singapore print media concerning this initiative. The majority reaction was adverse and focused on complaints that maids lived in family settings and therefore did not require time off, as might other workers. In addition, some suggested that if the maid's day off corresponded with the leave time of parents then who would look after the children and the grandparents while mum and dad enjoyed their Sunday? There was little or no appreciation of this provision as a universal employment right, or a labour market condition which applied to other workers in Singapore and then out of fairness and equity should be available to foreign domestic workers. The reaction of the electorate, reflected in the government's divesting of engagement and enforcement responsibility, reveals a deep seated attitude among employers and the beneficiaries of this labour market, that foreign domestic workers neither have nor merit equal rights to fundamental employment conditions.

There have been recurrent, regular and troubling instances of oppressed domestic workers, evidencing shocking reactions to the stress that they face at work, on top of the new and unfamiliar environment in which they find themselves. In 2009, an Indonesian domestic helper, Vitria Depsi Wahyuni, murdered her 87 year old employer whom she described as fussy, petty and demanding, and who had frequently subjected the maid to verbal and physical abuse that simmered frustration, anger and even hatred. Vitria has been sentenced to ten years' imprisonment after being convicted for manslaughter to which she had pleaded guilty.[35]

Where these foreign domestic workers are denied phone usage or other forms of contact with their family, or a day off to spend time with friends, their anxiety and depression are exacerbated by conditions of loneliness.

Similarly, in 2010, an Indonesian domestic helper, Nurhayati, killed the 12 year old disabled child of the family in which she was employed. In one of the notes left behind, Nurhayati wrote about how she wanted to escape her situation, but could not because of the lack of family and relatives in Singapore from whom she could seek help.[36] The psychiatric stress and emotional distress that this group of women undergo is

---

[35]   Yong and Sim (2012).
[36]   Lum (2012).

exemplified by the harm they cause even to themselves as a way of desperate escape. In 2004, an Indonesian domestic helper threw her employer's five month old child out the window from the 23rd storey apartment and then ended her life in the same fashion.[37] The conditions of job slavery and cultural subservience that these young women experience daily, without any of the frameworks of support with which they are familiar in their own social units, no doubt contribute to the violence of their reactions. Many have left their own children back home to seek a better life for them. It is hard to imagine the pressures which such sacrifice generates particularly when the women are required to provide extensive childcare duties. These dis-embedded and unsustainable conditions of living are often imposed on foreign domestic workers without countervailing conditions of trust and comity otherwise enjoyed by those around them, in particular between their employers and their families. Such workers are alienated by more than space and time from their own families[38] and then imprisoned within family settings in which they are institutionally and socially estranged. They work in a state of total social dis-embeddedness for poor pay and doing extremely long hours. The paradox of this estrangement and exploitation when contrasted with the close social bonds they may usually have enjoyed even in their relatively impoverished home situations takes a heavy toll on their well-being.

Despite so many of such stories of employer abuse and often despairing and self-destructive retaliatory action taken by foreign domestic workers which are becoming more frequent and media covered, the Singapore government has not considered this an urgent issue requiring more than meting out harsh punishments to delinquent foreign domestic workers, and less so to abusive employers. The employer/employee abuse cycle in the domestic setting indicates many features of dis-embedded market conditions and unsustainable social relations that tragically bridge both worlds.

The state leaves domestic worker employment agencies largely unregulated. These agencies 'sell' worker contracts without either acting in the interests of the worker or at that point and ongoing requiring of the employer certain standards of worker maintenance. The worker is disempowered through adverse contract terms, an absence of independent representation, exploitative work conditions which at the very least are

---

[37]   Agence France Presse (2004).
[38]   Some employers restrict the worker's telephone contacts with their families, and it is not contractual practice to enable family repatriation visits after a designated period of service.

less than expected for Singapore workers, and a failure of state oversight. The employer is left to determine the fate of their workers in all daily conditions, and generally makes decisions for worker welfare based on cost and self-interest.

Although foreign domestic workers differ on the issue of termination of work permits from migrant construction workers, whereby in theory domestic workers have available to them (through legislation) the option to transfer out of their existing employment, this is often an illusory protection, due to the fact that the original employer has to consent to the transfer. The pre-condition of employer consent to the request for transfer would therefore likely exclude situations of dispute regarding the workers' exercising the option to change their employers, which might be just the case when the worker's safety and life-balance are endangered.

THE DEPENDENCY RELATIONSHIP

So far we have talked about the unbalanced dependency relationship in the market from the perspective of migrant workers. However, as might be anticipated in a dis-embedded market economy where private property relations in a very broad economic sense rely on exploiting cheap labour, labour beneficiaries experience dependencies which may be different in a material sense but are no less economically unsustainable. In addition, the wider labour market can be negatively impacted.

Singaporeans, particularly working women with young children, are highly dependent on the foreign domestic worker market. In its debate whether to reduce the foreign domestic worker levy, the Singapore Parliament unashamedly acknowledged the 'important role [these workers play] in meeting the domestic needs of families … more notably those with elderly members, disabled persons or young children'.[39] With rising costs of living and a property market pushing already inflated property prices upwards, the growing pressures on married women to share in the financial burden of the family has led to an increase in the trend of families engaging foreign domestic workers to look after the house and the family – roughly one in every five households in the country of around five million people employ domestic workers from outside Singapore.[40] Such practices persist in Singapore even when young children in the family reach an age of maturity and childcare

---

[39] Singapore Parliamentary Reports, Mr Tan Chuan-Jin (25 February 2013) Reducing Foreign Domestic Worker Levy. Col 7 (Vol 90 Sitting 7).

[40] Neisloss (2012).

burdens might be alleviated. The recent 'viral' photo of a maid carrying the backpack of a young male family member returning to his national service barracks brought international derision over such a perpetual dependency.[41]

Further, in a country which politically and socially celebrates filial piety[42] and has even enacted legislation to empower aged parents to enforce rights of care against their adult children,[43] the phenomenon of maid-provided eldercare has become the true face of this doctrine. Again, through this facility and the proliferation of maid-provided child care, the state has been able to significantly transfer its welfare responsibilities to working parents, who then rely on the sweat of foreign domestic workers to ensure family stability and economic viability. The political and normative collusion to maintain such unsustainable market and broader social conditions is dangerously apparent in these mutualities of dependence, state/family unit/worker exploitation. Again there are adverse consequences for other market sectors. Arguably a reason for the slow and sporadic development of the early childhood sector in Singapore may reside in the maid-caregiver convenience.

Despite the persistence and expansion of these dysfunctional socio-demographic dependencies, they have not translated into a better valuing of the migrant worker market, even in terms of personal welfare, access to conventional employment rights protection or remuneration reflective of the crucial role these workers play in the maintenance of Singapore's economic and social security.

MAIDS ASSOCIATION

What we see as a crucial problem in the case of foreign domestic workers is the lack of access to justice through a representative body that shares their interests (as opposed to those of their employers or the agencies). In the case of the Chinese bus drivers who took industrial action in 2012 to protest about an increase in work days at no increase in salary, it was their non-union status that contributed to the determination that their strike was illegal. But despite the state's avowed encouragement for migrant workers to unionize,[44] in this situation the employer (Singapore

---

41   AsiaOne (27 March 2011).
42   Tsui (June 2010); National Family Council (2011); Basu (2010).
43   Maintenance of Parents Act (Cap. 167B, Rev. Ed. 1996).
44   Regarding the organization of industrial unions through the National Trades Unions Congress in Singapore, having NTUC's deep connections with

Mass Rapid Transit) had repeatedly denied the workers' requests for union membership approval.

One remedy against worker isolation, disempowerment and lack of representation (particularly for domestic workers) would be the establishment of an association to which these domestic and other migrant workers can have a constant recourse, and to which institutionally and as-of-right, an employer cannot prevent worker access to such a resource. At the meta level, this arrangement would be a tri-partite one where the association would necessarily and always act as a regulator in terms of ensuring that the behaviour of the employers, if suspect, was deliberated upon in a spirit of cooperation and consultation where the represented worker had much enhanced bargaining power.

MIGRANT WORKERS IN THE BUILDING AND CONSTRUCTION INDUSTRY IN SINGAPORE

Singapore's construction industry has played a key role in the country's socio-economic development and is in large measure the reason for the flourishing of this industry. Singapore offers major foreign construction conglomerates massive profit opportunities, significantly induced by the under-regulated supply of discounted migrant workers willing and able to perform the role as labour supply. A massive housing and construction boom, perpetuated by the state's aggressive involvement in property resumption, re-marketing and commercialization,[45] along with the state's heavy involvement in land tenure and marketing, and the iron-fist of state-controlled public housing and urban renewal, enables a lucrative commercial partnership between a few international construction giants, and the Singapore government.

However, this boom instead of creating a pool of public benefit, has through:

- the exclusion of locals from employment benefit,
- the repatriation of shareholder and company profit,
- the return of levies to state revenue, and
- the explosion in the housing market,

---

government, it could be said that independent organized labour in Singapore is a sham. It is sponsored by the government, in association with the large business interests, and validated by the citizens.

[45] Phang (2007).

benefitted those who possess large amounts of capital to finance these construction and development projects, and those who will possess commercial interests in the property estate that results.

A large proportion of these construction workers come to Singapore through unlicensed or unregulated employment agencies located in their home countries, or via their own informal networks of contacts such as friends and relatives. This complex and ungoverned networking has often led to and perpetuated a significant number of disputes over salary, agency fees, working conditions as well as living arrangements, with little effective recourse to dispute available to these workers, and no individual or agency taking responsibility. We argue that in whatever form, licensed or otherwise, because the state has failed to require local agents to take responsibility for agency negotiations off-shore, or to require eventual employers to confirm and enforce agency contracted conditions as contracting parties, agency is at the root of discriminatory private property arrangements. How can regular law give integrity to migrant labour market arrangements if parties can, with law's concession, deny the standard obligations that agency implies?

Special Pass Workers due to Pending Workplace Injury Claims or Disputes

Migrant construction and maritime workers are issued a Special Pass by the Ministry of Manpower in particular circumstances when their Work Permits are cancelled. This can happen if the employer terminates the employment of that worker, or if the Ministry of Manpower determines that the employer is in breach of his obligations towards the worker. In such situations, as the worker has a legitimate reason to stay on in Singapore to resolve a dispute or claim against the employer, or to obtain medical treatment and complete the work injury compensation process, they are issued this Special Pass.

Although the employers remain responsible for housing workers until the dispute or claim is resolved, in reality, few workers on Special Passes stay on in accommodation provided by employers, due to the incapacity to pay their expenses if their salary is suspended, along with common practices of expulsion from the premises and abuse by superiors.[46] For workers who are injured at work and have been given certified medical leave by doctors, they are entitled to receive a monthly stipend in the

---

[46]   Transient Workers Count Too (TWC2) (17 October 2013).

form of Temporary Incapacity Compensation from their employers.[47] The reality, however, is that employers do not honour such obligations because it is often the case that they no longer view these workers as in their employ.

Under such circumstances, it becomes impossible for these foreign workers to survive without seeking alternative employment. However, the current legislative framework in Singapore does not allow for that. Foreign workers who take on jobs without a work permit can be fined up to $20 000 and/or jailed for up to two years, while employers are liable to be punished with a fine of at least $5000 and up to $30 000 and/or be jailed for up to 12 months if convicted of hiring a foreigner without a valid work pass. As a result, a large number these migrant workers undertake illegal employment at a reduced wage in order to get by. Those operating within this informal sector of employment are not fully covered by labour laws, let alone social protection measures limited as these may be.

The realization in government that employers who circumvent these minimal dispute and welfare provisions push a greater number of migrant workers toward the informal employment sector has only led to official comments that it is 'Singaporeans [who] ultimately suffer when employers fail to pay the true costs of hiring foreign manpower or hiring foreign manpower that they are not entitled to', and that 'local workers will lose out in employment opportunities'.[48] The state in so doing creates greater tensions between the local population and foreigners working and living within the same country, without focusing on the real issue at hand – that is, the difficulties faced by this group of workers which leads them to undertake such illegal employment in the first place.

As evidence of the ambiguous situation of these transitional workers the state and not the employer takes responsibility for injured workers unable to resume work to ensure the existence of a social safety net. However, for those injured but continuing to work the employer retains the obligation. Even though there are requirements such as mandatory insurance to be purchased for the employee, these regulations are often flouted by employers and the Ministry of Manpower does not take serious action against these employers, despite its obligation so to act.

---

[47] Section 14A(1) and 14A(2) of the Work Injury Compensation Act.
[48] Singapore Parliamentary Reports, Tan Chuan-Jin (11 September 2012) Second Reading of the Employment of Foreign Manpower (Amendment) Bill. Col 17 (Vol 89 Sitting No. 7).

EXTORTIONATE AGENCY FEES

Not only is there a great variation in the amounts paid to agents by migrant workers for securing a job in Singapore, there are also differences in terms of when and how these payments are made, and by whom. Furthermore, some migrant workers have had to deal with a variety of 'agency' personalities, some of whom are not licensed by the government to be an agent. Putting aside the problems of these workers having to service the agent fees themselves (as opposed to the employers incurring the costs), agents sometimes continue to 'extort' from these workers even after they have secured employment, whether by tagging such demands to a delayed payment scheme or otherwise.[49]

The government has since introduced a cap on the recruitment/agency fees permitted to be charged by local employment agencies, with the Employment Agencies Act stipulating that the one-off payment of agency fees shall not account for more than 10 per cent of the migrant worker's first month's wage.[50] These requirements, however, are often not adhered to and there is lack of enforceability despite penalties for non-compliance.[51] In the circumstances of fee extortion the interests of the employment agency and the workers are diametrically opposed. Because the agent is the worker's first crucial stage of dependency, one where the job is available or it is not, there is a great potential for exploitation and deception to take place due to the enormous imbalance in power and the failure of law and its enforcement to intervene and rectify this imbalance or to construct the state and law as a countervailing contractual force.

Additionally, there are no such constraints imposed on employment agencies outside of Singapore. Where the states from which the bulk of the labour supply are targeted for provision, it begs the question why the government is reluctant to participate in multilateral agreements so that compatible rules would overcome the current futility in attempting to regulate local agencies who deny responsibility for the activities of their off-shore agents. Limits on recruitment/agency fees and service standards set in such ways would enable more causal and systemic regulation to tackle these exploitative practices irrespective of jurisdiction.

---

[49]   Transient Workers Count Too (TWC2) (24 June 2013).
[50]   Second Schedule: Employment Agency Rules.
[51]   Humanitarian Organisation for Migration Economics (HOME) and Transient Workers Count Too (TWC2) (June 2010), pp. 6, 17. Transient Workers Count Too (TWC2) (September 2006), pp. 10, 12, 14.

INEVITABLE SOCIAL CONSEQUENCES OF UNREGULATED AND UNSUSTAINABLE MARKET ECONOMY

In the sections above the chapter has identified the reasons workers are exploited in situations of dangerous dependency. The section following charts a recent incident where workers' frustrations at their disembeddness boiled over and social order was even momentarily challenged. It is not the riot and its reasons alone that are instructive against a background of exploitation. It is the reaction to this unrest and in particular the attitude of the state that reveals the nature of market unsustainability.

The background to the social unrest in Singapore fomented over the past two years despite Governmental denial,[52] that dysfunctional market exploitation motivated threats to public order such as not seen since the struggles to form the Republic. Regarding the broader social conditions, the relatively poor and unpredictable remuneration of these migrant workers are compounded by perceived discrimination and poor life/work qualities generating as yet unmeasured (and officially dismissed or minimized) discontent and resentment. The problems behind the apparent and dissonant exploitation of this labour force are conflagrated by the exclusionist social and political mores of the resident population. To this the Singapore government has reacted by fuelling frightened and xenophobic voters with talk of curbing the inflow of foreigners at the top-end of the income bracket rather than confronting the legitimate concerns of semi- and low-skilled workers, local and migrant. Meanwhile, foreign workers at the bottom-end are incensed but silenced by the power imbalance and the social exclusion which enables denial wholesale of their grievances.

China Bus Driver Strikes

In 2012, 170 public-bus drivers from the People's Republic of China staged a strike, the recourse to which is currently against the law in Singapore. The strike focused on exploitation by their employer, the SMRT (a major provider of public transportation in Singapore). This

---

[52] This position was supported by the narrow findings of a Committee of Enquiry into the Little India riots which located blame for the initial disorder on the immediate context of the death, such as the nationality of the victim and perceptions of his discriminatory treatment by authorities at the scene.

included unsatisfactory living conditions, a prohibition against joining a union, disparities in compensation and bonuses to the bus drivers (including two rounds of salary increments that excluded Chinese bus drivers), the change from a five-to-six-day work week without proper communication or variation in their contracts or remuneration, and the fact that the SMRT (the employer) held on to the passports of the drivers throughout their two-year period of employment.[53]

This form of industrial action, previously largely unheard of in Singapore, is made all the more remarkable by being initiated by vulnerable and otherwise defenseless migrant workers who would irrespective of outcome face long terms of imprisonment, corporal punishment and deportation.

Riot in Little India

More recently, on 8 December 2013, a civil disturbance involving almost 400 people took place in Little India (an ethnic Indian ghetto in Singapore, one of the few places of migrant construction worker recreation on their leave days). The street disturbance exploded following a fatal traffic accident involving a 33 year old Indian national construction worker and a private bus operator. The rioting workers were mainly Indian nationals, working as labourers in the construction, shipping and maritime industries.

The Singapore government, in dismissing arguments that these two events of public unrest were outcomes of discriminatory employment issues, is in a conscious process of political and social denial. The narrow dimensions of the rebuttal can only be designed to distance state economic policy and regulatory failing from debate or criticism. 'The workers who have been arrested in connection with the rioting incident are employed by different employers and housed in different locations. There is no basis to link their unlawful behavior to workplace issues', Singapore's Ministry of Manpower said in response to such allegations.[54]

However, the details of how the riot in Little India emerged tend to suggest otherwise. The private bus operator involved in the accident was one of the many buses which ferry foreign workers from Little India back to their dormitories after a Sunday's recreation and drinking. The victim, Sakthivel Kumaravelu, was told to get off the shuttle bus as it was

---

53   Tan (5 April 2013).
54   Wong (2013).

already full. He is said to have staggered off the bus, but not before pulling down his trousers. After the bus moved off and made a left turn into Race Course Road, Mr Kumaravelu was found pinned under one of its rear wheels. According to police investigations, Mr Kumaravelu was drunk and had walked or ran after the bus in 'an unsteady manner'. Thereafter he stumbled, tripped and fell onto the path of the rear tyre of the bus and was run over.[55]

Following the accident, the crowd outside the bus attacked the bus driver and the timekeeper with bottles, stones and dustbins. Police, civil defence and anti-riot force (consisting of special operations and Gurkha officers) were dispatched, and they similarly were attacked by the angry mob even as the victim's body remained pinned under the vehicle. A police car was overturned and set on fire, and concrete slabs, bricks, trash cans and fire bombs were flung at the vehicles.

Whatever the circumstances of the victim's death, it is important to realize the significance of being denied access to the bus. These buses are the only viable source of transport for workers back to their dormitories and if they do not return at a designated time they may have their salary docked or even face a termination of contract and repatriation. In the mind of perhaps an intoxicated man these consequences would explain his desperation to chase and re-enter the vehicle.

In addition, some witnesses suggested that tempers were inflamed by the careless and discriminatory official reaction to the victim at the scene by first lending medical assistance to the Chinese bus driver and leaving the body of the deceased under the vehicle for some time. It was even said that an unidentified officer kicked the prone corpse.

The Aftermath

A group of 25 workers have been charged with rioting, while 57 workers (all of which were Indian nationals except for one Bangladeshi) who took part in the riot have been repatriated to their home countries after having received stern police warnings and are disallowed from re-entering Singapore. This group of workers was deemed to have posed a threat to the safety and security of Singapore – conditions that allow the authorities to deport and ban them from entering the country again under the Immigration Act. Another group of 200 workers who were involved in the rioting but had a 'passive and incidental role' were issued formal police advisories. The 55 year old Singaporean bus driver who caused the

---

[55] Torrijos (2013).

fatal traffic accident was arrested for causing death by negligent act. These charges have since been dropped by public prosecution agencies.

What has been Said/Done?

The government put together a Committee of Inquiry to investigate the riot, but the Committee chose to take a rather short-sighted approach in focusing on the issue of restoration of control,[56] and the immediate social disorder context for ascertaining the cause of the riot, rather than looking at the broader issues of labour and immigration policies.[57] Further, several measures have been taken by various government agencies which, some might say inappropriately, target the issue of danger, rather than the context precipitating the social disorder. The police believe that alcohol consumption and intoxication in public areas contributed to the riots, imposing a six month long alcohol ban on the area and suspending private bus services to Little India for one week following the riot, in the hope of reducing the number of people ferried to the area. The Land Transport Authority put in place new bus queuing arrangements for the purposes of crowd control. Even more intrusively, the government and dormitory operators are contemplating organizing compulsory alternative weekend activities for the migrant workers and staggering leave days.

These measures implicitly lay blame for the social disorder on migrant workers who enjoy their limited free time in an urban ghetto where they feel safe and included. The Indian shop owners there provide food and drink to the workers at affordable prices and thereby supplement their otherwise simple businesses. Even the Chinese bus drivers have a financial stake in the community recreation which happens once a week in this small and contained cultural enclave in the city. Destroying this Sunday 'community', and further disempowering workers by removing a limited outlet of preferred recreation will only lead to further tensions, especially between workers and the police on patrol in Little India.

Beyond Little India, the local Singapore community, on the other hand, almost uniformly has reacted with shock, anger and a not un-typical call

---

[56] '... incidents like the Dec 8 riot can break out in a stable society, but it is important to have a well-trained Home Team that can deal with them in a measured and decisive way'. Prime Minister Lee Hsien Loong quoted in Goh (2013).

[57] 'I do not accept that we must straight away ask whether fundamental approaches or the whole way our society is organised needs to be re-thought immediately'. Prime Minister Lee Hsien Loong quoted in Goh (2013).

to send the workers home. Singapore civil society blames the rioters for threatening the ostensible security and stability of their country. This is all the more interesting when one reflects on the two guiding political precepts since the creation of the republic, being economic growth and racial harmony. Instead of urging the government to investigate what we believe to be the root causes of the unrest, that is, the systematic dis-embedding of the migrant worker community which now is exacerbated by the regulatory imbalance, Singaporeans are calling for more of what in fact is likely to perpetuate and deepen the risks to economic growth and social harmony.

Problematic Executive Decisions of Deportation

The executive's decision to deport 57 of the foreign workers allegedly involved in the riot draws into focus the paradox and contradiction resulting when executive and judicial decisions co-exist prioritizing the prevailing economic principle of market economy interests thereby and compromising the presumption of innocence. Seven of these deportees were initially charged but later had these charges withdrawn against them unilaterally by the prosecution, each with a Discharge Amounting to an Acquittal being granted by the Court. However, days after their acquittal, they were rounded up and were deported by the Ministry of Manpower.[58] M Ravi, the lawyer representing one of these deportees, Rajendran, tried to prevent this outcome by making representations to the Central Investigation Department and the Singapore Prisons Service, all to no avail. Ravi has since filed an application to quash the warning issued by the Attorney General, and to also set aside the deportation order issued by the Immigration and Checkpoints Authority of Singapore (ICA),[59] along with seeking a reinstatement of Rajendran's work permit.

---

[58] Similarly, following the strike by the SMRT bus drivers in 2012, 29 persons were deported without benefit of trial.

[59] Ravi is making the application on grounds that the actions of the authorities were a breach of natural justice and in breach of Section 33(2) of the Immigration Act which states that an appeal may be lodged with the Minister by anyone against whom a removal (deportation) order had been made. It is argued that Rajendran was not accorded this right under the law, and that the authorities' decisions were made arbitrarily and/or unreasonably. Rebutting the Law Ministry's contention that 'a foreign national who is subject to repatriation … has no right under our laws to challenge the repatriation order in court', Ravi argues that Section 39A of the Immigration Act does indeed allow the courts to review certain decisions made by the Minister or the Controller of the ICA.

The Senior Singapore Minister of State for Law, Indranee Rajah, has said that in challenging repatriation, the court process is 'inapplicable'. Such a position would therefore suggest that the precedence of executive discretion may deny the review jurisdiction of the courts. It would be fair for these workers to wonder, in a country which ascribes at least to a thin version of rule of law and to governance through separation of powers, how can an acquittal by the courts be so easily circumvented by arbitrary extra-judicial actions of the executive as seems to be the case here? If these seven men were acquitted, that would indicate such a doubtful degree of culpability to suggest that they pose no security threat, leaving the undesirability test for deportation in the Immigration Act unfulfilled. In deporting them, the Law Ministry claims it took 'firm and quick action' to avoid 'additional social and security risks' caused by a 'recurrence of an incident', with the Law Minister emphasizing the cost savings of repatriation decisions being administrative ones.[60] This explanation remains unconvincing at law, while vividly demonstrating the use of executive power over law for cost savings above justice. In terms of the state protecting exclusionist and discriminatory market interests there could be a more sinister explanation. These deportations despite acquittal send a chilling warning to the remaining migrant worker population – don't look to the protection of the law if the state decides that you have challenged market stability and the imposition of discriminatory social order.

While many Singaporeans see the employment opportunities offered foreign low-wage workers working as a privilege, the migrant labour market nevertheless carries reciprocal benefits, which have not been given sufficient emphasis and attention in the minds of the local community. Low-waged migrants, almost half the Singaporean workforce, contribute immensely in the short term to Singapore's wealth and the smooth functioning and growth of the economy. To deny these people the basic protections of due process as exemplified by this incident underscores that the conscious market exploitation which many migrant workers experience, is not even rationally tempered in the mind of Singapore civil society with a self-interested recognition of the need to tackle the seeds of worker unrest. This paradoxical attitude which

---

[60] 'If every case has got to go to court and a judge makes a decision, then repatriation decisions become judicial rather than administrative,' Shanmugam was reported to have said. 'Then every foreigner is entitled to stay here at taxpayers' expense, housed here at taxpayers' expense, it could stretch on a year or more'. See Loh (2013).

abounds among those who benefit in some measure from the dis-embedded market is perhaps the ultimate reason as to why the market is unsustainable.

CONCLUSION

There is much to draw from the creation and maintenance of private property arrangements which comprise the migrant labour market, in terms of our theory that such dis-embedded market conditions are unsustainable, and are so through the rejection of organic social bonding in favour of exclusionist individual wealth creation economies. However, for the purposes of evaluating law's failure and law's potential in terms of regulating for social bonding, it is useful to concentrate on the regulatory state as the sponsor of legal regulation. In what we have set out above the state can be seen as a self-interested player in the maintenance of dysfunctional property arrangements, and thereby the dis-embedded labour market economy.

(a) Too little law – the example of the one day leave for migrant domestic workers, and the requirements on wage payment reveal conditionality in law making which favours state and employer interests.

(b) Law too late – the opportunity for domestic workers to transfer their contracts, or for construction workers to seek limited residency rights in order to address industrial disputes are largely non-actionable legal protections in the face of employer intransigence and worker dependency.

(c) Limiting law's domain – with the state denying its inspectorial jurisdiction for migrant domestic labour when it comes to employment conditions in the home, law's enforcement capacity is selectively managed.

(d) Limiting legislation's capacity – by refusing to incorporate foreign domestic labour into employment legislation and limiting the reach of such legislation when it covers certain issues of construction labour contracting and not others adds to the discretionary powers of those who most benefit from discriminatory private property relations.

(e) Divesting sovereignty – the state's preference for requiring responsibility for worker repatriation, worker health coverage, workplace living conditions, and fundamental issues of worker's liberty to be

costed and determined by employers, creates unsustainable contexts
of dependency which the state can therefore refuse to ensure.

(f)   Denying law's common reach – the common conventions of agency
        do not exist through the executive's selective interpretation of
        migrant labour agencies' obligations, and as a consequence, the
        court's unwillingness to apply the law of agency as would be the
        case in other agency arrangements. This then has profound influ-
        ences over fundamental principles of contracting such as uncon-
        scionability and parity.

(g)   Denying law's actionability and enforcement – through divesting
        crucial enforcement functions, the executive has effectively
        removed judicial oversight of vital employment relationships and
        private property arrangements operating within this labour market.

(h)   Refusing to accept international legal conventions – Singapore's
        doctrine of autonomy means that when it comes to regulating
        migrant labour markets it chooses not to accept the binding nature
        of regional or international convention.

(i)   Lopsided approaches to enforcement – the state severely punishes
        worker over-stayers and delinquent maids who abuse their charges
        of care while at the same time showing leniency to negligent or
        abusive employers.

(j)   Distorting law's expressive function – when it comes to interpreting
        the conditions of industrial health and safety, or the absence of
        worker-centric concerns about pay and conditions, the state would
        have it that the law as it stands is more than adequate for balancing
        worker's interests and the facilitation of economic growth.

(k)   Duplicity in law's purpose – the government says that the increase
        in the foreign worker's levy is designed to reduce the number of
        workers recruited and therefore dependency. In the context of high
        demand for labour and a reluctance in local workers to do what
        migrants are contracted to do then the fee increase may simply be
        seen as a necessary increase in labour costs. This in turn benefits
        state revenue on which the reduction in the foreign labour quota (a
        more effective break on supply rather than demand) would have the
        reverse effect.

If we reflect these applications (or misapplications) of law against the
three M's matrix then the forces at work against sustainable social
bonding loom large. The state argues that its normative principle is to
under-manage the migrant labour market in order to advance its contribution to economic growth, which is good. However, as the critique of
the denial of rule of law conventions to the repatriated workers acquitted

of rioting suggests, cornerstone principles on which sound governance relies tend to be compromised by the state in order to further destabilize worker resistance and galvanize relationships of subservience and dependency for short-term economic and security justifications.

Mutualities of interest exist to the exclusion of labour power. The commodification of migrant labour at low cost has enabled the state to benefit from more women in the workforce, less demand for state-funded elder and child care, increase in consolidated revenue, reduced health provision costs through the hire of cheaper foreign professionals, and the private stimulus of the construction and maritime industries. The mutualized benefits for largely unregulated agencies and employers are obvious and compounded when despite limited cost-sharing the agents and employers have almost uninhibited control over terms and conditions and duration of employment. For local Singaporeans they are convinced that while migrants are below them in the pecking order, and somehow threaten their jobs, they are saved from shouldering responsibility for tasks that the migrant labourers discharge. Working parents can manage the skyrocketing costs of living by discounting the costs of domestic and health care. It is only the essential player in this market's social reality, the migrant worker, who can claim little mutualized benefit except for access to better-paid jobs whatever the conditions. However, in terms of individual integrity and social dignity, at what cost?

Finally, to the market and its sustainability. Whether it be through increasing wealth gaps, depressed low-skilled workers' salaries, destructive real estate price spirals, the cost to the wider economy posed by this labour market frame will eventually demand state intervention or civil society resistance. More immediate has been the realization that migrant worker tolerance can reach its limits and the fragility of a command-and-control state regulatory response would not be sufficient if the one million were to rise up against the rest.

6. Sustainable markets and community inclusion

INTRODUCTION

It would be too crude simply to follow the preceding chapter's critique of dis-embedded migrant labour markets with a discussion of market arrangements demonstrating the reverse characteristics of market bonding as opposed to the forces of dis-embedding. Instead, this chapter will explore examples of eco-tourism which reveal Polanyi's interest in economy as part of society. The essential economic priority behind dis-embedded market economies, as we revealed in chapter 3, has market forces no longer necessarily serving prevailing social needs, but rather imposing on society market conditions of wealth creation in preference to broader and more long-lasting supports for social bonding. In the previous chapter we established this imposition as both unsustainable in terms of the particular market economy in question, as well as the society on which it, in varying degrees, depends.

The purpose of this chapter is to demonstrate how market arrangements for the promotion of eco-tourism in Northern Thailand are preserving traditional communities and indigenous wildlife, which without the tourist dollar, may now be unsustainable in their customary forms.[1] In these examples there is a synergy between wealth-creating markets and integrated communities, in particular working elephants and the sensitive commercialization of traditional tribal lifestyles.

This chapter will discuss the manner in which communities and elephants have a shared salvation through the generation of a tourist market. In so doing the distinction will be drawn between tourism that exploits wildlife and commercializes culture, from those tourist forms which are committed to wildlife preservation and cultural integrity. We

---

[1] While recognizing its vigour, the chapter will not engage in the debate regarding what is legitimately sustainable when it comes to elephant park/refuge tourism. These debates are largely ideologically driven and work from differing notions of community and of the objects which should have priority in the sustainability project. These in our view are matters for local social consensus.

will argue that the latter is sustainable in a market sense because of its embeddedness within the societies that host limited tourist exposure,[2] as compared to exploitative tourist ventures which expose wildlife to harm and communities to cultural infection.[3]

In advancing the sustainability analysis we will return to the three M's 'market, morality and mutuality' matrix. Markets are discussed both as tourist projects, and also conservation vehicles for tribal communities and elephant habitat. Morality will shift from commercial profit to the social fundamentals of resource protection in cultural and environmental manifestations. Obviously, mutualities between the traditional land owners, their livestock, tourist promoters, state regulators and considerate tourists are crucial if economic sustainability for social survival is to be established and maintained.

Turning to the question of implementing any model or frame of sustainability over individual wealth creation/profit motivation, sociability becomes a tool for states and state governments to introduce laws and regulations, and policies which enable the different stakeholders, particularly those in less powerful positions measured against capitalist bargaining potential, to be able to carry on a dialogue with other actors on a more balanced terms. In this particular case-study, the collaborative shared interests at the heart of a sociability model empower local communities within Northern Thailand that may otherwise become the victim of exploitative enterprises.[4] The discussion that follows gives substance to this collaborative market experience. It recognizes in wildlife and cultural vulnerability with the advance of modernization, real communities of shared risk. Through cooperation between the conservation imperatives and commercial interests that underpin eco-tourism, risk is being turned into shared fate and some communities at least are taking responsibility for their sustainable futures. Where this is not the case, we will identify the reasons for the failure in the collaborative risk to fate transition.

On a larger scale, we might think of sustainable tourism as a strategy for sustainable social development, and for communal market relations. Together with employment opportunities and a lifestyle which brings with it livelihood,[5] eco-tourism involving the local communities can move a society or even a country forward toward sustainable localized commerce through a trickle down (or radiating out) effect in which the

---

[2] Picard and Wood (1997), p. 4.
[3] United Nations Environmental Programme website.
[4] Meekaew and Srisontisuk (2012).
[5] Ball (1989).

revenue generated from tourism, when reinvested into the local environment, can involve the building and strengthening of infrastructural
capacities.[6] This kind of self-reliant and mutually supporting economy, as
opposed to the dependency on subsidies and donations, or externalized
direct investments in other replacement industries which do not educate
and empower the local population, can be seen on a much wider level as
lifting local communities and their service regions out of unsustainable
growth lag/poverty.

ELEPHANTS AND THE SUSTAINABILITY CHALLENGE

In Northern Thailand elephants have had both a commercial and community value for generations. Historically, the elephant was employed in
transportation, military campaigns, logging and other heavy lifting occupations which were driven by very fundamental and localized economic
and sustainability interests.[7] As these activities diminished in their
commercial viability, elephants became a burden rather than a benefit for
communities in which they had been a feature. Along with the transition
of agricultural profile came the danger that tribal communities, like their
elephants, would no longer have a sustainable future and could break
down under the pressure of urban drift and modernization.[8]

   The symbolic and religious significance of elephants in Northern
Thailand should also not be forgotten.[9] Perhaps one reason for the deep
bonds between man and elephant in tribal cultures of the region was the
shared struggle for survival in the material and the mystical animist
worlds which both inhabited. Sustainable tourism, therefore, needs to
appreciate and reflect social, commercial and aesthetic synergies if risk to
fate is to be achieved.

   Communities in which sustainable elephant-centred tourism exists are
an essential extension of tribal societies which prize elephant caretaking
as a skill and vocation central to the preservation of the elephant as a
sacred animal and a commercial opportunity.[10] In today's world these
communities would be both financially and most probably culturally
unsustainable without tourism. This commercial reality is in part due to

---

   [6]   Dawson (2006).
   [7]   Mar (2007).
   [8]   Lohanan (2005).
   [9]   Choskyi (1988).
   [10] Elephant Conservation Center website.

the fact that the few critical local stakeholders within the wider tourism enterprise, such as the local workers at the elephant sanctuaries that maintain these animals and the local communities that are also a focus of the tourist experience, require economic and business frames to replace the fast disappearing agricultural occupations. Without a localized business base shifting from subsistence to cash forms both man and elephant would be forced out to search for paying work.[11] As the elephants became an unsustainable commercial burden they too would be ejected from the cultural and commercial mix. Like it or not, the elephants are equally dependent on other commercial and philanthropic stakeholders for their very basic survival needs. This dependency, however, can through humane inclusion, offer a dignified existence for the elephant in their domesticated and their natural habitats. Dignified inclusion is the crucial context in which dependency can prevail for sustainable rather than subjugated futures.

The tribes of man and animal in a modern world have become dependent on a market that can be both morally consistent with their traditions and mutualize their social values, or can destroy these for short-term profit, or will relegate the tribes and their elephants to an excluded lifestyle not dissimilar to that experienced by migrant workers (see chapter 5). Commercial dependency has the potential to sustain or destroy relative to the structure of the market, its moral location and the mutualities it serves.

In Bentrupperbaumer's discussion, four universal values emerge in regard to viewing wildlife in the tourism context:[12]

1. *doministic* view which sees these animals are under the dominion of people, emphasizing mastery, domination and control of the animals;
2. *utilitarian* view which values the animals only for their ability to provide benefit, whether social, economic or psychological to humans;
3. *moralistic* view which posits that the welfare and rights of animals are equally as important as those of the tourists; and
4. *protectionistic* view which endorses the use of wildlife tourism for the protection, conservation and preservation of animals.

---

[11]   Pimmanrojnagool and Wanghongsa (2001).
[12]   Bentrupperbaumer (2005).

These values can be aligned with our analytical matrix. Markets need to be managed by the societies which they should serve rather than the other way around. Even a utilitarian approach to wildlife management is only sustainable if the elephant is respected as a finite resource. In so doing the rights of the animal become inextricably connected to the morality and the sustainability of the market. Finally, a protectionist perspective is mutualized through the protection that community, wildlife, and tourist enterprise can offer each other, and risk moves to fate for the communities of mutualized interests.

What has been observed in the elephant tourism industry in Northern Thailand is an eco-centrism that keeps the society as a community afloat through the recognition (and sometimes respect) for the inter-dependency that the different stakeholders have with one another, and the appreciation of their environment as the finite context in which mutualities can be forged.[13] It would be careless to represent all elephant tourist ventures as moral, mutual or even embedded in a market sense. We can now reflect on those which do not exhibit such features as a further comparative substantiation of unsustainable commerce hard up against sustainable enterprise, and why so.

As anticipated above, in our writing on these eco-tourism markets we draw a distinction between two categories of tourism, both of which provide commercial benefit to its stakeholders:

- one which tends to exploit one or more of the stakeholders in some way for commercial benefit in a market sense, and where either moralities or mutual relationships are unsustainable; and
- the other, which respects the value of stakeholders beyond their commercial value. In these circumstances the market can be said to serve social rather than any dominant economic need. The morality of the enterprise is determined by the contributing stakeholders having the most significant 'buy-in' when it comes to sustainability. Mutual relationships are forged and maintained because of the embeddedness of the market in the communities of shared fate.

The former, more exploitative version of tourism has difficulty integrating within the communities that supply its attractions (as an industry) because of its reliance on external capital and essential commitment to external shareholder return. The supply chain along which this form of tourism runs has little interest in returning economic or social capital to

---

[13]   Miller (2004).

the communities it exploits. Such predatory tourist enterprises accept little or no social obligation to their domestic contributors, their health safety and cultural integrity. In this regard, if they have any interest in sustainability it is preconditioned by the driving motivation for economic growth and wealth creation external to the communities of service providers on which the tourism relies.[14] Sustainability is seen in terms of the tourist market rather than the environment in which the tourist opportunity essentially exists.

The latter category of enterprise which merits the classification *eco-tourism*, recognizes sustainability in the mutual social as well as economic relationships on which the viability of the endeavour depends. The supply chain is grounded in the community of essential service providers. The morality of the market cannot be degenerated into externalized wealth creation because the 'share-holders' are the communities, cultures and cohabitants that give this form of tourism its distinction. In fact one of the necessary requirements for the tourists attracted to this experience is to give back to the communities in which they share and to participate in the conservation of the lifestyles and livestock they have come to admire. The profit motivation therefore depends on rather than conceding to the sustainability ethos.

Eco-tourism determined through markets, mutualities and morality entails much more than being kind to elephants. Some philanthropic elephant sanctuary enterprises, in our view, are not sustainable because they disproportionately focus their enterprise on elephant welfare at the expense of other crucial community contributors. These operations tend to ignore the historical reality of a necessary commercial market favouring the mutual interests of livestock and livelihood. The morality of charity for elephants creates a dependency relationship which in many respects is as unsustainable as is externalized commercial exploitation.[15] By not recognizing the value of the interests of other stakeholders these enterprises may indeed be undermining the sustainability of elephant husbandry in contexts of mutualized social capital.

Our view of sustainability is that the market is a servant of society, and sustainability refers to more than just a simple arrangement for using the tourist dollar to help elephants and to aid the tribal communities in some philanthropic or dependency arrangements. Rather, the fundamental sustainability question is: how does tourism in that context empower social units that comprise elephants, people, habitat, culture?

---

[14]   Ashley and Roe (1998).
[15]   Ashley, Boyd and Goodwin (2000).

Even against the simplest measures of quality of life, with more socially integrated enterprises, concerns about market/social balance remain crucial in sustainability terms, and in this respect one cannot ignore economic indicators of wealth and growth. In our theorizing, however, economy and its health and advancement are no longer an externalized measure. Disengaged shareholders rather than social stakeholders cannot, in sustainable market relationships, claim priority over that product of sustainable markets.

As our research reveals, market balance entertains external investment and wealth and growth considerations, but locates these in a socially engaged middle ground, predetermined by the paramount interests of social stakeholders who the market serves; sometimes a delicate balance, as this form of eco-tourism demonstrates through its uneasy gradation between elephant exploitation and philanthropic sanctuary. The market median will give rise to a more sustainable social solution. The delicacy is clear even in more socially integrated enterprises, where for the sake of improved life quality for human inhabitants as this form of tourism embeds, the elephants might find their work burdens more taxing or human treatment of these animals might be more vigorous.[16]

SUSTAINABLE MARKET CONDITIONS

Returning to our three M's matrix, in this chapter markets, morality and mutuality are used in analysing how and why markets are a feature of, rather than a challenge to organic social bonding. In order to achieve this, wildlife and cultural preservation will be viewed both as economic and social frames. The sustainability of eco-tourism markets will be both a condition and consequence of the interaction between human and animal constituents, which in turn satisfy the particular entertainment and life experience preferences of environmentally conscious travellers.

Sustainability in this context is synergy rather than antimony. Eco-tourism relies on sustainable communities and at the same time is crucial in sustaining these communities. There would be no eco-tourism in Northern Thailand without the tribes and the elephants and it might be

---

[16]   There is a critique of elephant park operators who claim to manage their livestock in sustainable conditions but continue to ferry human passengers on elephant rides using chairs and strapping. There is evidence that the only safe way for humans to ride elephants is positioned on the neck above the ears, and one at a time.

fair to speculate that there would be few tribes and fewer elephants in the region without eco-tourism.

It is interesting to reflect on how elephants and tribal culture can either be degraded or enabled through different forms of tourist contact. In our sustainability model eco-tourism is no less concerned with commercial than environmental viability, but rather it re-invests profit into the wildlife, habitat and the cultures which it enjoys, and empowers the communities that host its activities through market inclusion to varying degrees on local stakeholder terms. This is model for market viability in the same manner as it sustains society through market viability. Market morality is wealth return rather than profit extraction. The mutuality of the market is socially embedded rather than externally directed.

The example of elephant-centred eco-tourism relies on a morality which values integrity, identity and investment. The market itself cannot exist (commercially or socially in any sustainable sense) without mutu-alities of interest which value profit as a mechanism to sustain society, and not society which sustains the profit of the market. The predatory market can and does operate alongside moral and mutualized markets but its future as with the future of the habitat it exploits is limited.

The central theme of this chapter is how economy serves society and how a particular market style is vital for the perpetuation of lives and lifestyles. In stark contrast with migrant labour markets, elephant-centred eco-tourism rests on the reality of a market maintaining society, and those working within the market benefitting from much more than merely the material profit it can achieve.

From Logging to Tourism

We begin by charting the recent historical course of the lifestyles of Thai elephants, and how elephant parks came to be the popular tourist destinations that they are today. In 1988, disastrous nationwide floods, which had been exacerbated by the soil erosion caused by logging, claimed the lives of 350 persons in the North Thailand region. As a consequence, the Thai government experienced tremendous international pressure to put a stop to such deforestation caused by logging activities in order to prevent further forest plunder for export markets, thereby averting future similar disasters as a consequence of erosion. Following the logging ban in 1989, the need for domesticated elephants fell drastically, with an ensuing dramatic decrease in the number of elephants in Thailand from 100 000 in 1900 to 4450 today.[17] The Thai elephant population was devalued, practically overnight, as agricultural and transport vehicles. Of these 4450 elephants currently in Thailand, approximately 1000 are wild while approximately 3450 are domesticated and as such may be the objects of this analysis.

The Asian elephant has since been classified by the International Union for Conservation of Nature as an endangered species,[18] with the Thai experience featuring as a microcosm of the decline of the Asian elephant. Northern Thailand, through the provision of semi-captive wildlife settings, hosts three-quarters of Thailand's contained elephant population. As it became illegal for the *mahouts* (professional elephant handlers) and their elephants to work in the forests, many were left unemployed. The mahouts have since switched focus to tourism as a source of income, with the elephants living in semi-captive environments to facilitate interactions between the elephants and the tourists. Mahouts, often from tribal societies beyond those in which the parks are located, have through the repatriation of their incomes, become the conduits for the survival of more far-flung and often remote tribal cultures. The sustainability net is therefore much expanded.

These semi-captive settings are known generically as elephant camps (*baang chang* in Thai). These elephant camps are run as businesses but are also in many instances a proxy solution for elephant conservation through providing care for domesticated elephants and preserving the culture of mahout life, which has a longstanding tradition in the Thai society. There are roughly 40 to 50 elephant parks in Thailand,[19] with seven major elephant parks in the northern part of Chiang Mai city, Mae Rim, Mae Taeng and Chiang Dao.

Elephants are in these market settings both wildlife and stock. In Thailand, legislatively, wild elephants fall within the conditions of the Wildlife Protection Act of 1992, which grants them basic protection from anthropocentric use. However, the domesticated elephants (in contrast with the wild elephants) are classified under the Draught Animal Act of 1939 as animals of burden, and are therefore considered private property possessing a value attributed to the creation of financial return for their owners. The commerce/habitat link is inextricable for elephant husbandry.

---

17 Snow (2008).
18 International Union for Conservation of Nature (2008).
19 Tipprasert (2002).

The hundreds of thousands of tourists that pass through the Northern area of Thailand and their elephant camps each year provide valuable revenue to the camp operators, the community, and the mahouts, in turn providing crucial benefit to the elephants through their commercial valuation.[20] This is supported by accounts of the camp owners that during the low season of tourist activity, the rented elephants that are not needed are often forced to wander the urban streets with their mahouts who sell food to onlookers, surviving on the little money made through such means.

Above and beyond these commonly identified actors within the elephant tourism industry, in our research, we observed that the development of a sustainable core tourism sector in the form described has in turn enabled the creation of a wider tourism-induced commercial sector,[21] viewed as important for the various members of the communities within which the elephant parks have chosen to locate themselves, and the support services that make these communities accessible. These villages or sometimes even tribal communities very often engage in souvenir production or mass cooking for tourists as an alternative to agricultural work, which used to be the livelihood of majority of these villagers, but has since diminished as a commercial option. In this chapter, both the core tourism sector and the tourism-induced sector described here can comprise community-based tourism and represent crucial stakeholders in the radiating tourism industry which is essentially reliant on the elephant for its survival.

In order to create and manage market sustainability with a social focus and mutualized wealth and growth priorities the eco-tourism market has had to rely on more than self-regulation. The role of the state in setting up conditions under which more organic regulatory frames might develop is worth brief reflection.

---

[20]   In saying this we do not intend to diminish the important, inherent dignity of the elephant which is recognized in Thailand as being perhaps more significant than its commercial value. All we are suggesting is that the preservation of elephants would be a much more difficult dependency project if their commercial value was denied.

[21]   This includes enterprises such as taxi transport, guide services, food and beverage provision, souvenir sales and photo memories, as well as the marketing of tribal culture and expeditions to local handicraft factories.

Mechanical Regulation – Does it Work?

While much of the literature on the elephant camps in Thailand criticizes the apparently overbearing focus on profit and cost issues (explored in chapter 5), and argues for the strengthening of normative guidelines for the management of elephant parks and the enforcement of the same, these allegations themselves merit critique. Many animal rights activists look at the operation of elephant camps only as businesses and identify problems with cost-savings on the part of these enterprises, calling for higher standards in relation to food, hygiene, safety, etc. For the elephant parks in Thailand, this 'regulatory pressure' is exerted in the hope of improving the conditions and lives of these Asian elephants. In chapter 1, we wrote about how regulation, particularly that which is mechanically imposed, may and often will backfire against its regulatory intent, if it does not complement regulatory principle and promote synthesis with medium-term and more sustainable organic regulatory initiatives. Such has been the by-product of some state-sponsored regulatory initiatives.

In 2002, when the Livestock Department in Thailand issued guidelines for elephant camps that established standards on issues such as elephant shelters, camp location, waste management, food and safety,[22] the owners of elephant camps initially responded by complying and embracing these standards. However, following active compliance on their part, these owners eventually drifted into more creative non-compliance. With the rising costs of doing business, they began cutting corners wherever they could, squeezing more money from the elephants as labour inputs, to counter-balance the costs they alleged in regulatory compliance. Furthermore, smaller elephant camps were finding it more difficult to cope with the compliance requirements, and therefore faced genuine challenges to sustainable commercial survival. The balance between habitat and market had moved away to some extent and in some sectors from the necessities of commercial viability.

Despite the commendable intentions behind these state-sponsored regulatory requirements, they created a regulatory paradox between guaranteeing uniform and enforceable standards of protection for the elephants working in the tourism sector, and increasing the costs of affordable enterprise which would drive smaller businesses out of the industry and force elephant camp owners to engage in cost-cutting which eventually proved damaging to the health and wellbeing of the elephants and their communities. We suggest that one solution to this paradox

---

[22] Department of Livestock Development (2002).

would be offered through more collaborative regulation that emerges organically through leveraging the interdependence that the different stakeholders within this identified community have one to another. This might take the form of employing and negotiating interest mutuality along with a transformed market morality to ensure sustainability through regulation. Stakeholders would measure the risks to sustainability of under-regulated elephant maintenance, and balance these against the risks to market viability from regulatory compliance costs. Collaboratively these community stakeholders would evaluate risk/benefit in a more social and holistic engagement and the fates both of the elephants and of the tourist market would be negotiated. Obviously the market as envisaged by the park entrepreneurs would require redirection from unsustainable and externalized profit margins to more realistic and responsible profit re-distribution and human/livestock capital valuation. In return, elephants would remain stock animals but with dignity rather than exploitation.

Exploitation vs Eco-tourism

As an alternative to the profit-driven elephant camp, we have identified at another extreme the elephant sanctuary featuring in Thailand's eco-tourism possibilities. These sanctuaries represent a peculiar kind of elephant habitat in which the owner buys in and acquires abused, abandoned and injured elephants, not for work but for their care. These elephants are more often than not injured as a consequence of their work either in the logging or tourism industry. No work is required of the recuperating elephants living in the elephant sanctuaries, and they do not perform a livestock role. Instead, these elephant sanctuaries draw tourists who pay for the opportunity to enjoy close interaction with these elephants in the stages of their care and rehabilitation. The tourist interaction would typically include programmes such as learning how to become a mahout, feeding, bathing and even nurturing elephants in circumstances where their injuries require special attention. These elephant sanctuaries provide food, veterinary care and adequate free time for the elephants to eat, drink, rest and bathe. While the sanctuaries exist for the elephants, at the same time they accept (sometimes begrudgingly and even dismissively) tourist visitation for the revenue that the tourism industry provides. This revenue is principally returned to the cost of elephant welfare and as such the elephant becomes the dominant stakeholder in the market enterprise. We suggest that such prioritization if it comes at the cost to the social sustainability of local communities and creates a medium-term dependency relationship between the philanthropic institution and its elephant herds, may be as unsustainable as the exploitative camps driven by externalized profit maximization.

Sitting in the middle of the spectrum from exploitation to sanctuary-centred eco-tourism are elephant parks which provide almost identical programmes consisting of an elephant ride, a rafting trip down the river on a bamboo raft, a buffet lunch, an oxcart ride, and an elephant show where the elephants kick soccer balls, dunk basketballs into hoops, play musical instruments, dance to music, and paint using paintbrushes held in the tips of their trunks. From the rides on the backs of these elephants through the nearby forests to the elephant shows, these elephant camps combine the different stakeholders, the elephants, the mahouts, the villager, the local service workers and the tourists to create a tourist experience based on a managed interaction mainly for mainstream tourist appreciation.

As we mentioned in an earlier section, at the exploitative end of the spectrum clandestine enterprises still operate where elephants are employed for illegal logging in situations where there is little care of their health and safety. These throw-backs to darker days of elephant exploitation have resulted in horrendous physical injuries to the animals and even psychological scarring[23] from the cruelty suffered in the course of such exploitative conditions.

Explaining Sustainable Markets

In researching the elephant parks in Northern Thailand as a sustainable enterprise case-study, we have been able to identify some market characteristics unique in this recently developing tourism market that complement our theoretical matrix. Through the application of the matrix to the analysis of market-centred social sustainability, the concept of sustainability as laid out in this book is demonstrated going beyond considerations of environmental responsibility and economic sustainability. The analysis reveals alternate market conditions that recognize the positive or negative social effects of crucial aspects of market activity, such as the impact on domestic economies from employing foreign labour at depressed wage levels, or in this case, tourism profits directed to the social benefit of local communities rather than to external capital investors.

---

[23]   Laohachaiboon (2010), p. 79.

An example of the potency of our analysis can be seen when reflecting on higher-level concerns for cultural sustainability:

- the tourist demand for an 'authentic' cultural experience can often be injurious to the local communities when their cultures are commodified, compacted and commercialized, and
- the diversification of local economic growth becomes mechanically constricted because those indigenous societies cannot move beyond tourism to find other more rewarding livelihoods.

This reveals another dependency relationship which endangers social sustainability. Market plurality, therefore, needs to be another moral and mutualized pre-condition for the social utility of the tourism market.

The analysis also identifies that in avoiding both exploitation and over-dependency, these four characteristics are significant sustainable market pre-conditions and conditions:

1. an integrated community of stakeholders through diversity and interdependence;
2. economic relationships that reflect a power balance which would foster social sustainability in the long run;
3. redistributing and repatriating the wealth and growth reaped from activities in which the multiple stakeholders have contributed; and
4. various stakeholders supporting rather than degrading or exploiting integration and mutuality for self-interest.

Once the moral of the market becomes shared profit, and the market relocates into the social, the analysis identifies the key to sustainability and what universalizes these market features well beyond the context of eco-tourism, as sustainable mutualities of interest which reveal and reflect the general good (see chapter 7).

INTEGRATION BETWEEN ELEPHANT MANAGEMENT AND LOCAL TRIBAL COMMUNITIES

In Northern Thailand, we have observed that contrary to accusations that eco-tourism pursuits necessarily alienate the local communities, rather that this is the unsustainable social outcome when foreign corporations and commercial interests, often in collaboration with the local government, infiltrate the local market provision (imposing unfair wages and exploiting the natural and livestock resources of local communities for external profit harvesting). If the elephant camps are more often than not owned and managed by the Thais, and some of the elephants living and working in the camps belong to members of the local community, then the conditions exist for profit repatriation and wealth re-distribution that is localized and socially sustaining. In this sense, the eco-tourism industry becomes a genuine and accountable source of income for the local communities, and is socially beneficial in that:

- these communities can continue to keep and care for their elephants, and
- manage and schedule work opportunities for their young people so that urban drift does not destroy regenerated village life.

In the Mae Taeng River area of Northern Thailand, two elephant camps rent 78 per cent and 82 per cent of their elephants respectively on a monthly basis, either from the members of the Karen tribal community or from Thais based in the northern and northeast of Thailand (Isaan).[24] These indigenous communities continue to live where their villages have traditionally been based, no longer being forced to resettle away from the elephant parks. Consistent with the desire for stable localized communities, we found that often the parks are built around tribal settlements with levels of elephant ownership (e.g. the hill-tribe villages) enabling the river raft/boat tour visitors to view, from a safe distance, tribal lifestyles without invading their privacy.

SUSTAINABILITY OF THE RELATIONSHIP BETWEEN ELEPHANTS, THEIR KEEPERS, AND THEIR COMMUNITIES

Although the local communities (and not the elephant camp) own the elephants, it is the mahouts who have the special expertise, vocation and lifestyle that enables them to bond with the elephant and to become intimately the elephant's trainer and guide. The mahouts typically come from Thai Yai, Karen or Burmese hill tribes, starting out as a young boy in the 'family profession' when he is assigned an elephant early in its life. Many of these mahouts belong to the indigenous hill tribe minority

---

[24] Kontogeorgopoulos (2009), p. 433.

communities which carry a respect for this profession, despite the mahouts having become a socially and economically marginalized group today.

The elephant and its mahout remain bonded to each other throughout their lives, in the consummate interconnection of habitat, occupation, nature and mystical spirituality. This unique intimacy has resulted in another level of dependent interconnection which can have sustainable outcomes for each stakeholder. The Thai park owners, managers and workers have come to depend on these hill tribe mahouts for the training and care of the elephants, forming a sustainable market mutuality as long as the mahouts and the Thais coexist in respectful and trusting market moralities. Unfortunately this is not always the case and petty racism and class division can endanger market sustainability. In addition, distrust and tension can arise from disproportionate market share. The mahouts are usually hired by the elephant owners at a low wage (around 3000–5000 baht (90–150 USD) p.a.). As a consequence of exploitative employment practices for the elephant trainers, these stakeholders have become reliant on sub-economies such as the tips from tourists for rides or photo opportunities which supplement their salaries. Despite informal supplementary labour power valuing, essential and sustainable wage labour requires balanced correspondence between essential market contribution and wage return which reflects skills and service, not race and class. Where the valuation of labour power does not reflect actual market contribution, the resultant dependency relationship (as with low priced migrant labour) is skewed and unsustainable. With a fairer distribution of enterprise benefit across stakeholder groups, the elephants will get more than bananas and peanuts. Handled by better-compensated mahouts, elephant welfare will be improved from the mahouts having less need to exploit their elephants through outside supplementary (and sometimes illegal or degrading) employment, or spending time away from the elephants under their care.

THE TOURIST DOLLAR TO SUSTAIN THE ENVIRONMENT AND CULTURE

In whatever form, the tourism industry has become a significant driver of the Thai economy. In one sense, the revenue generated from tourism can be used to sustain the local and regional environment and culture by paying to keep both healthy and alive.[25] This is justifiable from a business sense – the industry invests in its natural environment and living communities so that tourists come to experience a vibrant and convincing natural environment. In this market spirit, the elephant camps themselves hold great potential for tourist education regarding animal welfare and wildlife conservation. Through raising awareness amongst tourists, the dangers and problematic effects of industries such as the poaching of elephants for the ivory trade can be made known.

The largely domesticated elephant population in Thailand has few options for survival outside responsible tourism. Work in elephant camps is simply a preferable use of elephant occupation than illegal logging or street-wandering. Without tourism, even in less than perfect conditions, the life of these elephants would be much less sustainable.

On the other hand, for the domesticated elephant population in Thailand as a whole, the elephant sanctuaries positioned at the extreme end of an eco-tourism spectrum have little large-scale impact on sustainability. The sanctuary focuses on the small number of sick and injured or abandoned and abused. Because of the large natural space required by the elephants in which to work and roam in a stress-free environment, and the need to impose a cap on the visitor and volunteer numbers to ensure the kind of experience that the tourists look for in these sanctuaries, their costs are high and their elephant outreach limited. As a result, neither the elephant nor the tourist numbers can be increased significantly to support any larger proportion of the elephant population. Economies of scale say that the sanctuaries can contribute to but not replace other, more commercial forms, of eco-tourism markets.

The elephant camps, which are able to balance the priorities of caring for the elephants and making tourists happy, provide much greater potential to reach wider numbers of elephants, local people, service providers and tourists, as well as providing care for a more sustainable number of elephants. Furthermore, by essentially involving the local communities wherein the camps are located, the range and field of stakeholders potentially empowered through the operation of these elephant camps as eco-tour endeavours is spread wide. By prioritizing benefits to the local population as an integral part of any genuine eco-tourism venture, cultural disruption and environmental degradation which have been identified to be the biggest problems that accompany a

---

[25] This is particularly important in northern Thailand where cultures are diverse, races are many and the regional history is rich and distinct from the rest of the country.

booming tourism industry can be minimized.[26] The impact of such empowerment also ensures that the social and cultural dimensions of local communities are valued alongside environmental and economic dimensions. This empowerment framework operates on four different levels: psychological, social, political, and economic, and each as a field within sustainable markets contributes to their social embedding.[27]

EMPOWERING LOCAL COMMUNITIES

Empowerment, as Scheyvens (1999) understands, brings with it 'lasting economic gains' to the local community, the fair distribution of which is key to its social value. Furthermore, rather than commodifying tribal culture through tourism, but by recognizing instead its uniqueness and intrinsic value, the community and its culture as stakeholders in the tourist market would be more inclined to positively embrace the tourism industry and its effects. Together with that optimism, greater organic and collaborative control of the industry would allow the local community to gradually grow to be more self-reliant, taking pride in their own traditions and culture. As Scheyvens states 'Eco-tourism which is sensitive to cultural norms and builds respect for local traditions, can therefore, be empowering for local people'.[28]

As it would be overly idealistic to assume that all within the stakeholder community would undoubtedly and unproblematically share in the production and benefits of the eco-tourism, as with the mahouts, regulation must first recognize distribution and repatriation inequalities in the market. Regulation for this purpose, stimulated by principles of fairness, would ensure that market inequalities are not exacerbated by the introduction of an otherwise foreign and suddenly lucrative industry to which all will not have opportunity access. Communitarian equilibrium also has to develop and be supported as a market morality by such regulatory empowerment, and fair representation of needs and concerns of the different actors and interest groups within the community has to be a market outcome. This can be done by enhancing access for the variety

---

[26]   This assumes that the local populations have been educated to the dangers of degradation and share for their benefit in conservation ideologies and practices. These are additional conditions of morality and mutuality on which the sustainable market depends.

[27]   Scheyvens (1999).

[28]   Ibid, p. 248.

of different actors to decision-making processes, such that a consensual market governance can be achieved.

Scheyven's empowerment framework also enables us to analyse the impacts of eco-tourism on local communities, so that these effects can be singly addressed. While conventional ideas of eco-tourism as environmentally responsible tourism do reflect on the impacts of travel on environments and peoples, there are certain unreconstructed commercial conditions which must be better understood and then repositioned into the sustainability frame in moving forward:

> We recognize, and have sought to make sense of, [eco-tourism's] appeal ... to unlock new forms of self-realization, sentiment, entitlement, enrichment. This notwithstanding the fact that it carries within it a host of costs and contradictions: that it has both insurgent possibility and a tendency to deepen prevailing lines of inequality, the capacity both to enable and to disable, and the power both to animate and annihilate.[29]

While the recent literature relating to eco-tourism emphasizes *responsible tourism* (where individuals, organizations and businesses are asked to take responsibility for their actions and the impacts of their actions on the environment), this market morality may represent minimum returns in the immediate term, for either the environment or the local communities. Externally constructed and imposed responsibility regimes are as likely, without close local consultation, to ignore the 'needs' or 'wants' that crucial local stakeholders expect from the tourism market. Differences in perspective are likely to arise at crucial points in the supply chain regarding the nature and characteristics of responsible relationships. For instance, tourism operations may think that they are complying with and promoting responsible behaviour through opening up more and more opportunities for tourist engagement with the environment. Without meaningful dialogue amongst those who share a common fate in the sustainability exercise, even sensitive market expansion may expose important areas of sanctuary or communal privacy to tourist gaze and the risk of commodification. As suggested earlier collaborative regulation of the interactions between key stakeholders is prefaced on responsibility and does not require its external imposition.

Going even further from a collaborative form of regulation, we can consider embedded market mechanisms where the local community's ownership and husbandry of the area and the environment becomes the primary value, prized above any commercialization. In the Philippines,

---

[29]   Comaroff and Comaroff (2009), Conclusion, pp. 139–50.

for instance, a new law puts local communities in charge of maintaining protected areas, with the income generated from such activities within these areas being funnelled back into an administrative body run by the local communities. This creates a revolving fund for eco-tourism projects that explicitly involves local stakeholder interests and helps build their capacity for engaging in work that stands as a source of income and sustainable lifestyles for these tribal communities.[30]

In our work, by prioritizing sustainability, we move the concept of eco-tourism further to one which ensures that the benefits of sustainable market enterprise be returned to all members of a community, thereby bringing long-term economic stability to those involved.

CONCLUSION

Eco-tourism has been applauded for re-building local economies and preserving eco-systems, and has been preferred by those concerned with such values over other forms of travel, in order to present an authentic experience in preserved natural environments for tourists to enjoy and contribute to. That said, these preferences come with their own set of consequences, many of which may be positive for social sustainability but through the impact of modernization, may challenge the continuity of cultural lifestyles and values. These are issues necessary for communities to grapple with as much as are the struggles for subsistence survival. We will not presume to offer solutions for cultural resilience as to do so may be another threat to the decision-making integrity of local stakeholders and their communities. What we have advanced in this chapter are reasons as to why organic sustainability through market synthesis is both preferable and capable of sustainable futures for those involved.

The chapter has presented a theoretical framework for building sustainable markets, by prioritizing interdependence and relationships amongst different stakeholders, ensuring fair and equal access, and preserving a balance such that there is no one stakeholder or interest group that dominates the interests of the others. How can this aspiration be ensured? In answering this question we return to our earlier chapters (chapters 1 and 2), and the concept of mutualizing interests. Making each and every participant in the community understand their interdependencies as members of different social and market groupings is the initial step

---

[30] Ranada (2013).

toward crafting sustainable economies which serve sustainable communities. The time of self-regulation for self-interest has passed, and for
communities of shared risk (unsustainable economic and social futures)
to move forward to communities of shared fate (accepting the challenge
of market repositioning away from externalised wealth and growth
valuation), regulatory transformation is required to create 'safe economic
and social spaces' wherein the shift to sustainability can be explored.

In their preface to the new edition of *Reclaiming Development* Chang
and Grabel talk of the transformation of global economic policies to
recognize the pre-eminence of 'equitable, stable and sustainable economic development'.[31] The neoclassical paradigm that the market is the
natural form of social organization ensuring individual freedom can be
realised through the reverse direction of prevailing development
models.[32] Sustainable eco-tourism does not reward the standard risk
profiles which characterize exploitative tourist enterprises. The environment is regulated for sustainability through a morality of stakeholder
engagement and empowerment. Mutualized relationships naturally arise
from embedded market arrangements. Markets are required to first
service the social needs of livestock conservation and of social and
cultural preservation before considerations of wealth and growth which
themselves are sustainably embedded in essential frameworks of social
bonding.

---

[31]   Chang & Grabel (2014), p. xxvi.
[32]   As our book has previously suggested this means a shift away from a
cognitive and normative economic monoculture.

7.   The truth of growth

DOING IT DIFFERENTLY

In a recent opinion piece entitled 'How to get back to strong, sustained growth' Klaus Schwarb, the father of the World Economic Forum, concluded:

> Ultimately, however, the path to sustained growth requires not only new policies, but also a new mind-set. Our societies must become more entrepreneurial, more focused on establishing gender parity, and more rooted in social inclusion. There is simply no other way to return the global economy to a path of strong and sustained growth.[1]

Despite the reformist invective this futurist thinker seems unable to escape the mind-set which he targets for change. Growth is economic and sustainability is about economies and the wealth they produce. In the same article Schwarb concedes:

> The global growth slowdown is taking place against the backdrop of rising economic inequality, owing to labour's declining share of national income – a worldwide phenomenon arising from globalisation and technological progress … Systems that propagate inequality or that seem unable to stem its rise contain the seeds of their own destruction.

This destruction arising as it will within an interdependent world, can never be averted or even modified until regulatory frames work for social rather than economic sustainability. Such is our book's sustainability message. As the tensions in many market economies currently demonstrate, these forms of economically driven sustainability are not productively interdependent from wider social sustainability. Rather, the ultimate and prioritized focus on economic growth in a world of finite resources and capital and labour-denuding technologies will always undermine organic social bonding.

---

[1]   Schwab (2014).

This conclusion reiterates how through using regimes of regulation for social bonding rather than exclusionist (and increasingly illusive) economic growth missions, law can work to advance social justice rather than individualist economic gain, through the social responsibility of stakeholders and thereby promote collective liberty. These, we argue, are the principles, relationships and outcomes of Polanyi's embedded markets.

There has been a lot of recent crisis 'talk' about global sustainability[2] but few legal scholars have endeavoured to chart a path along which law can advance embedded social sustainability rather than wealth and gain through private property relations.[3] This lacuna may be both because of a prevailing belief that there is no answer in either traditional economic or legal scholarship[4] to the inequality of the market or even more naively in some uncritical retention of confidence that the market is naturally fair. Whatever position is preferred, policymakers and regulators seem loath to move away from a law's role in propping up a failing economic model and spend their energies on the *holy grail* of maintaining sustainable economic growth and wealth creation. This book has presented another way.

SUSTAINABLE SUSTAINABILITY?

The governing theme in this book is the emergence of sustainability as a new global regulatory principle. As has been developed in the last two case-study chapters, what gives this shift in regulatory principle its particularity is the assertion that law's regulatory function in protecting and advancing private property rights can either retard or promote crucial economic and social relationships essential for sustainable social bonding.

In the analysis which has gone before, sustainability is viewed as organic social bonding and regulation therefore becomes a mechanical and organic force for bonding which is socially embedded. Social

---

[2] Kanninen (2012). This analysis of the consequences of global warming in particular again focuses the regulatory reform agenda on an urgent and complete overhaul of the prevailing global economic model.

[3] If there is discussion concerning law's role it is primarily in the context of sustainable economic development.

[4] Particularly in the traditions of neo-liberal economics and law, and of the economic analysis of law in the Chicago style.

solidarity and resultant sustainability is arguably a general good.[5] General good can become the driver for new approaches to legal regulation of private property relations. For instance, in a discussion of intellectual property rights (IPR) and their influence over South World development, specifically in terms of the neo-liberal dogmatic correlation between the protection of IPR and the generation of new knowledge, Chang and Grabel challenge any such contemporary private property rights valuation in that:[6]

> There are many cases where ideas have been generated without monetary gain in mind. In such circumstances we might consider the idea of public or communal property rights. One example of this type of public property right occurs in the open software programmes (sometimes called freeware) that are available on the Internet. The principles behind open software are straightforward: it is shared freely with the public at no charge; users can improve upon it; and the users are expected to share the improved software with the public. The only proviso is that no one can exploit the software for commercial gain. From a neo-liberal perspective, open software is illogical insofar as it involves a significant investment of ideas for reasons other than monetary gain.

If there was to be a subtitle for our thinking on shifting regulatory principle it is just that; *for reasons other than monetary gain.*

By looking as we have at the South World, and at transitional societies and economies that serve social needs, the regulatory importance of social bonding is more apparent than is currently recognized in North World regulatory states.[7] For our purposes here, the focus of our regulatory attention through the case-studies that comprised the last two chapters is the manner in which private property relationships act as forces for and against social bonding, and the case-study of migrant labour in particular was employed to explore South/North intersections specifically in terms of private property relations as an unsustainable exploitation of labour power.[8]

The critical consequence of this analysis is to more richly investigate law's essential role in regulating private property relationships as a

---

[5] Cotterrell (1996).

[6] Chang and Grabel (2014), p. 94.

[7] Krippner et al (2004).

[8] We use the notion of 'power' to represent labour as a dynamic and it should not be confused with any assumption of the empowerment of labour relations. Such empowerment, we argue, is only possible through a repositioning of private property relations enunciated in contracts of employment.

precursor to arguing for a repositioning of law's regulatory purpose.[9] This will be done from a unique perspective as far as contemporary private law theorizing is concerned; that of social sustainability and contract inclusion.

Regarding the relationship between private property rights, repositioned regulatory principle, and market embeddedness, sustainability is the primary purpose for regulation which then in turn develops and maintains markets that are directed towards economic outcomes which service social bonding. The veracity of this transition can be tested in the context of contemporary crises in global regulation and governance priorities[10] that reveal the pressing need for shifts away from individualized wealth creation and exponential economic growth at any price, as the driving motivation for regulatory determinations.[11] This framework for transition, as the recent international financial meltdown and its aftermath vividly demonstrate (see chapters 2 and 3), will not be painless. To date legal regulation has not assumed much more than a reactive or curative role in this journey. This arguably being so, we conclude that by reshaping the regulatory principles motivating law's influence over private property rights and protections (and in our case-study concerning migrant labour, activating law's regulatory involvement through such motivations), social and economic sustainability can be promoted in market settings[12] which would thereby ensure more enduring social locations for dis-embedded markets like labour force and for exclusionist regulatory paradigms such as law.[13]

The labour force case-study establishes that through considering mechanisms of social bonding in transitional and developing economies,

---

[9]   This is currently the subject of an extensive research grant proposal which we intend to develop as the next monograph in this series.

[10]   Findlay (2013a), chapters 5-8.

[11]   This is not to be confused with the movement for sustainable wealth creation even though we agree with its emphasis on 'recapitalising' social capital. See Singapore Institute of Directors (2008). Rather it involves a fundamental redirection in regulatory principle, see UNESCO (1997).

[12]   Again in this brief discussion we cannot pause to develop our conceptualization of markets and market settings. Our thinking is shaped by the caution that in perceiving markets in terms of their social embeddedness, we should not take the market itself for granted (Krippner et al (2004), p. 110). The market is a theoretical entity in its own right. Markets are social objects and for the purposes of this project markets provide a framework for the exchange of value through identified social bonds.

[13]   See the discussion of market economies and social embeddedness in chapter 3.

and contrasting these with the regulatory features which dislocate North World market economies, it is possible to speculate on how regulation can advance sustainability in a new economic model. For the purposes of this book any such new model, when it comes to the use of legal regulation over private property relations, will value conditions of social bonding and economic responsibility[14] in a similar way that wealth creation and growth have been the regulatory values of the global economic system now under strain.

What does all this have to say for a more specific appreciation of law and its regulatory utility in emerging and transitional economies, such as many of those in South East Asia? An important dimension of unsustainable market economies is exclusionist and oppressive private property relationships, endorsed by law, which protect the massive wealth gaps that threaten to strangle Asia's emerging markets. Alternatively we argue that legal regulation can be transformed to assist in making private property arrangements more inclusive, accessible and generally beneficial, thereby contributing to the essential social bonds which establish and ensure sustainable market economies.

Sustainability and Economic Distortion – Income Inequality

There are many economic and social factors which challenge sustainability. Consistent with our interest in the legal regulation of private property relations, being one such factor, we argue:

● Wealth and income gaps with regard to either unsustainable economic growth or its continuation share a curious relationship. In many emerging Asian economies, for instance, economic growth has depended on the exploitation of cheap labour, and resultant wealth gaps growing in the large part from the exploitation of such labour power, can lead to a general suppression of wages and a depression in consumer markets, or even a fundamental deterioration in labour relationships.
● Social dis-embeddedness which is class-based and identified in wealth gap distinction impairs social capital, undermines crucial trust arrangements on which organic markets depend, and eventually leads to social disorder.

---

[14] Courts enforce legal values such as justices as an 'expression of requirements for stable social interactions and for predictable expectations in social relations' (Cotterrell (2010).). See also Cotterrell (1996), p. 17.

The 2013 World Economic Forum, Global Risks Report identified 'severe wealth gaps and unsustainable government finances as the biggest economic threats facing the world'.[15] In an IMF Staff Discussion Note[16] entitled 'Inequality and Unsustainable Growth: Two Sides of the Same Coin?', it was observed:

> The relationship between income inequality and economic growth is complex. Some inequality is integral to the effective functioning of a market economy and the incentives needed for investment and growth. But inequality can also be destructive to growth, for example, by amplifying the risk of crisis or making it difficult for the poor to invest in education. The evidence has also been mixed: some find that average growth over long periods of time is higher with more initial equality; others find that an increase in equality today tends to lower growth in the near term ... The empirical literature on growth and inequality, however, has missed a key feature of the growth process in developing countries: namely, its lack of persistence. Per capita incomes do not typically grow steadily for decades ... Inequality still matters, moreover, even when other determinants of growth duration – external shocks, initial income, institutional quality, openness to trade, and macroeconomic stability – are taken into account ... attention to inequality can bring significant longer-run benefits for growth. Over longer horizons, reduced inequality and sustained growth may thus be two sides of the same coin.

Through an analysis of the unexpected connections between income inequality and environmental degradation,[17] researchers have concluded that:

> income inequality has been extensively correlated with health and social problems: life expectancy, obesity, mental health, drug use, educational performance, teenage births and violence to name a few ...[18] It may be, as Coburn has argued, that income inequality is itself *the result of the basic social, political and economic characteristics of a given society which also affect the quality of the environment* (our emphasis).[19] Characteristics such as the prevailing economic ideologies, cultural values like individualism and materialism, as well as attitudes toward consumption, work and the importance of protecting the environment are all likely to influence national policies which affect both income distribution and environmental quality. Breznau's analysis of survey data from five countries showed that those with egalitarian values are the most likely to support government services designed to reduce

---

[15]   Hirschler (2013).
[16]   Berg and Ostry (2011).
[17]   Haupt and Lawrence (2012).
[18]   Wilkinson and Pickett (2010).
[19]   Coburn (2004).

inequality. Conversely, those who support *economic individualism*[20] and neo-liberal economic policies are the least likely to favour such a role for government ...[21] Generally speaking, those who hold pro-market/individualist worldviews do not endorse pro-environmental values and behaviours; the reverse holds true for people who maintain pro-environmental (sustainability) values.[22]

The *Financial Times* (through the chief economist of the Asia Development Bank) identified that the rapidly growing wealth gap threatens Asia's 'growth miracle':

> Over the past 20 years, the gap between Asia's rich and poor has widened so that the richest 1 per cent of Asian households now account for 6 per cent to 8 per cent of expenditure. Income inequality has widened in China, India and Indonesia, the countries that have powered the region's economic growth. Taking developing Asia as a unit, the Gini coefficient – a common measure of inequality – has increased from 39 per cent to 46 per cent. Had it only remained stable, another 240 million people would have escaped poverty ... Widening inequality threatens the sustainability of Asian growth. A divided and unequal nation cannot prosper. Rising inequality can lead to instability and poor political choices, as governments facing populist demands opt to curry favour – for example, with inefficient subsidies on fuel or food – rather than promoting long-term sustainable growth.[23]

Emerging markets transiting from the South World face a growing threat from unsustainable market stimuli and under-regulated market growth. In chapter 5 we singled out the exploitation of cheap labour as both a key factor in Asia's recent economic growth and, in the wider perspective, the suppression of general wages which this distorted labour market feeds. Where migrant labour sustains construction and real estate development, local labour either eschews or is excluded from such an employment band. As a result the unskilled labour market for local workers is contracted, and the price of that labour is constrained through comparison with prevailing salaries in the construction (and domestic services) sectors where migrant labour dominates. On the other side of the market, real estate development is an artificially lucrative investment as a

---

[20] Economic individualism – a cultural orientation that emphasizes the values of individual autonomy, self-reliance, and achievement and is associated with support for capitalism and laissez faire market economics and preference for a limited role of government in the economy. Breznau (2010).
[21] Arikan (2011).
[22] Heath and Gifford (2006); Steg and Sievers (2000).
[23] Rhee (2012).

consequence of high margins of return ensured through suppressed labour value.

The World Economic Forum *Global Competitiveness Report 2013– 2014*[24] positions Singapore, for instance, second to Switzerland in world rankings. At the same time Singapore is measured as having the highest income gap in Asia.[25] This widening income gap is a natural side effect of the Singapore government's under-regulated pro-growth policies. Aligned with this the global recessions from 2007 witnessed the depression of unskilled workers' salaries while inflating those of skilled workers, and the reliance on a migrant workforce was accommodated in transitional economies with limited domestic labour potential in areas of crucial workforce demand. Due to the widening income gap and its connection with employment status, work determines class. From the perspective of social bonding the widening income gap is inclined to inflict negatively on social cohesion and undermine community trust largely because of a labour demarcation politicized through skewed arguments against the presence of foreign workers, and their impact on domestic employment conditions and possibilities. The popular devaluation of foreign workers in transitional economies already unsustainably reliant on their labour power, has distracted the economic analysis away from unfair investment (or non-investment) in social capital, the unsustainability of which will challenge the stability of the society.[26]

As the Singapore experience shows (see chapter 5), these conditions overheat all levels of real estate commerce creating wealth bubbles, over-extended credit gearing and barriers to access which produce conditions of unsustainable economic inequality and eventual social unrest.[27] It is argued that along with the advance of technology and the

---

[24] The *Global Competitiveness Report 2013–2014* assesses the competitiveness landscape of 148 economies, providing insight into the drivers of their productivity and prosperity. The Report series remains the most comprehensive assessment of national competitiveness worldwide.

[25] A 1,494,200 Non-Resident population as at year 2012; see Saw (2013).

[26] Uslaner and Brown found a correlation between the amount of trust and the amount of income equality. It can be explained that people can gain a sense of security from high income equality therefore they are expected to trust each other. A related study by Putnam (2000) also demonstrated that economic equality tends to lead to a high level of social capital (or 'connections among individuals'). People will show a tendency for engaging with others and hence strong social connectedness and civic engagement can be forged; see Uslaner and Brown (2002).

[27] In Singapore this has recently manifested in anti-foreigner sentiment, focused on the assumption that migrant labour challenges local employability,

eradication of poverty, the promotion of 'employment friendly' workforce regulation is crucial for contracting the wealth gap and creating a future for sustainable economic growth through a more balanced labour market where value and exchange are more aligned.

In drawing to a close our consideration of sustainability as the new regulatory principle some limited but critical observations on determining wealth as monetary value and material gain are necessary on which to build our arguments for repositioning regulatory relationships and outcomes (see chapter 2). Crucial to understanding sustainability, in terms of regulatory repositioning, is rethinking social wealth away from monetary value as dependent, inextricable and integral measures.

Wealth through Pricing Labour Power Subordinated to Capital

Market economies are not a reciprocity system such as those which often predominate in subsistence economies (discussed more fully in chapter 3). In the current global economic model money-based market economies proliferate, not systems based on reciprocity and redistribution. The prevailing wealth measure in such market economies is valued against the prices returned in marketing surplus exchange. Even in the simplest subsistence societies, market economies operating with money as a fictional unit of exchange (not essentially dependent on other more socially grounded measures of worth or value – see chapter 3) transact surplus production and trade in the resources (such as labour) which in turn produce surplus exchange. This process, we concede is not essentially destructive of social bonds. Rather it is when the production of surplus exchange is purposed for external wealth creation more than general social good, that these markets undermine their social location (see chapter 6).

As Dale concludes for subsistence societies with lesser market economies and no inclination to return surplus into capital investment, '... in the absence of the subordination of labour-power and the main instruments of production to capital, market trade may develop and flourish but a market economy will not'.[28]

We assert that, for instance, in valuing the price of labour as it is subordinated to capital, in money terms, both labour and the markets it sustains are socially dis-embedded. The process of subordinating labour

---

and migration upsets established racial balance. Concerning the former it takes no account of the critical economic reliance on migrant labour in the present workforce frame. See Tan W. (2013).

[28] Dale (2010), pp 179–80.

to capital and the consequent valuing of wage labour in terms of money opens up vast opportunities for dislocation from any realistic social valuation of labour in terms of subsistence productivity. In practice this is so when the price of labour depends on the profit returned to capital investment, through the exchange of surplus. Social bonding is dangerously exposed in wage labour economies contracting to such a degree that generations are becoming disenfranchised from opportunities for economic sustainability serviced by even the unbalanced wealth returns that wage labour offers.

As labour power is dis-embedded from its social value through its subordination to capital, then the price of wage labour may be more determined by the interests of those who manage capital than by more predictable and organic determinations such as productivity. In our example of Singapore's migrant labour workforce, we identified the unsustainable disconnects between under-priced labour power and wealth gaps consequent on capital exploitation, which currently legal regulation can assist. This in turn endorses the later-argued position that market dis-embeddedness challenges mutuality and morality through its unsustainable character.

Obviously such a fundamental rethink in market valuing will not happen without regulatory effort. To date in market economies as we have addressed them regulatory regimes such as the legal protection of private property relations are both ensuring unsustainable value frameworks and are missing the possibility through transformation to be powerful forces in the revaluing project.

Market Regulation: Law's Failing?

As an example of law's failing as a transformational regulator, it is informative to return to how the migrant worker/agent/employer/government/civil society dynamic in transitional economies relies on the maintenance of exclusionist and repressive private property arrangements. This reliance is made clearer through examining how law can address its failings when applied across the interests of all contracting parties, and thereby suggesting the need to include and make accessible within law's protections crucial conditions of the workforce market that at present are repressive and exclusionist of labour power's interests (discussed in chapter 5). In so doing it will be the absence of law perhaps more than its discriminatory protective dimension which is a feature of its regulatory purchase.

Transacting migrant labour in a dis-embedded market economy often relies on social and economic contexts of dis-embedding that are sequential and recurrent. The labourer and the agent situated in his home country (the home agent) negotiate terms which are usually exploitative of the worker and his family sponsors, and these terms are often illusory. The worker embarks on a relentless passage of obligation wherein he is required to invest relatively large capital outlay for tenuous immigration status and employment contracts. The status of the home agent is certainly not as a representative of the worker's interests even in the negotiation of the original contract terms of engagement. It is also not clear in the practices of the many off-shore and on-shore agents or of any eventual employer (nor are the duties and obligations of these agencies even generally confirmed by the state through law) whether the agency connections from home to host jurisdiction can be enforced by the worker in any legally recognized contractual conveyance.

There are already in the fabric of contract/agency law in most jurisdictions conventional avenues for law to regulate the transaction of labour in migrant dis-embedded market settings. However, from law's application (or absence) in migrant labour agency relations in too many market settings, the notoriously unbalanced platform is contract relationships. Recognizing this, states and governments regularly introduce legislative restrictions on critical contract stages in order to rebalance the commercial and market inequality which characterizes the property relations between employer/agent/employee. Even where there are minimal provisions covering say workplace health and safety, the impotence of the worker at both the contract and daily workplace stages makes them appreciate no choice but to accept sub-standard safety environments.[29] The regulatory situation is predictably and tragically devoid of effective intervention through the force of law. There is rarely extra-territorial legal reach from the host jurisdiction over the actions and representations of the home agent. Added to the absence of law connecting through agency arrangements, the potential employer to the on-shore agency, and these agents to the home employment provider, even the force of common law contractual obligation is not ensured.

---

[29] A study by the Workplace Safety and Health Institute, Singapore found that when future lifetime costs are included, 'the total cost of work injuries and ill health was estimated to be S$10.45 billion … with S$2.31 billion (22.1%) borne by employers; S$5.28 billion (50.5%) born by workers; and S$2.87 billion (27.4%) born by the community'; see Workplace Safety and Health Institute (2011). In 2012, 56 workers were fatally injured at work, 588 workers sustained major injuries at their workplaces, and 10 469 workers suffered minor injuries; see Workplace Safety and Health Institute (2012).

Take as an example of legal residualism and regulatory reticence, the manner in which the law in Singapore interprets what are matters for contractual attention. The distinction drawn between *legislated matters* (matters relating to non-payment of salary or overtime wages, working hours and illegal deductions from the worker's salary)[30] and *non-legislated matters* (disputes relating to the working conditions, contractual conditions, the job scope, and the amount of salary),[31] can only be made sense of if the private property relations so regulated are skewed by legislated law away from the worker and towards employer/agency interest. The reason for this conclusion rests in the apparent illogicality of distinctions such that salary payment may have legal protection but not salary terms.

Law's failing here is measured against social sustainability evidenced through a more mutualized consideration of contractual standing, terms, interests and bargaining power. Rather, if the evaluation is it seems in market economies at present with the regulation of many migrant labour markets, then the purpose of legal regulation in favour of employers interests is successfully if unsustainably achieved through law's differential and discriminatory advancement of employer contractual interests, mediated through the facility of the state.

We argue, however, that even when viewed against its conventional normative ascription to parity, clean hands and fair consideration for offer and acceptance, and thereby through reciprocity, legal regulation in migrant workforce contracting is failing. Undue influence, unfair terms and unconscionability abound and go largely unpunished. This is the daily experience of NGOs who process migrant workers' complaints.[32]

Privity of contract is a reason for this state of affairs and may also hold the key to its remedy. At present inclusion in the benefits of contractual advantage and protection are limited to parties to the contract. In practice this exclusionism is extended by the preferential positioning of employer interest, and the tolerance of perpetual breaches of limited worker

---

[30]   Sections 21 (non-payment of salary), 27 (unauthorized deductions) and 38(4) (overtime salary) of the Employment Act (Cap. 91).

[31]   'Some 600 statutory employment claims (e.g. non-payment of salary or overtime pay, unauthorized deductions made from salary etc.) are processed every month, which are resolved through conciliation or adjudication by the Labour Court. More than 90% of such cases are settled within 1 month. For non-statutory contractual grievances related to the workplace (e.g. dissatisfaction with employment terms, wages, job scope), workers should raise the matter with the company or their unions who can take up their grievances.' See Tan (2012).

[32]   See for instance Batistella (1993).

protection through the state's blind eye or hands off approach to inspection and enforcement. A reconsideration of privity through widening access, inclusion, protection, actionability and accountability may transform the contract into a mechanism of more balanced rights protection and social bonding; this would reposition the contract as regulator of private property interests through rights marginalization and individualised interest, at the cost of mutuality, to a framework for more sustainable workforce social bonding.

Law's Repositioned Regulatory Role – Centrality of Contract

To this end we will offer a brief consideration[33] of ways other than individualized rights protection and wealth generation, whereby law's command of private property can advance common good and contribute to social sustainability. Returning to our migrant workforce case-study, generally the current state of legal regulation is a combination of:

- limited and illogically discriminatory legislative protection (of such things as wage payment, working hours and agency), with vague or only individually actionable enforcement provisions;
- an absence of legislative protection for determining terms of contract;
- an absence of detailed regulation of employment agency practise through licensing, and no extra-territorial claims over offshore agents;
- lack of clarity in agency relationships particularly with employers;
- a regime of 'warnings' (often not recorded) rather than prosecutions for first offences;
- immigration legislation which works against workers' recourse to private justice, particularly where employers exercise their powers of contractual termination and forced repatriation;
- no provision for assisted legal representation;
- labour court structures that provide procedures and remedies which do not favour workers' interests, and do not offer equivalent standards of justice provision as other levels of judicial tribunals;
- lax inspectorate, enforcement and prosecution practices by agencies delegated with secondary legislative responsibility to police workers' rights and workplace health and safety obligations;

---

[33] A fuller analysis of these frames will need wider empirical study employing the theoretical considerations in this book.

- executive enforcement cultures that favour the interests of employers, for fear that otherwise investment preference may be adversely affected; and
- while worker and workplace insurance schemes may be available, employer cultures often deter injury reporting or claims against the insurer.

In such an environment it is obvious that legal regulation and its calibration are designed to advance employer interests at the expense of labour force rights protection.

The challenge for repositioning is to address this interest imbalance, even if for no other reason than medium-term market sustainability, by levelling out in particular contractual issues of obligation, rights and actionability. Law needs to have a more holistic presence. Its expressive function must clearly declare an interest in redressing imbalance.

The regulatory actors essential for redressing currently unsustainable employment practices would primarily be those who presently benefit from the private property interest imbalance: the employer, the agent, the state, and civil society. Each, individually and collectively, should be required through legal regulation to shoulder identified responsibilities in the regulatory transition, and for ensuring its ongoing viability. These responsibilities would largely be consistent with the normative expectations covering legally endorsed contractual relationships.

CONCLUSION

The cynic might argue that if the regulatory conditions for sustainability remove the capacity for unsustainable market economies to exploit migrant labour to the advantage of employer/state private property interests, then the attraction of the market will disappear along with the market itself. If, as is the case with economies where an appropriately skilled local labour reserve and technology can take over the labour power requirements of the industry now using migrant labour, then this is an indication of social embedding and a return of the market economy closer to the bonds of organic labour balance.[34] Regularly in unsustainable emergent markets neither of these economic or social preconditions

---

[34] The down side of such repositioning is that in the short term migrant workers will gradually be denied even the exploitative benefits of wage labour which offers much better returns than could be expected in their home economies. For the sake of medium-term sustainability we say that such dependency

for such a transition are in place in the short- to medium-term. That being so, repositioning less powerful stakeholders interests within more embedding market forces will be a governance challenge for legal regulation in the medium term.

Underpinning the belief in a transition of regulatory principle from individualist wealth creation to sustainable social bonding is the critique that for too long conventional regulatory thinking (and law's application within it) has not ventured far beyond economic paradigms.[35] The shift in principle to sustainability defined as broad social bonding within which market economies can return greater organic social connection requires that legal regulation see economic issues and economies as frameworks of specific social bonding. The great transformation into a *market society* provoked such a diremption, and the division of society into state and market where the apparatus of a political democracy saw itself as in constant conflict with the businesses elites. Prioritizing economic actions and interactions above all other types of interpersonal social activity conditioned individual human beings to conceive themselves as behavioural agents within a framework that prized rational self-interest above all else. Assisting this emphasis, instead of affirming its role in carrying socially responsible normative principles into being through the indispensability of a mutualized moral perspective, the law confines its role to supporting the market as a value-free, technical instrument. In so doing, social and political considerations have been subordinated as law effectively sanctions the amoral orientation of economic life and life as a whole.[36]

Calls for stricter regulatory oversight consequent on the numerous recent economic failures in (or lack of) market accountability has prompted society to question the capabilities of its political leaders. In Polanyi's terms this initiates a countermovement as trust in elected representatives or world leaders evaporates due to market dysfunction.

---

regimes neither address the failings of labour markets in the home and the host economies. As with any form of indentured or exploitative labour market arrangements, rectification is an economic challenge for the home economies. In addition, wider considerations of family and community sustainability will be better addressed when domestic workers are not forced through economic necessity to leave their own children and care for others, and construction workers can contribute to the infrastructure development of their own towns and cities.

[35] 'It is a reality that all actors are engaged in multiple diverse and complex patterns of social action and interaction which go uncaptured in economics'; see Perry-Kessaris (2011).

[36] Dale (2010), p. 102.

The global governance dimensions of such regulatory irresponsibility are now playing out in a massive political re-ordering across the globe.

Recognizing the responsibility of law in regulating private property relations which fuelled market failure as well as challenging social confidence in established governance frames, our argument has attempted to redirect the global regulatory focus from world to world, towards a reconsideration of the meanings and values of crucial market variables such as labour power. Central in this transition is law's expressive and facilitative influences which can move private property rights and obligations in the direction of sustainable social relations.

Bibliography

Agence France Presse (19 December 2004) Maid Jumps to Death After Dropping Baby Off Apartment Building, accessed on 25 May 2014 at http://www.singapore-window.org/sw04/041219af.htm.

Agh A. (1990) The Hundred Years' Peace: Karl Polanyi on the Dynamics of World Systems. In K. Polanyi-Levitt (ed.) *The Life and Work of Karl Polanyi: A Celebration*. Black Rose Books, Montréal.

Amin S. (1974) In Praise of Socialism. *Monthly Review* (September) cited in K. Polanyi-Levitt (ed.) (1990) *The Life and Work of Karl Polanyi: A Celebration*. Black Rose Books, Montréal.

Anon (1999) Agenda 21: Programme of Action for Sustainable Development. *BGCI* 3/2, accessed on 21 May 2014 at http://www.bgci.org/worldwide/article/0011/.

Appleby J. (1978) *Economic Thought and Ideology in 17th-Century England*. Princeton University Press, Princeton, NJ.

Arikan G. (2011) Economic Individualism and Government Spending. *World Values Research* 4/3, 73–95.

Arrow K. (1974) *The Limits of Organization*. Norton, New York.

Ashley C., Boyd C. and Goodwin H. (2000) Pro-poor Tourism: Putting Poverty at the Heart of the Tourism Agenda. *Natural Resource Perspectives* 51, 1–6.

Ashley C. and Roe D. (1998) Enhancing Community Involvement in Wildlife Tourism. *International Institute for Environment and Development Wildlife and Development Series No. 11*.

Ashworth A. (2000) Testing Fidelity to Legal Values: Official Involvement and Criminal Justice. *The Modern Law Review* 63/5, 633–59.

AsiaOne (27 March 2011) National Serviceman Needs Maid to Carry His Backpack, accessed on 21 May 2014 at http://news.asiaone.com/News/AsiaOne+News/Singapore/Story/A1Story20110327-270356.html.

AsiaOne (6 August 2011) Missing Migrant Workers Hunted Down in Singapore, accessed on 21 May 2014 at http://news.asiaone.com/News/AsiaOne+News/Singapore/Story/A1Story20110806-293029/2.html.

Balbus I. (1973) *The Dialectics of Legal Repression: Black Rebels before the American Criminal Courts*. Russell Sage Foundation, New York.

Ball R.M. (1989) Some Aspects of Tourism, Seasonality and Local Labour Markets. *Area* 21/1, 35–45.

Basu R. (March 2010) 'Filial Piety' Law May Soon Get More Bite. *The Straits Times*, accessed on 22 May 2014 at http://app.msf.gov.sg/Portals/0/Summary/pressroom/MediaCoverage/Mar2010/filial_piety_law_may_soon_get_more_bite_st16.pdf.

Batistella G. (1993) The Human Rights of Migrant Workers: Agenda for NGO. *International Migration Review* 27/1, 191–201.

Bedford O. and K. Hwang (2003) Guilt and Shame in Chinese Culture: A cross-cultural framework from the perspective of morality and identity. *Journal for the Theory of Social Behaviour* 33/2, 127–44.

Bentrupperbaumer J. (2005) Human Dimension of Wildlife Interactions. In D. Newsome, R. Dowling and S. Moore (eds) *Wildlife Tourism.* Channel View Publications, Clevedon, UK, pp. 82–112.

Berg A. and Ostry J. (2011) Inequality and Unsustainable Growth: Two Sides of the Same Coin? *International Monetary Fund Staff Discussion Note,* SDN/11/08 (8 April 2011), accessed on 21 May 2014 at http://www.imf.org/external/pubs/ft/sdn/2011/sdn1108.pdf.

Berger A. and Bouwman C. (2009) Bank Capital, Survival and Performance around Financial Crises, accessed on 21 May 2014 at http://fic.wharton.upenn.edu/fic/papers/09/0924.pdf.

Bernard P. and Boucher G. (2007) Institutional Competitiveness, Social Investment and Welfare Regimes. *Regulation and Governance* 1, 213–29.

Berthoud G. (1990) Towards a Comparative Approach: The contribution of Karl Polanyi. In K. Polanyi-Levitt (ed.) *The Life and Work of Karl Polanyi: A Celebration.* Black Rose Books, Montréal, pp. 171–82.

Bienefeld M. (2007) Suppressing the Double Movement to Secure the Dictatorship of Finance. In A. Bugra and K. Agartan (eds) *Reading Karl Polanyi for the Twenty-First Century: Market Economy as a Political Project.* Palgrave Macmillan, Basingstoke, UK, pp. 13–31.

Birmingham R. (1970) Breach of Contract, Damage Measures, and Economic Efficiency. *Rutgers Law Review* 24, 273.

Black J. (2002a) *Critical Reflections on Regulation.* London School of Economics and Political Science, London, UK, accessed on 21 May 2014 at http://eprints.lse.ac.uk/35985/1/Disspaper4-1.pdf.

Black J. (2002b) Regulatory Conversations. *Journal of Law and Society* 29, 163–95.

Black J. (2010) Managing the Financial Crisis – The Constitutional Dimension. *LSE Law, Society and Economy Working Papers 12/2020,* accessed on 21 May 2014 at http://www.lse.ac.uk/collections/law/wps/WPS2010-12_Black.pdf.

Block F. (2003) Karl Polanyi and the Writing of 'The Great Transformation'. *Theory and Society* 32, 275–306.

Block F. and Somers M. (1984) Beyond the Economistic Fallacy: The holistic social science of Karl Polanyi. In T. Skocpol (ed.) *Vision and Method in Historical Sociology.* Cambridge University Press, Cambridge, pp. 47–84.

Boettke P. (1994) The Reform Trap in Economics and Politics in the Former Communist Economies. *Journal des Economistes et des Etudes Humaines* 5/2/3, 267–93.

Borzaga C. and Becchetti L. (2010) *The Economics of Social Responsibility. The World of Social Enterprises.* Routledge, London.

Braithwaite J. (2005) *Markets in Vice, Markets in Virtue.* Federation Press, Sydney.

Braithwaite J. (2006) Responsive Regulation and Developing Economies. *World Development* 34, 884.

Braithwaite J. (2008) *Regulatory Capitalism: How It Works, Ideas for Making It Work Better.* Edward Elgar Publishing, Cheltenham, UK.

Braudel F. (1979) *The Wheels of Commerce.* University of California Press, Berkeley, CA.

Breznau N. (2010) Economic Equality and Social Welfare: Policy Preferences in Five Nations. *International Journal of Public Opinion Research* 22/4, 458–84.

Bruner J. (1990) *Acts of Meaning.* Harvard University Press, Cambridge, MA.

Buckley C. and Wang A. (21 December 2011) China Premier Tells Banks to Support Firms, accessed on 25 May 2014 at http://uk.reuters.com/article/2011/12/21/china-economy-wen-idUKL3E7NL09520111221?feedType=RSS&feedName=rbssFinancialServicesAndRealEstateNews&utm_source=feedburner&utm_medium=feed&utm_campaign=Feed%3A+reuters%2FUKBankingFinancial+(News+%2F+UK+%2F+Financial+Services+and+Real+Estate.

Bugra A. (2007) Polanyi's Concept of Double Movement and Politics in the Contemporary Market Society. In A. Bugra and K. Agartan (eds) *Reading Karl Polanyi for the Twenty-First Century: Market Economy as a Political Project.* Palgrave Macmillan, Basingstoke, UK, pp. 173–89.

Cardoso F. and Faletto E. (1979) *Dependency and Development in Latin America.* University of California Press, Berkeley, CA.

Chang H.J. and Grabel I. (2014) *Reclaiming Development: An Alternative Economic Policy Manual.* Zed Books, London, UK.

Chin D. (3 July 2010) Safety Issue in Construction Despite Efforts. *The Straits Times.*

Choskyi V.J. (1988) Symbolism of Animals in Buddhism. *Buddhist Himalaya* 1/1.

Coburn D. (2004) Beyond the Income Inequality Hypothesis: Class, Neo-liberalism, and Health Inequalities. *Social Science & Medicine* 58/1, 41–56.

Cohen S. (1985) *Visions of Social Control.* Polity Press, Cambridge, UK.

Comaroff J. and Comaroff J. (2009) *Ethnicity, Inc.* Chicago University Press, Illinois, Chicago.

Cotterrell R. (1996) *Law's Community: Legal Theory in Sociological Perspectives.* Clarendon Press, Oxford, UK.

Cotterrell R. (2010) Justice, Dignity, Torture, Headscarves: Can Durkheim's Sociology Clarify Legal Values? *Socio & Legal Studies* 20/1, 3–20.

Dale G. (2010) *Karl Polanyi: The Limits of the Market.* Polity Press, Cambridge, UK.

Dawson J. (2006) How Ecovillages Can Grow Sustainable Local Economies. *Communities* 133, 56–61.

Department of Livestock Development (2002) *Gan Battipat Ngan Tammatratan Bang (Camp) Chang (Standard Operation Guidelines for Elephant Camps.* Department of Livestock Development, Bangkok.

De Soto H. (September 1993) The Missing Ingredient: What Poor Countries Will Need to Make Their Markets Work. *The Economist.*

De Soto H. (2000) *The Mystery of Capital: Why Capitalism Triumphs in the West and Fails Everywhere Else.* Basic Books, New York, NY.

Dobransky S. (2012) Book Review of *The Origins of Political Order: From Prehuman Times to the French Revolution. American Diplomacy* (February), accessed on 25 May 2014 at http://www.unc.edu/depts/diplomat/item/2012/0106/bk/book_dobransky_origins.html.

Dubash N. and Morgan B. (2012) Understanding the Rise of the Regulatory State of the South. *Regulation & Governance* 6/3, 261–81.

Durkheim E. (1893) *The Division of Labour in Society.* Free Press, New York.

Durkheim E. (1897) *Suicide: A Study in Sociology.* Free Press, New York.

Dworkin R. (1997) *Taking Rights Seriously.* Harvard University Press, Cambridge, MA.

Ebner A. (2010) Transnational Markets and the Polanyi Problem. In C. Joerges and J. Falke (eds) *Karl Polanyi, Globalisation and the Potential of Law in Transnational Markets.* Hart Publishing, Oxford, UK, pp. 19–41.

Elephant Conservation Center website. Status of Lao Mahouts, accessed on 14 May 2014 at http://www.elephantconservationcenter.com/index.php/en/explore-the-center/center-facilities/mahout-vocational-center/187-mahouts-status.

Elliott L. (25 January 2012) Davos: a Sanatorium for Those in Denial of Capitalism's Ills. *The Guardian,* UK, accessed on 14 May 2014 at http://www.guardian.co.uk/business/2012/jan/25/davos-sanatorium-capitalisms-ills?INTCMP=SRCH.

Epstein R. (1978) Book Review: The Next Generation of Legal Scholarship. *Stanford Law Review* 30, 335.

Estache A., Rossi M. and Ruzzier C. (2002) The Case for the International Coordination of Electricity Regulation: Evidence from the Measurement of Efficiency in South America. *World Bank Research Working Paper Series 2907*, accessed on 14 May 2013 at http://info.worldbank.org/etools/docs/library/64608/wps2907.pdf.

Ewing J. (20 December 2011) A Fight to Make Banks More Prudent. *The New York Times*, New York, NY, accessed on 14 May 2014 at http://www.nytimes.com/2011/12/21/business/global/a-fight-to-make-banks-hold-more-capital.html?pagewanted=all.

Findlay M. (1999) Crime and Social Development. In M. Findlay (ed.) *The Globalisation of Crime: Understanding Transitional Relationships in Context.* Cambridge University Press, Cambridge, UK, pp. 20–57.

Findlay M. (2007) Misunderstanding Corruption and Community: Comparative Cultural Politics of Corruption Regulation in the Pacific. *Asian Criminology* 2/1, 47–56.

Findlay M. (2008) *Governing through Globalised Crime.* Willan Publishing, Cullompton, UK.

Findlay M. (2013a) *Contemporary Challenges in Regulating Global Crises.* Palgrave Macmillan, Basingstoke, UK.

Findlay M. (2013b) *International and Comparative Justice: A Critical Introduction.* Routledge, Abingdon, UK.

Findlay M. (2 August 2013c) Culture of Corruption Pervades NSW Inc. *The Sydney Morning Herald*, accessed on 21 May 2014 at http://www.smh.com.au/comment/culture-of-corruption-pervades-nsw-inc-2013080 1-2r23r.html.

Findlay M. (forthcoming) Fictional Assets and Governing Market Failure. *Economics and Society.*

Findlay M. and Lim S. (forthcoming) Relevance of the Regulatory State in North/South Intersections. *International Journal of Social Economics* 41/7.

Fiske A, Kitayama S., Markus H. and Nisbett R. (1998) The Cultural Matrix of Social Psychology. In D. Gilbert, S. Fiske and G. Lindzey (eds) *The Handbook of Social Psychology.* McGraw-Hill, New York, pp. 915–81.

Fourcade M. and Woll C. (2013) Introduction to Moral Categories and Financial Crisis. *Socio-economic Review* 11, 601–5.

Fukuyama F. (March 2007) *Observations on State-building in the Western Pacific*, accessed on 21 May 2014 at http://fukuyama.stanford.edu/files/working_papers/WP_State-Building.doc.

Fukuyama F. (2011) *The Origins of Political Order*. Farrar, Strauss and Giroux, New York.

Gilardi F., Jordana J. and Levi-Faur D. (2006) Regulation in the Age of Globalization: The Diffusion of Regulatory Agencies Across Europe and Latin America. *Ibei Working Papers*. Institut Barcelona, Barcelona.

Godwin W. (1986) *The Anarchist Writings of William Godwin*. Freedom Press, London, UK.

Goetz C. and Scott R. (1977) Liquidated Damages, Penalties, and the Just Compensation Principle: A Theory of Efficient Breach. *Columbia Law Review* 77, 554.

Goh C.L. (25 December 2013) First Priority is to Find Cause of Little India Riot: PM Lee. *The Straits Times*, accessed on 21 May 2014 at http://www.straitstimes.com/breaking-news/singapore/story/first-priority-find-cause-little-india-riot-pm-lee-20131225.

Grabosky P. (2012) Beyond Responsive Regulation: The Expanding Role of Non-state Actors in the Regulatory Process. *Regulation & Governance* 7/1, 114–23.

Granovetter M. (1985) Economic Action and Social Structure: The Problem of Embeddedness. *American Journal of Sociology* 91/3, 481–510.

Guérin D. (ed.) (2005) *No Gods, No Masters: An Anthology of Anarchism* (trans. P. Sharkey). AK Press, Oakland, CA.

Harvey D. (2005) *A Brief History of Neo-liberalism*. Oxford University Press, Oxford.

Haupt J. and Lawrence C. (2012) Unexpected Connections: Income Inequality and Environmental Degradation. *Shaping Tomorrow's World*, accessed on 21 May 2014 at http://www.shapingtomorrowsworld.org/hauptInequality.html.

Heath Y. and Gifford R. (2006) Free-Market Ideology and Environmental Degradation: The Case of Belief in Global Climate Change. *Environment and Behaviour* 38/1, 48–71.

Henham R. and Findlay M. (2002) Criminal Justice Modelling and the Comparative Contextual Analysis of Trial Process. *International Journal of Comparative Criminology* 2/2, 162–86.

Hettne B. (1990) The Contemporary Crisis: The Rise of Reciprocity. In K. Polanyi-Levitt (ed.) *The Life and Work of Karl Polanyi: A Celebration*. Black Rose Books, Montréal, pp. 208–20.

Hettne B. (2006) Re-reading Polanyi: Towards a Second Great Transformation. In K. McRobbie and K. Polanyi-Levitt (eds) *Karl Polanyi in Vienna: The Contemporary Significance of the Great Transformation*, Black Rose Books, Montréal, pp. 61–72.

Hirschler B. (2013) Wealth Gap, Debt Top Risks Ahead of Davos. *Reuters*, accessed on 21 May 2014 at http://www.reuters.com/article/2013/01/08/us-davos-risks-idUSBRE90709K20130108.

Hobbes T. (1983) *De Cive: The English Version*. Clarendon Press, Oxford, UK.

Honneth A. (1995) Crime and Ethical Life: Hegel's Intersubjectivist Innovation. In A. Honneth (ed.) *The Struggle for Recognition: The Moral Grammar of Social Conflicts*. MIT Press, Cambridge, MA.

Howard R. (1993) Cultural Absolutism and the Nostalgia for Community. *Human Rights Quarterly* 15, 315–38.

Ho D. (1976) On the Concept of Face. *American Journal of Sociology* 81/4, 867–84.

Hsu F. (1948) *Under the Ancestor's Shadow: Chinese Culture and Personality*. Columbia University Press, New York.

Hu H. (1944) The Chinese Concepts of 'Face'. *American Anthropologist* 46, 45–64.

Human Rights Watch (December 2005) Maid to Order: Ending Abuses against Migrant Domestic Workers in Singapore, p. 38.

Humanitarian Organisation for Migration Economics (HOME) and Transient Workers Count Too (TWC2) (June 2010) Justice Delayed, Justice Denied. The Experiences of Migrant Workers in Singapore.

International Herald Tribune (22 December 2011) Banker Pushes to Defuse Global Threat. New York, NY, p. 1.

International Union for Conservation of Nature (2008) IUCN Red List of Threatened Species, accessed on 21 May 2014 at http://www.iucnredlist.org/search/details.php/7140/sum.

Jones R. and Tsutsumi M. (20 February 2009) Sustaining Growth in Korea by Reforming the Labour Market and Improving the Education System. *Economics Department Working Paper No. 672*, Organisation for Economic Co-operation and Development, accessed on 21 May 2014 at http://search.oecd.org/officialdocuments/displaydocumentpdf/?doclanguage=en&cote=eco/wkp(2009)13.

Jordana J. and Levi-Faur D. (2004) *The Politics of Regulation: Institutions and Regulatory Reforms for the Age of Governance*. Edward Elgar, Cheltenham, UK.

Kanninen T. (2012) *Crisis of Global Sustainability*. Routledge, London.

Kapstein E. (1982) Resolving the Regulator's Dilemma: International Co-ordination of Banking Regulations. *International Organization* 43, 323–47.

Kontogeorgopoulos N. (2009) Wildlife Tourism in Semi-captive Settings: A Case Study of Elephant Camps in Northern Thailand. *Current Issues in Tourism* 12/5-6, 429–49.

Krasner S. (2004) Sharing Sovereignty: New Institutions for Collapsed and Failing States. *International Security* 29/2, 85–120.

Krippner G. *et al.* (2004) Polanyi Symposium: A Conversation on Embeddedness. *Socio-Economic Review* 2, 109–35.

Krugman P. (2009) *The Return of Depression Economics and the Crisis of 2008*. W.W. Norton & Co, New York and London.

Krugman P. (18 December 2011) Will China Break? *The New York Times*, accessed on 21 May 2014 at http://www.nytimes.com/2011/12/19/opinion/krugman-will-china-break.html?_r=0.

Laffont J. (1994) The New Economics of Regulation Ten Years After. *Econometrica* 62/3, 507–37.

Laohachaiboon S. (2010) Conservation for whom? Elephant Conservation and Elephant Conservationists in Thailand. *Southeast Asian Studies* 1/1, 74–95.

Leith W. (27 December 2008) Still Looking for a Free Lunch. *The Guardian*, accessed on 21 May 2014 at http://www.guardian.co.uk/books/2008/dec/27/return-of-depression-economics-paul-krugman.

Levi-Faur D. (2004) Comparative Research Designs in the Study of Regulation: How to Increase the Number of Cases Without Compromising the Strengths of Case-oriented Analysis. In J. Jordana and D. Levi-Faur (eds) *The Politics of Regulation*. Edward Elgar Publishing, Cheltenham, pp. 177–99.

Levi-Faur D. (2005) The Global Diffusion of Regulatory Capitalism. *The Annals of the American Academy of Political and Social Science* 598, 12–32.

Leys C. (1980) Neo-conservatism and the Organic Crisis in Britain. *Studies in Political Economy* 4, 41–63.

Liew H. (29 September 2010) 100 Pregnant Maids Sent Home a Year. *The Straits Times*.

Lie J. (1997) Sociology of Markets. *Annual Review of Sociology* 23, 341–60.

Loh A. (27 December 2013) Comment: Why deport the acquitted in Little India riot? *Yahoo! News*, accessed on 21 May 2014 at https://sg.news.yahoo.com/blogs/singaporescene/deporting-acquitted-052222758.html.

Lohanan R. (2005) The Elephant Situation in Thailand and A Plea for Co-operation. *Food and Agriculture Organization of the United Nations Corporate Document Repository*, accessed on 21 May 2014 at http://www.fao.org/docrep/005/ad031e/ad031e0r.htm.

Lum S. (10 October 2012) Indonesian Maid Jailed 20 Years for Killing Disabled Girl, accessed on 21 May 2014 at http://www.thejakarta globe.com/archive/indonesian-maid-jailed-20-years-for-killing-disabled-girl/.

MacKenzie D.W. (2005) Oskar Lange and the Impossibility of Economic Calculation. *HES Meetings*. Puget Sound.

Mar K. (2007) The Demography and Life History Strategies of Timber Elephants in Myanmar. *Thesis submitted to the University College London*, accessed on 21 May 2014 at http://www.zsl.org/sites/default/files/document/2014-01/demography-life-history-strategies-elephants-Myanmar-khyne-mar-2007.pdf.

Marx K. (1852) Letter to Weydemeyer. In *Jungsozialistische Blätter* accessed on 25 May 2014 at https://www.marxists.org/archive/marx/works/1852/letters/52_03_05-ab.htm.

Marx K. (2005) *Early Writings*. Penguin, London.

Marx K. and Engels F. (1867) *Das Kapital: A critique of political economy, Volume 1*. Verlag von Otto Meisner, Germany.

Mccaulay S. (1963) Non-contractual Relations in Business: A Preliminary Study. *American Sociological Review* 28/1, 55–67.

Meekaew N. and Srisontisuk S. (2012) Chiangkhan: Cultural Commodification for Tourism and its Impact on Local Community. *International Proceedings of Economics Development & Research* 42, 34–7.

Melossi D., Sozzo M. and Sparks C. (eds) (2011) *Travels of the Criminal Question: Cultural Embeddedness and Diffusion*. Hart Publishing, Oxford.

Michnik A. (12 November 1990) The Two Faces of Eastern Europe (trans. A. Husarska). *The New Republic*.

Miller G. (2004) *Living in the Environment: Principles, Connections and Solutions*. Brooks/Cole-Thompson Learning, Belmont, CA.

Ministry of Manpower website, Foreign Workforce Numbers, accessed on 12 November 2013 at http://www.mom.gov.sg/statistics-publications/others/statistics/Pages/ForeignWorkforceNumbers.aspx.

Ministry of Manpower website, Labour Force Satistical Information, accessed on 12 November 2013 at http://stats.mom.gov.sg/Pages/Labour-Force-Summary-Table.aspx.

Mises L. (1928) Neue Schriften zum Problem der sozialistischen Wirtschaftsrechnung. *Archiv für Sozialwissenschaften*, Volume 60.

Mizanur R.M. (2006) Foreign Manpower in Singapore: Classes, Policies and Management. *Asia Research Institute, Working Paper Series No. 57* (February), p. 3.

Morgan B. and Yeung K. (2007) *An Introduction to Law and Regulation*. Cambridge University Press, Cambridge, MA.

National Family Council (2011) *State of the Family Report 2011*. National Family Council, p. 1.

Neisloss L. (24 May 2012) Call for Action as Singapore Maids Fall to Their Deaths, accessed on 21 May 2014 at http://edition.cnn.com/2012/05/23/world/asia/singapore-maids-deaths/.

Nisbet R. (1969) *Social Change and History: Aspects of the Western Theory of Development.* Oxford University Press, London.

Nozick R. (1974) *Anarchy, State, and Utopia.* Basic Books, New York, NY.

Omarova S. (2011) Bankers, Bureaucrats, and Guardians: Towards Tri-partism in Financial Services Regulation. 37/3, 621–74, accessed on 25 May 2014 at http://papers.ssrn.com/sol3/papers.cfm?abstract_id= 1924546.

Orton W. (1930) The Atomic Theory of Society. *The American Political Science Review* 24/3, 628–37.

Pearson H. (ed.) (1977) *Karl Polanyi: The Livelihood Man.* Academic Press, New York.

Perez O. (2002) Using Private-Public Linkages to Regulate Environmental Conflicts: The Case of International Construction Contracts. *Journal of Law and Society* 29/1, 77–110.

Perry-Kessaris A. (2011) Reading the Story of Law and Embeddedness through a Community Lens: A Polanyi-meets-Cotterrell Economic Sociology of Law. *Northern Ireland Legal Quarterly* 62/4, 401–13.

Pfanner E. (24 January 2012) Gates to Pitch His Charity Work at Davos. *The New York Times,* accessed on 21 May 2014 at http://dealbook. nytimes.com/2012/01/24/gates-to-pitch-his-charity-work-in-davos/.

Pfanner E. (25 January 2012) Wealth Gaps Are Growing Globally, and So Is Unease. *International Herald Tribune,* New York, p. 1.

Phang S. (2007) The Singapore Model of Housing and the Welfare State. *Housing and the New Welfare State: Perspectives from East Asia and Europe.* Research Collection School of Economics, Singapore Management University, accessed on 21 May 2014 at http://ink.library. smu.edu.sg/soe_research/596/.

Picard M. and Wood R.E. (eds) (1997) *Tourism, Ethnicity, and the State in Asian and Pacific Societies.* University of Hawaii Press, Honolulu.

Pimmanrojnagool V. and Wanghongsa S. (2001) A Study of Street Wandering Elephants in Bangkok and the Socio-economic Life of their Mahouts. *Proceedings of the International Workshop on the Domesticated Asian Elephant 5-10 February 2001 (Bangkok, Thailand), Food and Agriculture Organization of the United Nations,* pp. 35–42.

Polanyi K. (1944) *The Great Transformation: Economic and Political Origins of Our Time.* Rinehart, New York.

Polanyi K. (2005) Uber die Freiheit. In M. Cangiani, K. Polanyi-Levitt and C. Thomasberger (eds) *Chronik der grossen Transformation.* Vol 3, Metropolis.

Polanyi K, Arensberg C. and Pearson H. (eds) (1957) *Trade and Market in the Early Empires: Economies in History and Theory.* The Free Press, Glencoe, UK.

Polanyi-Levitt K. (1990) The Origins and Significance of *The Great Transformation*. In K. Polanyi-Levitt (ed.) (1990) *The Life and Work of Karl Polanyi: A Celebration*. Black Rose Books, Montréal, pp. 111–23.

Posner R. (1979) Utilitarianism, Economics and Legal Theory. *Legal Studies* 8, 103–40.

Prado M. (2008) The Challenges and Risks of Creating Independent Regulatory Agencies: A Cautionary Tale from Brazil. *Vanderbilt Journal of Transnational Law* 41/2, 435–503.

Proudhon P. (1866) *Théorie de la propriété*. Librairie Internationale, Paris, France.

Proudhon P. (1890) *What is Property? An Enquiry into the Principle of Right and of Government*. Howard Fertig Publisher, New York, NY.

Proudhon P. (1927) *Solution du Problème Social* (ed. – H. Cohen). Vanguard Press, New York, NY.

Proudhon P. (2011) *Property is Theft! A Pierre-Joseph Proudhon Anthology* (ed. – I. McKay). AK Press, Oakland, CA.

Putnam R.D. (2000) *Bowling Alone: The Collapse and Revival of American Community*. Simon and Schuster, New York, NY.

Ranada P. (4 October 2013) New Law Empowers Local Communities for Ecotourism. *The Rappler*, accessed on 21 May 2014 at http://www.rappler.com/nation/40553-protected-areas-ipaf-ecotourism.

Randles S. (2010) Karl Polanyi: The Limits of the Market. Times Higher Education, October 2010, accessed on 22 May 2014 at http://www.timeshighereducation.co.uk/books/karl-polanyi-the-limits-of-the-market/413836.article.

Rawls J. (1971) *A Theory of Justice*. Harvard University Press, Cambridge, MA.

Rawls J. (1999) *The Law of Peoples*. Harvard University Press, Cambridge, MA.

Rawls J. (2001) *The Law of Peoples*. Harvard University Press, Cambridge, MA.

Rawls J. (2008) *Lectures on the History of Political Philosophy*. Harvard University Press, Cambridge, MA.

Reed G. (2001) The Mystery of Capital: A ReAL Review by Gerard Reed.

Rhee C. (2012) Inequality Threatens Asia Growth Miracle. *Financial Times* (7 May 2012), accessed on 21 May 2014 at http://www.ft.com/intl/cms/s/0/fba71e2c-9607-11e1-9d9d-00144feab49a.html#axzz2htIfpfmW.

Robbins L. (1935) *An Essay on the Nature and Significance of Economic Science*. Macmillan and Co, London.

Rodrigues J. (2013) Between Rules and Incentives: Uncovering Hayek's moral economy. *American Journal of Economics and Sociology* 72/3, 565–92.

Rousseau J. (1766) *Du Contrat Social ou Principes du droit politique.* Marc-Michel Bousquet, France.

Saw S. (2013) Implications of Demographic Trends in Singapore. *Institute of Southeast Asian Studies Perspective* (2 January 2013), accessed on 21 May 2014 at http://www.iseas.edu.sg/documents/publication/ ISEAS%20Perspective%202013-1.pdf.

Sayer A. (2000) Moral Economy and Political Economy. *Studies in Political Economy* 61, 79–103.

Scherer A. and Palazzo G. (2011) The New Political Role of Business in a Globalized World: A Review of New Perspectives on CSR and its Implications for the Firm, Governance and Democracy. *Journal of Management Studies* 48/4, 899–931.

Scheyvens R. (1999) Ecotourism and the Empowerment of Local Communities. *Tourism Management* 20, 245–9.

Schick A. (1998) Why Most Developing Countries Should Not Try New Zealand Reforms. *World Bank Research Observer* 13/8, 1123–31.

Schwab K. (2014) How to get back to strong, sustained growth. *The Malay Mail*, accessed on 22 May 2014 at http://www.themalaymail online.com/what-you-think/article/how-to-get-back-to-strong-sustained-growth-klaus-schwab.

Scott C. (2004) Regulation in the Age of Governance: The Rise of the Post-Regulatory State. In J. Jordana and D. Levi-Faur (eds) *The Politics of Regulation: Institutions and Regulatory Reforms for the Age of Governance.* Edward Elgar, Cheltenham, UK.

Selznick P. (2002) *The Communitarian Persuasion.* Woodrow Wilson Centre Press, Baltimore.

Sen A. (2009) *The Idea of Justice.* Allen Lane, London, UK.

Shleifer A. (2010) 'Efficient Regulation. In D. Kessler (ed.) *Regulation versus Litigation: Perspectives from Economics and Law.* University of Chicago Press, Chicago, IL, pp. 27–43.

Sim M. (18 September 2008) Temporary Housing Still Needed. *The Straits Times.*

Singapore Institute of Directors (2008) Managing the Five Capitals for Sustainable Wealth Creation!, accessed on 22 May 2014 at http:// www.sid.org.sg/uploads/bulletin_sub/documents/196_feature6.pdf.

Singapore Parliamentary Reports, Tan Chuan-Jin (11 September 2012) Second Reading of the Employment of Foreign Manpower (Amendment) Bill. Col 17 (Vol 89 Sitting No. 7).

Singapore Parliamentary Reports, Mr Tan Chuan-Jin (25 February 2013) Reducing Foreign Domestic Worker Levy. Col 7 (Vol 90 Sitting No. 7).

Singapore Parliamentary Reports, Tan Chuan-Jin (21 October 2013) Daily Average of Non-residents in Singapore over the Past 12 Months. Col 34 (Vol 90 Sitting No. 23).

Singapore Parliamentary Reports, Tan Chuan-Jin (12 November 2012) Non Resident Population in Singapore. Col 28 (Vol 89 Sitting No. 10).

Smith A. (1776) *The Wealth of Nations.* Penguin, Baltimore.

Snow M. (5 February 2008) Someone Isn't Enjoying the Ride. *Washington Post*, B02.

Somers M. (1990) Karl Polanyi's Intellectual Legacy. In K. Polanyi-Levitt (ed.) *The Life and Work of Karl Polanyi.* Black Rose Books, Montréal, pp. 152–60.

Soros G. (30 October 2009) Soros: The Way Forward. *Financial Times*, London, UK, accessed on 22 May 2014 at http://www.ft.com/cms/s/2/2ee0b622-bfeb-11de-aed2-00144feab49a.html.

Standing G. (2007) Labour Recommodification in the Global Transformation. In A. Bugra and K. Agartan (eds) *Reading Karl Polanyi for the Twenty-First Century: Market Economy as a Political Project.* Palgrave Macmillan, Basingstoke, UK, pp. 67–93.

Stanfield J. (1989) Karl Polanyi and Contemporary Economic Thought. *Review of Social Economy* 47, 266–79.

Stanfield J. (1990) Karl Polanyi and Contemporary Economic Thought. In K. Polanyi-Levitt (ed.) *The Life and Work of Karl Polanyi: A Celebration.* Black Rose Books, Montréal, pp. 195–207.

Steg L. and Sievers I. (2000) Cultural Theory of Individual Perceptions of Environmental Risks. *Environment and Behavior* 32/2, 248–67.

Tan C. (2012) Recognising the Contributions of Foreign Workers in Singapore. *Ministry of Manpower Singapore*, accessed on 22 May 2014 at http://www.momsingapore.blogspot.sg/2012/12/recognising-contributions-of-foreign.html.

Tan Chuan-Jin, Acting Minister for Manpower & Senior Minister of State, National Development, Reply to Parliamentary Question on Foreign Worker Levies Collection, Notice Paper No. 369 Of 2012 For The Sitting On 12 Nov 2012, accessed on 22 May 2014 at http://www.mom.gov.sg/newsroom/Pages/PQRepliesDetails.aspx?listid=64.

Tan J. (5 April 2013) Former SMRT bus driver: Why we went on strike (Part 1). *Yahoo! News*, accessed on 22 May 2014 at http://sg.news.yahoo.com/former-smrt-bus-driver–why-we-went-on-strike–part-1–135100687.html.

Tan W. (2013) Concerns Raised at Forum on Racial Relations. *TodayOnline* (12 September 2013), accessed on 22 May 2014 at http://www.todayonline.com/singapore/concerns-raised-forum-racial-relations.

The Jakarta Post (2 November 2013) Wages Rise as Strike Goes On. *The Jakarta Post*, p. 1.

Thiruvengadam A. and Joshi P. (2012) Judiciaries As Crucial Actors in Southern Regulatory Systems: A Case Study of Indian Telecom Regulation. *Regulation & Governance* 6, 327–43.

Tipprasert P. (2002) Elephants and Ecotourism in Thailand. In I. Baker and M. Kashio (eds) *Giants on Our Hands: Proceedings of the International Workshop on the Domesticated Asian Elephant, Bangkok, Thailand.* FAO Regional Office for Asia and the Pacific, Bangkok, pp. 157–71.

Torrijos E. (8 December 2013) Deceased Foreign Worker in Little India Riot Tripped and Fell After Being Ejected from Bus: Police. *Yahoo! News*, accessed on 22 May 2014 at http://sg.news.yahoo.com/fire–rioting-taking-place-in-little-india–reports-152651999.html.

Transient Workers Count Too (TWC2) (September 2006) Debt, Delays, Deductions: Wage Issues Faced by Foreign Domestic Workers in Singapore.

Transient Workers Count Too (TWC2) (24 June 2013) Nearly Half of Workers Interviewed Paid Agents before Getting Confirmation of Jobs, accessed on 22 May 2014 at https://twc2.org.sg/2013/06/24/nearly-half-of-workers-interviewed-paid-agents-before-getting-confirmation-of-jobs-2/.

Transient Workers Count Too (TWC2) (26 July 2013) Mixed Progress on Maids' Day Off, accessed on 22 May 2014 at http://twc2.org.sg/2013/07/26/mixed-progress-on-maids-day-off/.

Transient Workers Count Too (TWC2) (17 October 2013) Our Stand: Housing Workers Who Are On Special Passes, accessed on 22 May 2014 on http://twc2.org.sg/2013/10/17/our-stand-housing-workers-who-are-on-special-passes/.

Tsui D. (June 2010) 'Father & Son' television commercial. *National Family Council Annual Report 2009/2010*, p. 34.

Tucker R. (1978) *The Marx-Engels Reader.* Norton, New York.

UNESCO (1997) Educating for a Sustainable Future, accessed on 22 May 2014 at http://www.unesco.org/education/tlsf/mods/theme_a/popups/mod01t05s01.html.

United Nations Environmental Programme website. Tourism's Three Main Impact Areas, accessed on 22 May 2014 at http://www.unep.org/resourceefficiency/Business/SectoralActivities/Tourism/TheTourismandEnvironmentProgramme/FactsandFiguresaboutTourism/Impactsof Tourism/EnvironmentalImpacts/TourismsThreeMainImpactAreas/tabid/78776/Default.aspx.

United Nations General Assembly (March 20, 1987) Report of the World Commission on Environment and Development: Our Common Future. Transmitted to the General Assembly as an Annex to document A/42/427 – Development and International Co-operation: Environment;

Our Common Future, Chapter 2: Towards Sustainable Development, accessed on 22 May 2014 at http://www.un-documents.net/ocf-02.htm.

Uslaner E.M. and Brown M.M. (2002) Trust, Inequality, and Political Engagement. *2002 Annual Meeting of the American Political Science Association*, Boston, MA.

von Mises L. (1972) The Anticapitalistic Mentality. Libertarian Press, Inc, Grove City, PA, accessed on 22 May 2014 at http://mises.org/etexts/anticap.pdf .

Wade R. (2014) Foreword. In H.K. Chang and I. Grabel (2014) *Reclaiming Development: An Alternative Economic Policy Manual*. Zed Books, London, pp. i–xxv.

Wallerstein I. (2000) Globalization or the Age of Transition? A Long-term View of the Trajectory of the World-system. *International Sociology* 15/2, 249–65.

Weber M. (1930a) Asceticism and the Spirit of Capitalism. In M. Weber (ed.) The Protestant Ethic and the Spirit of Capitalism. Allen and Unwin, London, pp. 102–25.

Weber M. (1930b) *The Protestant Ethic and the Spirit of Capitalism*. Allen and Unwin, London.

Weber M. (1947) *The Theory of Social and Economic Organization*. (trans. A.M. Henderson and Talcott Parsons). Oxford University Press, New York.

Weber M. (1978) *Economy and Society* (xx edn). University of California Press, Berkeley, CA.

Wilkinson R. and Pickett K. (2010) *The Spirit Level: Why Equality is Better for Everyone*. Penguin Books Ltd, New York, NY.

Wong C.H. (9 December 2013) Singapore Riot Signals Foreign-Labor Strains. *Wall Street Journal*, accessed on 22 May 2014 at http://online.wsj.com/news/articles/SB1000142405270230474430457924782360454 40160.

Woolcock M. (1998) Social Capital and Economic Development: Towards a Theoretical Synthesis and Policy Framework. *Theory and Society* 27/2, 151–208.

Workplace Safety and Health Institute (2012) Workplace Safety and Health Report, accessed on 22 May 2014 at http://www.wshi.gov.sg/files/Workplace%20Safety%20and%20Health%20Report%202012.pdf.

Wyatt E. (20 December 2011) Fed Proposes New Capital Rules for US Banks. *International Herald Tribune*, New York, NY, accessed on 22 May 2014 at http://www.nytimes.com/2011/12/21/business/fed-proposes-new-capital-rules-for-banks.html.

Yong A. and Sim B. (10 March 2012) Maid, 16, Gets 10 Years for Killing 'Demanding' Boss, accessed on 22 May 2014 at http://www.asiaone.

com/print/News/Latest%2BNews/Singapore/Story/A1Story20120308-
332337.html.
(2013) Discussion Forum – Moral Categories in the Financial Crisis.
Socio-economic Review 11, 601–27.

LEGISLATION

Article 8 of the European Convention on Human Rights.
Fifth Amendment to the United States Constitution.
Fourth Schedule: Conditions of Work Permit/ Visit Pass for Foreign
    Worker, Employment Act (Cap. 91).
Maintenance of Parents Act (Cap. 167B), Singapore.
Part VA of the Land Titles (Strata) Act (Cap. 158) (Rev. Ed. 2009).
Penal Code (Cap. 224, Rev. Ed. 2008).

Index